C000052419

# AND THEN THE
# DARKNESS

Sue Williams is an award-winning journalist and columnist. She has written for all of Australia's leading newspapers and magazines, as well as having her own opinion segment on a TV show. Born in England, she has also worked in print and TV in the UK and New Zealand and spent many years travelling around the world.

She has written seven other books: *Powering Up* (co-authored); *Getting There: Journeys of an Accidental Adventurer*; *Peter Ryan: The Inside Story*; *Mean Streets, Kind Heart: The Father Chris Riley Story*; *Apartment Living: The complete guide to buying, renting, surviving and thriving in apartments* (co-authored); *Death of a Doctor: How the medical profession turned on one of their own*; and *World Beyond Tears: The ongoing story of Father Chris Riley*.

# AND THEN THE
# DARKNESS

Peter Falconio and Joanne Lees went into
the outback together. Only one came out alive.
This is the whole true story…

# SUE WILLIAMS

JOHN BLAKE

Published by John Blake Publishing Ltd,
3, Bramber Court, 2 Bramber Road,
London W14 9PB, England

www.blake.co.uk

First published in hardback in the UK in 2006

First published in Australia in 2006 by ABC Books for the Australian Broadcasting Corporation,
GPO Box 9994, Sydney, NSW 2001

ISBN 1 84454 267 X

All rights reserved. No part of this publication may be reproduced, stored in a
retrieval system, or in any form or by any means, without the prior permission
in writing of the publisher, nor be otherwise circulated in any form of binding
or cover other than that in which it is published and without a similar condition
including this condition being imposed on the subsequent publisher.

British Library Cataloguing-in-Publication Data:

A catalogue record for this book is available from the British Library.

Design by www.envydesign.co.uk

Printed in Great Britain by William Clowes Ltd, Beccles, Suffolk

1 3 5 7 9 10 8 6 4 2

© Text copyright Sue Williams 2006

Papers used by John Blake Publishing are natural, recyclable products made
from wood grown in sustainable forests. The manufacturing processes conform
to the environmental regulations of the country of origin.

Names have been changed, or witheld, where requested.

For Jimmy,
always a warm light
even when the world is
cold and dark

## ACKNOWLEDGEMENTS

FOR THE FALCONIO FAMILY, this is one of the most tragic stories that's ever been told. They've been remarkable for the courage and dignity with which they've borne the loss of a treasured son, and much loved brother. Many thanks to you all for your help with this story. May you one day find the closure you so desperately need.

For Joanne Lees, it's also been a nightmare. I want to thank her family, her neighbours, her many friends and work colleagues, both in the UK and Australia, who spoke to me about her and her ordeal.

And, of course, it's been a grim experience for the family and friends of Bradley Murdoch. I'd like to thank his mum and dad particularly for talking to me, his girlfriends, his friends and former workmates.

The other people who've worked so long and hard to bring this ordeal to an end have been the many police officers in the Northern Territory and around Australia who did their tireless best to unravel the mystery, and try to solve it. For their help and co-operation with this book, as well as their priceless insights into the tragedy, I also offer my sincere thanks.

And to the bit players all around the UK and Australia who helped with my research, the people whose lives were touched by this dark journey far into the brutal heart of this beautiful country, I wish to record my gratitude.

CONTENTS

# PROLOGUE

THE SUN WAS JUST KISSING the horizon when Joanne Lees suddenly jerked the Kombi van's steering wheel to the left and jammed on the brakes. There was a yell from the back and a head appeared in the rear-view mirror. 'What's up?' asked the dark-haired young man who'd been sleeping on the back seat, pushed down to form a bed. 'Why are you stopping?' Joanne heaved the creaky handbrake and gestured through the window at the turquoise Australian sky, already shot with streaks of gold. 'The sunset,' she replied. 'Let's watch.'

Joanne and her boyfriend Peter Falconio scrambled out the doors and leaned back against the old orange van. They'd been driving for two-and-a-half hours since heading north from Alice Springs and this was their first break. Joanne tilted a bottle of water to her lips, and Peter rolled a joint, then lit the end. They could have been anyone: just two more overseas backpackers doing the time-honoured trip around Australia; a young couple having a taste of outback adventure before returning to Britain to settle down to careers, marriage and kids.

As the heavens turned a rosy pink and bronze against the fierce burnished ochre of the earth, Peter slipped an arm around Joanne's shoulders and passed her the joint. She smiled at him. It was one of those rare perfect moments on this, their dream trip around the world. Joanne fiddled with her camera, lined up the sunset and took a picture.

As soon as they'd finished, she slipped back behind the wheel and drove the Kombi across the road to the Ti Tree Roadhouse and service station. While Peter pumped the petrol, Joanne went into the cashier to pay and buy more cold drinks and snacks for the drive ahead. Their final destination was Darwin, some 1300 kilometres away, but Tennant Creek lay just 300 kilometres up the road, with its own wonders – the awesome

1

Devil's Marbles. They'd been told to try and see the massive rock formations at dawn in order to experience the full eerie impact. If they could, they would. Tonight they planned to pull over somewhere by the side of the road only when they grew too tired to keep going.

By the time Joanne returned, Peter was sitting behind the wheel, ready to set off on the last stage of their journey. It was nearing 7 p.m. when they pulled away, back into the barren featureless landscape that stretches far beyond any horizon the eye can see. They'd only been driving for around twenty minutes when Joanne spotted two small rings of fire on the left, five or so metres from the bitumen road. Peter started to brake.

'What are you doing, Pete?' Joanne asked.

He shrugged. 'I just thought we should put them out. The fire might spread.'

Joanne peered into the fading light. 'They look weird,' she said, shivering as she caught a chill through the open window. 'They look almost as though ... they've been started deliberately ...'

Peter laughed. 'What – out here? But we're the only ones here!'

Joanne didn't seem to hear him, and touched his knee. 'Keep driving,' she urged. 'I don't like it. It could be some kind of trick ... or trap.'

Peter noticed an edge of fear to her voice, and stopped laughing. This kind of lonely terrain with its mood of utter desolation was enough to spook anyone. He smiled fondly over at her, put his foot on the accelerator and moved smoothly back into fourth gear. 'Okay,' he said, gently. 'We'll keep going.' He said nothing when they saw two more fires further up the road, and they drove past in silence.

Less than an hour later, Peter noticed bright headlights behind him and slowed to let the vehicle overtake. As it drew level, however, it braked to the same speed as the Kombi. With the road so long and straight and empty of traffic, there was little danger. Peter looked to his right and saw the driver gesturing at him. He wound down the window and heard the man shouting something about sparks coming from the exhaust.

Joanne glanced past Peter through the gloom of the gathering dusk at the other driver, and didn't like what she saw. The man, in a baseball cap and check shirt and with his dog sitting up in the passenger seat beside him, was still jerking his finger towards the back of their vehicle. She saw Peter put his foot on the brake and suddenly, inexplicably, felt scared.

'Don't stop, Pete, don't stop!' she begged. 'I don't like it.'

Peter looked at her quizzically, but kept the pressure on the brake. 'We have to see what it is,' he said. 'It'll only take a minute.' He pulled up on the gravel shoulder, and the white four-wheel-drive ute with its green canopy stopped behind them. Peter got out and went to see what the problem was. He came back to ask Joanne to rev the engine, smiled at her, and returned to behind the Kombi.

And then the darkness enveloped him, and Joanne Lees never saw her boyfriend Peter Falconio again.

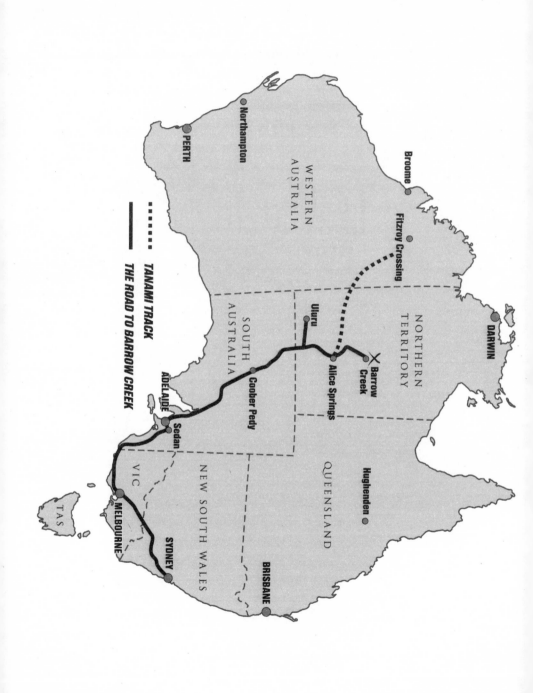

# PART ONE

# LEAVING HOME, SWEET HOME

# CHAPTER ONE

# From An English Country Garden

AS KIDS GROWING UP IN the historic villages on the outskirts of the teeming British Midlands town of Huddersfield, both Peter Falconio and Joanne Lees were always warned to stay close to home. Their early years were coloured by snatches of whispered conversations between adults about the horrors of the 'Moors Murderers' who tortured and killed youngsters out on the bleak, windswept hills nearby. Their childhood was spent in fear of the mysterious 'Yorkshire Ripper', who preyed on lone women. By the time that killer was eventually unmasked, thirteen women lay dead, and a whole generation had grown nervous about venturing far from home alone.

'It had a real effect on everyone's psyche,' says a contemporary of Joanne's from the same village. 'You grew up being told never to talk to strangers, never to hitchhike anywhere, never to stop for people. It takes you a long time to un-learn those lessons.'

Sometimes, it's better not to try.

PETER MARCO FALCONIO WAS born on 20 September 1972, and grew up in the nineteenth-century village of Hepworth, Holmfirth, 10 kilometres south of Huddersfield. A jumble of weavers' cottages and old stone buildings clinging to the emerald hillside, it was once an idyllic place. Today, however, developers have marched in with their smart new housing estates and mock Victorian façades have steadily engulfed the original buildings. The Falconios' two-storey, four-bedroom detached house is built of creamy stone and is neat and well-kept but is now encircled by newer homes. Where once Peter's mother, Joan, used to look out over the washing-up to vast swathes of endless green, she now stares straight into the white brick of the end house of the new estate. 'It used to be much nicer,' she says sadly. 'We were on our own with great views until they built *that*. But what can you do?'

A few kilometres east lies New Mill, another small village scattered around a busy crossroads. It's here that Peter Falconio's father, Luciano, a short, nuggety Italian migrant, ran the local post office. A cheery man with silvery hair, a ready smile and a strong accent, he and his four sons – Nick, five years older than Peter; Paul, three years older; Peter; and finally Mark, six years younger – were well-known around the area, all helping, at various times, to deliver the morning and evening newspapers. 'They were also noticeable because of their striking dark Italian looks,' says neighbour Richard Ainley. 'They really stood out.' The lads hung around the town square, meeting friends and chatting to girls, rather than joining, like some of the other neighbourhood kids, the local cubs or scouts. 'They weren't goody goodies like me,' says Ainley. 'But they were all a really nice family.'

Joan, not much taller than Luciano, with soft greying wavy hair, glasses, a strong Huddersfield accent and a permanently worried expression, was kept busy tending to the needs of four growing boys and a strong-willed husband who believed in raising their kids with old-fashioned discipline and respect. 'I've known Luciano for fifteen to twenty years,' says local councillor Donald Firth. 'He's been here a long time now. He's a very forthright gentleman who speaks his mind, and his wife stays very much in the background. I've enormous respect for him and his family, as does everyone here.'

Over the years, Hepworth's become more a part of the neighbouring, and much bigger, village of Holmfirth which tourists used to visit for the quaintness of an older, bygone England, and the good walking of the Brontë Country in the heart of the nearby Pennines. Nowadays they're more likely to come to see the sights made famous by Britain's longest running TV sitcom, BBC TV's *Last of the Summer Wine*, which is set in the village. Minibus tour guides point out 'Sid's Café', 'Compo's bar', 'Clegg's cottage', and the church where Compo was buried. These days, the tours also include pointing out the house of Peter Falconio.

BORN A YEAR AND FIVE days after Peter on 25 September 1973, Joanne Rachael Lees grew up just 7 kilometres away in the small village of Almondbury. Like Hepworth, Almondbury's an uneasy hotchpotch of the old and the new – in one part of the high street stand original buildings like the old blackened weavers' cottages and one of the UK's last surviving blue police phone boxes, from the days before radio communications. The two-lane road, however, is choked with traffic, and around the corner are grim three-storey 1950s council tenements, with washing fluttering from mean balconies. Here, kids scream as they ride bikes up and down, and women glumly shuffle behind pushchairs with more squealing children. There's one shabby pub, The Lion; a bottle shop; a newsagent and a Pop In Centre which people wait forlornly outside every morning waiting for opening time. At the end of the row of flats are two houses huddled together. The furthest one, a modest two up, two down, belongs to Joanne's family.

Joanne and her single mum, Jenny, who never stayed in contact with Joanne's father much beyond their daughter's birth, moved into the house after Jenny met neighbour Vincent James while helping him put up a garden shed. Joanne was devoted to her mum, but soon warmed to the pale, lean man with the tired eyes and habit of chain-smoking his own roll-ups. By the time Jenny and Vincent married in 1983, Joanne was calling him 'Dad', and was delighted when her half-brother, Sam, was born in 1986. The four lived together quietly in the house with their dog Jess. It was dingy, but homely, small and cluttered with ornaments and trinkets and photographs on every surface, and half-a-dozen noisily ticking clocks, with others chiming on the quarter hour. Holidays were spent in a caravan by the seaside.

'We were very close from the start, and she and her mum were devoted to each other,' Vincent James told *Real* magazine in 2002. 'Joanne could have refused to accept me as her dad, but it was never a problem. My stepdaughter was the perfect little girl – she seemed to do everything right.'

THERE ARE ASPECTS OF LIFE in this part of England that have changed little in hundreds of years. Although most of the great textile mills that fired the industrial revolution have long been driven out of business by cheaper imports, and the main shopping strips of Huddersfield are today peppered with loan offices, charity stores and one-pound shops, people born in these close-knit working-class communities still continue to live, love, work, raise their families, retire and die where they were born. Many have rarely travelled as far afield as London, let alone overseas, and most would see scant reason to do so. Staying close to family, friends, neighbours and familiar routines is the norm; a desire to travel is regarded with suspicion, and moving any distance away almost a betrayal. The pubs are the hub of social life, with Huddersfield having one of the highest numbers per head of population in Britain. There are still traditional, wood-lined lounges warmed by authentic log fires, but the sticky, plastic bars, noisy with the electronic bleeps and crashing of pokie machines, are steadily taking over. But they all have their place. Ask anyone the way to anywhere, and their directions – 'Turn left at the Sycamore Inn, then go past the Lion and when you see the White Hart, go right there' – sound more like a pub crawl.

'Generations after generations live in the same place,' says one local, Mark Koh. 'When I moved from one village to a town 14 kilometres away, people were: 'Oh God! What a shame!' I left school twenty-one years ago now, and yet 90 per cent of the people in my school wouldn't have moved more than 10 kilometres away.'

Why would anyone leave anyway, when everything one needs can be found in Huddersfield? With a large influx of migrants post-World War II from the Caribbean and the Indian subcontinent making up the shortfall in the textile trade, even foreign cuisine is well catered for. In every row of shops there'll be a curry and chip takeaway alongside the local specialty greasy Joe's, selling liver and onions with gravy and chips. In Huddersfield's high street, there's even a fast-food Indian that locals have nicknamed 'McSingh's'.

Homes are affordable, although wages are modest, and the kind of low-skill jobs offered by businesses like call centres are plentiful. It's kept the area stolidly working-class and these origins are routinely celebrated, with a determination never to look above, or beyond, one's station.

Huddersfield is the home of British rugby league, for instance, after the tumultuous breakaway with the more middle-class union, and longtime Labour Prime Minister Harold Wilson was born there. The affection isn't always a two-way street though; he moved at the age of sixteen to Liverpool.

But most locals stay, and few seem to mind the relentless rain that leaves the washing flapping forlornly on clotheslines strung out even in the front gardens for days. Grey dreariness is only noticeable, after all, if you have something with which to compare it. But to be fair, it has its rewards, too. On good summer days, the undulating hills beyond the villages glow green in the sunlight with brilliant rugs of bluebells and dog roses; sheep graze contentedly and squirrels dart and play. Couples sit in parked cars playing loud music around the region's highest point, the 270-metre Castle Hill, and the more adventurous copulate hurriedly in the scrub.

JOANNE AND PETER MET IN 1996 at Huddersfield's biggest nightclub, Visage, when she was twenty-two and he, twenty-three. With a large student following, the club down by the old converted mills was known for drinks that weren't too dear, determinedly middle-of-the-road music and a relaxed atmosphere. Peter spotted Joanne with a couple of her friends standing near the bar and liked what he saw. With her black, glossy hair cut into a neat bob just above her shoulders, a flawless complexion, baby blue eyes, rosebud lips and a dazzling white smile, she looked like a porcelain doll. She seemed shy, but she danced well, and they soon fell into easy conversation.

Joanne, in turn, was charmed by this handsome, dark stranger. With his short cropped hair, soft brown eyes, easy-going manner and old-fashioned gentlemanly courtesy, he was sweet and funny. She'd been out with plenty of boys before, but Peter struck her as different from the rest. He was passionate about what he was doing, determined to succeed, ambitious and confident. Even more attractive, however, was his appetite for life beyond the confines of their villages. He'd already been overseas a few times, on skiing trips to Italy and France, and seemed restless for change.

'So what do you plan to do?' she asked him curiously.

'Aha!' He grinned back at her. 'I won't always be staying here, that's for sure. I want to travel. I want to get out there and live life …'

Joanne smiled back. Working in a travel agency, she had itchy feet too, but had never roamed far, torn between the desire for adventure and the cosy comfort of staying close to home and her beloved mum. But that evening her imagination was fired like never before, and for the next three months the pair were inseparable.

Joanne had been an average student, plodding and methodical, diligent but uninspired, working hard enough to do well, but impatient to leave school and start earning a living. At Almondbury Junior, a pretty little place tucked away off a main road, she didn't make much of an impression on either her fellow students or teachers. At her next school, the sprawling Almondbury High – a run-of-the-mill comprehensive with 800-odd pupils – she didn't particularly stand out either.

'You know, it's funny, but no-one recalls her – even the teachers who took her in classes,' says teacher Yvonne Ainley. 'I think she was simply never exceptional. She was an ordinary girl. Very ordinary.'

While Joanne was popular with her classmates, she concentrated more on her social life than on her studies. When she left school and went on to college to take her A levels, she worked part-time as a barmaid and, at one point, as a bacon packer in a local factory to pay for nights out and nice clothes in which to enjoy them all the more. After her final exams, she found a job in the local branch of the Thomas Cook travel agency. She was ideally placed to discuss travel plans with Peter.

AT WOOLDALE JUNIOR AND THEN Holmfirth High, Peter Falconio was known as a bright boy who did the minimum amount of work to get by. He wasn't lazy, it was just that his attention always seemed to be elsewhere. He had a lively mind that flitted from one thing to the next without wanting to spend too much time on any one thing in particular, and generally preferred entertaining his classmates, and taking part in various tearaway adventures, to hunching over his books. He was smart, but not particularly academic, clever in a much more pragmatic way: good at solving problems, thinking his way around difficulties, and relying on his charm to get him out of sticky situations.

'Educational-wise, he was one of the brightest ones,' says a friend of the family, Ken Sims. 'But he's also been in and out of trouble like many of the youngsters. He's veered from straight and narrow a bit in the past. It was never anything serious, just a bit of bother from time to time. He was always an adventurous kind of lad, much more so than his brothers. And he was always very high spirited.'

Peter got through his school exams at the age of sixteen but, unsure what to do next, decided he'd have to go on to college in order to make any kind of decent living. At first, he applied for a catering course at Huddersfield Technical College, but quickly discovered it wasn't for him. He then reapplied for the BTEC national diploma in construction, a qualification accepted by the construction industry for entry into employment at a technician level, or by universities as an entry requirement. The course is held in a charmless modern annex to the college, but tutor Stephen Jones sensed how keen Peter was, especially when he ran into problems transferring his grant from catering to his next choice. Week after week, he waded through the paperwork, and wrangled with the authorities until, finally, he reached an unusual decision. To hell with it: he'd pay for the course himself.

'It was very unusual, but he was so determined,' says Jones. 'He felt the only way out of his financial problems was to get a job and earn money to pay for everything himself. I really admired him for that.'

Peter found part-time work in a bowling alley and behind the bar in the nearby nightclub Hotshots, and started the course at the age of eighteen. He did well in all three. At the nightclub they were impressed at how self-assured and quick-thinking he was whenever there were problems; at the bowling alley, they found him an extremely personable and amiable attendant; and on the course, his tutor took an instant liking to this ambitious young man.

'He had a big personality, and always a smile, and ready for a laugh,' says Jones. 'He was also very upfront and confident. He seemed a lot more mature than his years too, and was a very insightful person. He was quite assertive and always ready to take charge of the situation whenever there were problems. He organised a bowling trip for his fellow students and, when they tried to charge him double what he'd been quoted, he stood his ground and argued until he got what he wanted. He wouldn't be swayed.'

After Peter successfully finished the course, he began work as a surveyor, bought a small cottage of his own close to his family and planned his next career move. No-one who knew him was in any doubt that, whatever it would be, he'd make a success of it. 'He was someone who could negotiate his way out of any problem,' says Jones. 'He had such confidence, such charm, and could be a real bullshitter when he wanted to be. Others his age might be vulnerable, but he was certainly not. When he left here, I couldn't help feeling he had a great future ahead of him. He was so full of life, and he seemed absolutely immune to anything bad ever happening.'

If only.

# CHAPTER TWO

# In An Australian Wilderness

BRADLEY JOHN MURDOCH WAS A mistake from the moment of conception. His parents, Colin and Nancy, were battlers who'd assumed, edging into their forties with two growing sons aged fifteen and eleven, that the tough times were behind them. The arrival of a new, unplanned baby on 6 October 1958 changed everything.

The family lived in a small three-bedroom fibro house in Northampton, a rough-and-ready town 475 kilometres north of Perth in Western Australia. Nestled between scarred hills with most of its housing spread out and fronting dirt or roughly-tarred roads, it has the despondent air of having been overlooked by the outside world. And that's because it largely has.

One hundred and fifty years ago, Northampton was a thriving industrial centre with the country's first lead mine and a rich seam of copper. The ore was transported to Geraldton, 50 kilometres to the south, by the first government-built railway in WA. But eventually the mines were exhausted and the railway closed the year before Bradley was born. The town came to rely instead on its fertile farmlands on the edge of the region's wheatbelt. In years of plentiful rainfall, the area thrived; in drought, everyone suffered. Locals, anxious to develop a fledgling tourism industry to supplement earnings from the land, tried to woo visitors from the bustling coastal towns of Port Gregory and Kalbarri, both set in picturesque wildflower country nearby. It was a hard ask. Visitors to the area could easily miss Northampton completely, since the scenic route north peels off the highway 200 metres before the town. Those who ventured in found a place that still closed up on weekends and sometimes at lunchtimes, offering little in the way of attractions. With three pubs and three churches, the only other diversion was The Mechanics Institute, a large tin shed where dances were sometimes held. Even new residents to the area found the place cliquey, with some families now proudly into their third generation in the district reminding more recent 'blow-ins' of their pioneer heritage. The local café displays a sign that reads, 'No cappuccinos here'. It's a proud boast rather than an embarrassed apology.

Town newcomer Heidi Sommer-Stinson, who used to run a restaurant in the village centre before opening Northampton's first B&B, despairs at how resistant to change the town is. 'Change is a threat to this place,' she says. 'People don't like change or ever doing anything differently. There's a lot of stillbirths because there's still a lot of inbreeding, and it's all very small-minded.'

Across the hills and over the nearby Greenough River, the neighbouring town of Mullewa is a study in contrast. The bigheartedness of the inhabitants gives it a warm easy-going air, and when they suffer drought, the townsfolk get together to share what they have. In Northampton, it's quite the opposite. 'People hoard,' Sommer-Stinson says. 'They don't pull together. There's no generosity of spirit at all. Everyone's compartmentalised into those who have wealth and those who have nothing. People are very, very competitive.'

Bradley Murdoch's parents fell into the narrow middle ground, and found it suited them well enough. They weren't farmers, and they definitely weren't wealthy, but both had skills that enabled them to become indispensable in time to both camps. Colin, tall and strong with wavy brown hair, was a skilled mechanic who could fix anything and everything. He had a reputation as someone who could get any piece of old farm machinery working again, whether it involved a simple overhaul, or an innovative patchwork of parts from other pieces of junk he kept in his shed to the side of the house. He was affordable too. Many farmers couldn't buy new equipment, and those who could invariably preferred not to. So a man like Colin Murdoch, eager to please and happy enough tinkering around to find the most economical way to start a clapped out tractor or replace the engine in a rusted old ute, was a godsend.

Nancy was no slacker, either. As the only hairdresser in town, she set up shop in the bathroom and kitchen of their family home on West Street. Customers would enter through the lounge, and be led into the neat but faded kitchen beyond. For their hair to be washed, they'd be walked through to the next room, the little bathroom and shared laundry. Nancy was always immaculate, her blonde hair bouffanted high above her head in the style of the time; and wash and sets, with a bi-monthly perm, became her stock in trade. The house, already crowded when her two eldest sons were home from school, often also had a local sitting in the kitchen with her hair in curlers, reading a magazine and chatting with Nancy through a shared cloud of cigarette smoke.

The couple were popular in the town, and not only because of their respective trades. They were seen as a close family, firm but fair with their sons; battlers who worked hard and minded their own business. The two oldest boys were good mates, born within four years of each other: Robert in 1943 and Gary in 1947. Adding to Colin and Nancy's difficulties, however, was the fact that Robert was born without an ear. Nicknamed 'Speedy', presumably because his disability made him the opposite, he was a sickly child who was constantly in and out of hospital for operations, one of which saw him fitted with a prosthetic ear.

Gary, on the other hand, was as hale and hearty as his brother was poorly. 'He was a big blustery fellow, but Robert was very quiet, like his dad,' says John Drage who grew up next door to the family. 'But I liked Gary. He was pretty level-headed. He was all right.'

Bradley's arrival at the Geraldton Regional Hospital wasn't a terribly welcome event. Neither Robert nor Gary were particularly interested in a baby brother, and Nancy was worn out already with the demands of the three males in the house. Both she and Colin had believed their days of washing nappies and losing sleep at night were over.

BRADLEY GREW UP COMPETING WITH his brothers for his parents' attention since Nancy was often too exhausted to give her youngest son much time, and Colin always seemed to be too busy. As a little boy, Bradley therefore spent long hours sitting in his dad's shed, breathing in the scent of diesel and oil, patiently watching his father fix trucks and repair machinery, eagerly handing him his screwdriver, a wrench or nails whenever he was allowed. The skills he picked up in that shed, repairing engines, cannabalising parts of vehicles to add to others, finding inventive solutions to mechanical problems, as well as his parents' fierce work ethic, were to stand him in good stead for the rest of his life.

His brothers resented him from the word go. Their house was too small for four, let alone five, and Robert didn't like having to share his windowless bedroom with his kid brother. The wooden floorboards shook as the two eldest raced around the house; their mother frequently screamed for quiet when Bradley tagged along to try to join in. Children in those days made their own entertainment, so the three were often thrown together out of necessity. Robert and Gary would tend to brush Bradley off as a nuisance, and gradually he developed a swagger of false bravado to hide his misery and annoyance. Neighbours grew used to seeing the three boys racing out to the woods to go rabbiting, Gary in front, Robert following, and Bradley trailing along despondently behind, glowering resentment.

'Brad grew up a real rebel,' says neighbour Drage, now 60, who used to collect toy cars with Robert. 'He'd be defiant, kind of: "I'm going to do what I want!" He was a bit of a loner. He was too young for his brothers, really, so he had no-one to play with.' Bradley had started off life as an outsider even within his own family. It was a slight he was never to forget, or forgive. 'All that family were very nice,' Drage adds. 'But Brad was always a pain in the bum. He was surly and trying to get his own way. He was going right off the rails.' It didn't help either that Gary was so popular, with lots of friends and casual acquaintances who'd ask him to join in their activities. It seemed only to underline Bradley's isolation, and the role that was quickly becoming his: as the misfit, and the rebel without any cause but his own.

He lumbered his way through school with scarcely a second glance. What was the point of all that English and maths when he'd already decided to become a mechanic like his dad? Teachers at the local primary school, Northampton District, were fighting a losing battle to get the kids interested in the world beyond the district's farms and small businesses. The school was well-equipped for a small town, with basketball courts, a row of handbasins in the playground, and the obligatory tall watertank, but today the school sits empty, with another built out of town, just up the highway, further displacing the heart of Northampton. Bradley did just enough to get by each day in class. 'He battled to get through school,' says his dad Colin. 'He liked sport, but not lessons.' Teacher Bob Johnson remembers his brother Gary fondly, but not Bradley. 'Gary was a nice kid, everyone knew him. But Bradley ... no-one really had much to do with him. He was a loner.'

Outside school, it was easier to get the other kids' attention. Bradley was a big boy, tall and strong for his years. 'He was always a fighter,' says his dad. 'He was a very good fighter.' To others, he quickly became known as a bully. Old schoolmates remember a thickset kid who found it easy to intimidate others and often infuriated teachers with his insolence. Secretly, Bradley delighted in the kind of attention he craved but was never able to get at home. Family life there was becoming more fragmented – his parents were beginning to despair of their youngest, and found him more and more difficult to control. Bradley was angry and resentful that they seemed to lavish so much time and money on Robert, and he envied Gary the freedoms he was able increasingly to claim for his age. Bradley felt his brothers were always labelling him a pest, and trying to brush him off. He felt increasingly distanced from his parents, too, who seemed very old, and the gulf between them only widened over the years.

Bradley was later to claim there was trouble in Northampton between white kids and Aboriginal kids, and that his father Colin was often used by the police to spy on the black community. As a result, says Bradley, he was regularly beaten up by black children. No locals, however, have any recall of such disturbances, some going so far as to say that relations between the two groups were always extremely civil. Rather more locals, indeed, remember Bradley picking on black kids, but most will say that smaller white kids copped it too.

As he entered his teens, Colin and Nancy found it even harder to control their youngest son. Robert was working for the CBH Group, which stores, handles and markets grain, and Gary had started his own truck business, and, with the older boys away, there was no-one left to act as a check to Bradley's behaviour. 'They were such good parents to those boys,' says one elderly local. 'But that's just no guarantee these days to how kids'll turn out.'

When Bradley turned twelve, Colin and Nancy decided to make a last ditch effort to keep their youngest son on the rails. Perhaps feeling guilty they hadn't paid him more attention, and possibly worried at the way he was turning out, they made a monumental decision. Although they'd been happy in Northampton, there was no high school in town, and they decided to move to Perth so Bradley could attend high school there, rather than commute to Geraldton every day. He could start with a clean slate, wouldn't be out of their sight for so much of the day, and they could do more to try to keep him on the straight and narrow, they reasoned. It was an eleventh hour bid to save their youngest son from spending the rest of his life on the wrong side of the thin blue line. But it was to be totally in vain.

Bradley didn't want to leave the familiar surroundings where he felt comfortable and in control. It was a wrench to move from the only home he'd ever known and a shock to be suddenly the new kid in a huge, unfamiliar city. In Northampton, he knew how far he could push things; in the big smoke, he knew no-one, and he felt vulnerable and lonely. He compensated, as before, in the only way he knew how: by shouting louder and striking first. Dave Headley, a schoolmate from Perth's Como Senior High, remembers Bradley as a bully with a mean streak that made him unpredictable and dangerous to the younger kids and irritating to the bigger ones. 'He didn't seem to fit in with any particular group, he just seemed to be a bit of annoyance to a lot of people. He seemed to get a bit of pleasure out of other people's misfortunes. You never wanted to trust him. He had a bit of a short fuse too.'

Almost friendless at school, and isolated within his own family, Bradley began to feel even more alone and adrift. It seemed he'd always been on the outside looking in. And for the first time he began to feel angry that he was being excluded by everyone. Very angry.

# CHAPTER THREE

# Leaving Home

PETER FALCONIO WAS A YOUNG man full of the confidence that he could do anything and everything he had a mind to try. He'd been working and earning good money since leaving Huddersfield College but he really wanted to move higher, and faster. He knew a university degree would give his career an enormous boost. His girlfriend Joanne Lees was supportive; she loved her job as a travel agent, but saw how restless her boyfriend was becoming and didn't want to hold him back. He looked around at courses, and settled for one at Northampton, the county town in the East Midlands of England after which Bradley Murdoch's hometown had been named. But when he got there, he realised he'd made a mistake, so he quit after a year, and transferred to Brighton University, on England's south coast, which had just been upgraded from a Polytechnic, to do a BSc Honours degree in building and construction management.

'There were all these little snags, he just didn't move smoothly from one point to the next,' says old Huddersfield College tutor Stephen Jones. 'But he had a strong personality and always got through. He was always questioning what he was doing and if he felt if it was wrong, he had to do something about it.' He was eventually accepted into Brighton and, with the course starting in September 1996, there was one more big decision to be made: what to do about his relationship with Joanne. Over the year they'd been together, they'd grown very close. They'd gone on holiday together to Edinburgh, Italy, Greece and Jamaica, and had enjoyed wonderful times, and Joanne's mum Jenny adored Peter and felt they were good together. 'The more we saw of him, the more we thought he and Joanne seemed the perfect match,' says her stepfather Vincent James. 'They'd laugh at the same things, go to pop concerts together. They were like best friends.'

They complemented each other well, too. Peter was outgoing, confident and likeable, and was also solid, dependable and strong. For someone like Joanne who'd spent her early years without a father, these were immensely attractive qualities. He was extremely close to his family too, which Joanne, growing up with only her mother for so many years, also loved. In addition, although Peter wasn't over-intellectual, he was smart and, so focussed on what he wanted to achieve and determined to get there, he inspired confidence. Joanne, on the other hand, was quiet and reserved. When she was with people she knew she was livelier, but to casual acquaintances her shyness often came across as coolness.

'She changed a bit after she started going out with Pete,' says a friend, Jenny Mackie. 'I think he was very supportive and caring, and she kind of blossomed. She was devoted to him, and he always treated her as if she was up on a pedestal. He changed too. He calmed down a bit when he met her. Before, he was always looking ahead at what was next, and could be a bit of a lad. But he became more settled somehow. They were both obviously very happy together.'

Peter knew a degree could set him up for a good career as a construction site manager – Brighton University had an excellent reputation and graduating students were usually snapped up by the big construction companies – so he moved south for his first year of college, but travelled back the 400 kilometres to Huddersfield whenever he could to visit Joanne. It wasn't an ideal arrangement and in the holidays before starting his second year he asked Joanne if she'd consider leaving Huddersfield and setting up home with him. She was torn: she'd been close to her mum since they'd lived alone together so long before Vincent arrived, and Jenny was unwell, suffering from painful rheumatoid arthritis, a chronic inflammation of the lining of the joints. Yet at the same time Joanne longed to break free of the restrictions of small-town life, and Brighton had a reputation as an exciting place for young people. With a great live music scene, a large number of pubs, a lively political scene and a busy shopping centre, it had justifiably earned the nickname 'London-by-the-sea'.

And then, of course, there was Peter, her soulmate and best friend. He was so strong, determined and impulsive, she had no idea where he might be leading her, but she knew the journey would be exciting. He was a restless spirit, someone who'd never plump for the easiest or most comfortable option, and someone who'd never be content in one job, or one place, for the rest of his life. She was much more conservative and ordinary by comparison but, when she compared her mum and stepfather's insular lifestyle with Peter's free-wheeling outlook, there was no competition.

Joanne took a deep breath, smiled and nodded her assent. It was a big step, but she felt sure it was the right one. Nothing would part them now.

WHEN JOANNE TOLD HER BOSS at Thomas Cook about her plans, he was happy to arrange a transfer to one of the agencies in Brighton. She'd proved herself a good worker and was always bright, pleasant and friendly on the front desk. With that brilliant smile and easygoing manner, customers warmed to her.

Her mum took it harder. She was upset that Joanne was moving so far away – a few hundred kilometres felt like the ends of the Earth to people in those parts – but she liked Peter and had confidence in him to look after her daughter. She knew it could prove an important move for them both. She gave them her blessing.

The couple found a flat they could afford between the university and the beach, 1.5 kilometres from the first, and 2 kilometres, most of it uphill, due north from the main pier. That tattier part of Ditchling Road, one of the steepest streets in Brighton, is filled during term-time with students who flock there for the old semi-detached villas subdivided into affordable flats or, where they were demolished in the 1960s, the purpose-built apartments erected in their place. Joanne and Peter's one-bedroom flat was small, on the second floor of a large three-storey corner house converted into a small block of five units, but it was cosy. Sometimes even too cosy. The walls were paper-thin and often you could hear every fight, and making-up, the neighbours had. 'Sometimes I felt like I knew Joanne and Peter well, just from hearing them in the bathroom and bedroom,' says then-neighbour Robert Snow. 'But we were all very friendly, anyway. I'd say, "All right, mate!" whenever I saw him. She was a lot quieter. I'd usually only get a little smile from her. Generally, they kept themselves to themselves. Everyone does around here, really.'

The pair usually did their socialising around the university with the other students, at the cheap, subsidised student bars. For money was tight, even though Joanne was working full-time, and Peter again had various part-time jobs to help support his studies. Joanne had quickly settled into her new job at the Thomas Cook agencies in both London Road and North Street. The North Street branch was popular, being between two of Brighton's most famous landmarks, the old Clock Tower built to commemorate Queen Victoria's golden jubilee, and the stunning Royal Pavilion used by the Prince Regent as his private pleasure palace. Arriving at work there always gave Joanne a great buzz, but the other office in London Road also had its advantages. It was always busy, being right on the main road, and was much closer to home, just a fifteen-minute walk away. It helped too that Joanne had made good friends with many of the staff. One of her closest friends in Brighton, Tina Smith, says Joanne surprised everyone early on. 'When she first arrived, she was quite quiet and shy,' she says. 'But with a drink, she could suddenly be really lively. It was such a difference!'

Peter was also enjoying his time in Brighton. The course was everything he'd hoped it would be, and he was working hard and receiving good marks. He'd opted to take the sandwich course, working in the construction industry for the second year of his four-year course and, studying full-time for his final year, from September 1999 to June 2000, his tutors were delighted with his progress. 'Peter was a very determined young man,' says Dr Kassim Gidado. 'But he was also very good-natured. He would take on other people's problems and try to help them out too. He was a real team-player which is something we encourage. He could motivate people and if you wanted to get something done, you'd go to Peter. He was great at getting people to work together to meet deadlines. He had a very, very bright future. We could see he was going to be a real high-flier.'

But Peter wasn't in any desperate hurry to embark on his new career. He and Joanne had been secretly planning a one-year trip around the world as soon as his course finished. They'd started talking about it in 1998, and grown more and more excited as time went by. Joanne brought home brochures from the travel agency for them to pore over, together with recommendations from workmates and past customers. While Peter sat with his books in the evenings, Joanne worked out all the best destinations. When he'd pushed his last assignment for the day finally aside, they talked through all their ideas and plotted their ideal routes. And at night, they'd lie in each other's arms and dream of far-flung golden beaches, distant mountains, crowded foreign cities and great deserted stretches of the romantic outback.

# CHAPTER FOUR

# A Bad Seed

WHILE PETER FALCONIO AND JOANNE LEES worked hard to build a future for themselves in the south of England, it seemed to some that Bradley Murdoch was hell-bent on sabotaging his. He was becoming more and more involved with Australia's infamous outlaw motorcycle gangs, the hard men alleged to be heavily embroiled in organised crime, a big slice of the country's drug market and violence against the police – and each other. 'We know, and you know, that murder after murder, rape after rape, drug deal after drug deal, shootouts in our city, shootouts and bombings in our suburbs are directly related to outlaw bikie gangs,' declared South Australian Premier Mike Rann in frustration at their increasing level of activity.

After leaving school in 1973 at the age of fifteen, Murdoch had drifted. He'd spent time doing odd jobs in Perth before wandering back up north to Geraldton, near his hometown of Northampton. He picked up work as a mechanic, putting to good use those hours he'd spent watching and learning from his father. But in his spare time, he began to get involved with the area's bikies. Former neighbour John Drage still remembers the night he took on a visiting bikie from a rival gang and 'belted the hell out of him'.

The death of his eldest brother Robert soon after pushed Murdoch even closer to the edge. Robert had endured so many operations and had been sick for so long, it seemed almost as if he'd finally given up the fight. 'We all thought the doctors had killed him,' said Drage. 'They'd mucked about with him so much, it had made him too weak.' Although Murdoch had never been that close to Robert, his death shocked him.

On top of this, Murdoch's childhood interest in guns had never left him, and he grabbed every opportunity to use, or own one, even if it were stolen. His first brushes with the law were always over guns. His first court convictions, in 1977 and 1978, were for firearms offences, once for going armed into a public place.

Murdoch knew it was time for a change, however, when, in March 1980, during a spell working at the world's largest lead smelter, Pasminco, in Port Pirie, South Australia, he was involved in a road accident which resulted in the death of a motorcyclist. Blame was placed squarely on Murdoch and, convicted of causing death by dangerous driving, he was slugged with a suspended prison sentence. It was a timely wake-up call, and the close brush with jail penetrated his rough, tough exterior. He was at a crossroads: he could continue the way he was, and almost certainly end up in jail; or he could make a bid for a better, different kind of life.

He decided to leave the area that he knew so well and try his luck somewhere completely different. He chose the coastal town of Albany, on the southernmost tip of WA. One of the most isolated settlements in Australia, and the state's oldest town, it overlooks one of the biggest natural harbours in the world on one side and, on the other, stares towards the spectacular Stirling and Porongurup Ranges, some 400 kilometres south of Perth. With rugged granite cliffs dropping down to the cold ocean, and brisk winds blowing straight off the Antarctic, it felt the perfect kind of place for a fresh start. And for a while it was. Murdoch fell in love with Albany's wild unpredictability. There were a couple of good surfing spots, a lot of open stretches of water, and good fishing, particularly off the rocks, from which the unwary were occasionally swept to their deaths. Rents were among the cheapest in the state, there was plenty of work for mechanics and drivers, since most food and fuel was trucked into the area, and the agricultural and logging industries always needed help. In addition, Albany had the lure of being a long, long way from anywhere that really counted.

Murdoch liked the town's transient lifestyle too. 'Many people are sent here for work for short periods, like teachers and bank staff, and there's always a lot of tourists,' says long-term resident Craig Drummond.

'Everyone's looking for a totally different place, but it doesn't suit everyone.' In previous years, Albany had been an important whaling station and, as a kid, one of its most famous former inhabitants, the writer Tim Winton, remembers standing at the water's edge watching, with horror, the slaughter of the gracious giants with harpoons and grenades while the sea at Frenchman's Bay frothed pink with blood and scavenging birds. The whaling ceased in 1978, just a couple of years before Murdoch's arrival, and most of the excitement in town had gone with it. As a result, Murdoch soon drifted back into the company of the bikies who passed through on their regular runs.

Bikie culture is bigger in WA than in any other part of the continent and, with so many more bikies per head of population, the state has seen a great deal of club violence and inter-gang warring. Five clubs dominate the Australian stage – the Bandidos, the Rebels, the Hell's Angels, the Coffin Cheaters and the Gypsy Jokers – with the latter formed in 1969 through the help of the then Sydney chapter of the Hell's Angels, until the Angels launched a takeover bid and the two became sworn enemies. According to Professor Arthur Veno, bikie expert and author of *The Brotherhoods*, the Gypsy Jokers have the highest profile in WA and SA, where a number of the most violent incidents over the years have taken place. Two Gypsy Jokers were charged with murder after the former Perth chief of Criminal Investigations and anti-gang warrior Don Hancock – whom they wrongly suspected of shooting dead a club member in the WA mining town of Boulder – was killed, with a friend, in a car bomb in a quiet Perth street in September 2001, just days before the inquest was due to take place. A Gypsy Joker who confessed to his part in the bombing, and broke the gang code of silence to implicate his sergeant-at-arms, received fifteen years' jail, while his boss was acquitted.

'The outlaw motorcycle clubs consider themselves to be among the last bastions of free people, free from the straight world,' says Veno. 'Many club members see themselves as modern cowboys, the outlaw heroes of the Wild West.'

IN 1980, ON 14 JULY – a date that would later crop up in circumstances no-one could ever have predicted – Bradley Murdoch married a Perth local, a quiet, pretty girl clearly overwhelmed by his presence. He was twenty-one and, at 191 centimetres (six foot four) with a broad chest and powerful arms, cut an impressive figure. He was never out of work either. Those skills as a mechanic, together with his resourcefulness and inventiveness in cobbling together quick fixes on the cheap, made him a model employee. His wife thought she had the perfect catch too, and in 1986 presented him with a baby son. Murdoch, however, wasn't ready to play happy families and he started spending more and more time away from home, and often disappeared for days on end.

His bikie mates turned him on to other job opportunities. Many of the gangs at that point were getting into security work and Murdoch was the ideal candidate. He discovered it wasn't necessary to work nine to five and leave with dirty hands any longer. With his build and temperament, it was easy to pick up the kind of work that tends to attract aggressive young men full of bluster and belligerence. He began work as a nightclub bouncer. While it suited him for a while, it wasn't long before he grew restless. Clubs were trying to clean up their acts and were demanding stricter standards of behaviour from their staff. They were instructing their bouncers to reason with troublesome punters rather than to hustle them out of the door with a show of muscle, recruiting more women and implementing stricter dress codes.

Besides, he was growing bored. Albany is beautiful, with great beaches, good swimming and fishing, and wondrous scenery, but for a young man in his prime, it's hardly dynamic. Murdoch found it tough adjusting to the demands of a wife who wasn't happy that he wasn't sitting on the sofa with her every evening, and still less the needs of a small, crying baby. This wasn't the life he'd envisioned for himself at all. He wanted thrills, he decided, even if they did come with spills. He phoned an old bikie mate in Bunbury and asked him if he knew of any work going. The man, again thought to be a Gypsy Joker, asked him if he fancied driving trucks up north. The work was hard and involved long hours, but it paid well.

'Yep, count me in,' replied Murdoch. He felt it was time to really stretch his wings. 'When can I start?'

FOR THE NEXT FIFTEEN YEARS Murdoch drove trucks around WA and the Northern Territory, leaving his wife at home bitter and disillusioned, and his young son without a father. Today, she leads a quiet life, and hasn't had any contact with her ex-husband for years. 'I don't want to see him either,' she says. 'He's nothing to do with us. He wasn't interested in being a family. We're better off without him.'

Up in his cab at the wheel of a massive truck, pulling as many as three trailers at a time in a road train and thundering across the deserted Australian outback with a gun often at his side, Murdoch felt like a true road warrior, all-powerful and all-conquering. He was the king of the road, a real Mad Max with the gravel spitting beneath his wheels, the sun in his eyes, and the cry of freedom in his heart, needing nobody and nothing.

God help anyone who got in his way.

# CHAPTER FIVE

# The Great Trip

IT'S SAID THAT AUSTRALIA HAS more enemies of humankind than anywhere else on the planet. If it's not 100-tonne roadtrains careening through the outback that get you, it could be sharks, crocodiles, or any one of the ten most venomous snakes on earth. Then there's the lethal red-back spiders that lurk under outdoor toilet seats, the fierce sun that can kill a traveller stranded in the outback without water or shade within two hours, and the perilous riptides that catch you in the ocean and spit you out too far from land ever to hope to swim to safety. When Joanne Lees and Peter Falconio broke the news to their families that they were planning a once-in-a-lifetime trip to Australia via Asia, their parents were understandably anxious. Aside from the natural dangers, Australia had enjoyed a reputation as one of the safest destinations in the world but, back in 2000, when the pair were planning their visit, several horrific incidents had recently tarnished the country's near-pristine image.

Seven other bright-eyed young backpackers had also once planned such trips. Their bodies were subsequently found, horribly disfigured and tortured, buried in shallow graves in the lonely Belanglo State Forest in southern New South Wales. Their killer Ivan Milat with the help of possibly one accomplice who is still at large, had picked them all up hitch-hiking, tied them up, blindfolded and gagged them, then raped the women and used them all as a gruesome target practice. After a long police hunt he was eventually caught and given seven life sentences in July 1996; one for each murder.

Earlier that year, a lone gunman had opened fire one sunny Sunday afternoon at sleepy Tasmania's Port Arthur and massacred thirty-five people – many of them tourists. Twenty more were injured, and their assailant, Martin Bryant, aged twenty-nine, was arrested as he ran from the scene, his clothes on fire. He was given thirty-five life sentences, with a recommendation never to be released.

Then, in Sydney, twenty-two-year-old Dorset university graduate Gawen Whalley, in Australia on a working holiday, was stabbed to death by a thirteen-year-old boy said to be prone to violent mood swings. Whalley had been camping with friends.

Just as the memories of these horrors started to fade, and even as Peter and Joanne were putting the finishing touches to their travel plans, yet another terrible tragedy unfolded. A few minutes after midnight on 23 June 2000, a raging fire swept through a backpackers' hostel in Childers, Queensland. Sixty-nine people managed to crawl their way to safety through the choking black smoke, but tragically fifteen did not. Four of the dead were British. Itinerant Robert Long, who'd been kicked out of the same hostel earlier, was convicted of starting the fire and sent to jail for life. That blaze brought back terrible echoes of the 1989 arson at the Down Under backpackers' hostel in Sydney's Kings Cross which killed six. And, worryingly, just three days after the Childers fire, another hostel in Kings Cross went up in flames, this time thought to have been caused by a faulty heater. No-one, thankfully, died.

So it was little wonder that Joanne's mum, Jenny James, was nervous. 'When they eventually announced they were giving up their jobs and the flat to go travelling, we were excited for them,' said her husband Vincent. 'Of course, like any parents, we were also concerned about their safety.' Quite apart from the big headline-grabbing crimes, there were also those lone events that send a shiver down the spine of any parent whose child might be planning a trip to Australia: like the young Essex pharmacist Susan Zack who was murdered by 'a friend' she met in Cairns; or London postman Brian Hagland, a cousin of British TV soap *EastEnders* star Sid Owen, who was killed in Bondi when he fell under a bus while being bashed by a street thug. Then there were the unsolved mysteries, perhaps the most agonising of all, where the parents were left waiting and wondering. American tourists Thomas and Eileen

Lonergan took a day's diving trip in 1998 to a popular spot at the Barrier Reef off Queensland's Cairns – and never returned. It's thought they were left behind by their boat, and they perished on the reef. Similarly, no-one is sure what happened to young English tourist Daniel Nute who disappeared in 1997 on a six-hour hike up Mount Sorrow in dense Cape Tribulation rainforest in the State's Far North, nor the fate of environmentalist Celena Bridge from Carlisle, 160 kilometres north of Huddersfield, who vanished from the same state while on an outback bird-watching trip the following year.

But while Jenny worried, Joanne and Peter tried to allay her fears. They were made of sterner stuff, they reassured her, and no harm would come to them. Yes, a number of young tourists had died in the past, but those kind of tragedies could happen anywhere. They weren't planning to hitchhike, and Peter was eminently sensible about taking risks. Besides, the number of tragic incidents was small when you considered the 750,000-odd international backpackers that visited Australia each year, a quarter of them British. And, on TV, Australia was looking so glorious in the run-up to the Sydney 2000 Olympic Games. They would be fine.

Their travel plans had to be delayed in any case following Peter's graduation. Just as he was finishing the course, he was asked if he'd like to finish off a project he'd been doing in his sandwich year. It was an exciting opportunity, and his dad was keen for him to take it up. 'Me and his brother, we dissuade him,' recalls Luciano. 'We said why don't you keep your job?' So Peter asked Joanne, apologetically, if she'd be prepared to hang on a few more months. She agreed, and the new date for their departure was set for 15 November 2000.

They spent their extra time in Britain saving hard, and watching the Games on TV, excitedly anticipating their forthcoming trip. England was enduring its wettest autumn since 1766 and they were both growing sick of the incessant rain. A dark, sodden November felt like the perfect time to be heading off overseas and they couldn't wait to see the sun again. Joanne was also looking forward to spending time alone with Peter; in between work and his studies, it sometimes felt like they rarely relaxed. They'd grown close and she had no doubts their relationship could withstand whatever trials and tribulations their travels flung at them. 'Because I was living away from my family, Pete had to be everything to me,' she says. 'He had to be my family, my boyfriend and my best friend. And he was. Pete meant the world to me, really. He was my future.'

Peter slipped a medallion of St Christopher, the patron saint of travellers, around his neck to keep him safe as friends kept calling to tell them how envious they were of their adventure. 'Sydney looks so beautiful,' Karen Biggins remembers telling them. 'I wish I could come with you. You're going to have the time of your life. It's going to be something you'll never forget.'

FLYING INTO KATHMANDU ON THE first stop on their grand tour, Joanne and Peter craned their necks to glimpse the mighty snow-tipped Himalayas out of the window of the plane. Below lay the tiny mountain kingdom of Nepal, home to the world's tallest mountain, Everest. Some of the most scenic, challenging and thrilling walking trails on earth beckoned. The pair loved Nepal, and spent a few days in Kathmandu before heading off on a trek in the nearby Annapurna region. Both had come well-equipped with good hiking shoes and light, casual clothes and, already keen walkers, made easy work of the tracks. With snow-capped peaks towering above them, crystal clear lakes below, fast-flowing rivers thrusting through deep gorges and stunning Tibetan monasteries and pretty little villages, they were enchanted. It was their first real experience of a world far from home, and they were struck by the warmth and friendliness of the Nepalese people, the cultural diversity of the country and its raw natural beauty.

From Nepal they flew to Singapore, then caught a bus into Malaysia, travelling north past lush palm plantations and thick jungle into southern Thailand. From there, they continued by train, stopping off at a picturesque beach resort along the way to celebrate Christmas in the sun, and visiting the tiger sanctuary at a Buddhist Temple at Karnchanaburi, where they experienced the thrill of feeding milk to a young orphaned cub. Every few days, they'd email or call home to let everyone know they were fine – and having the time of their lives. Heading back to Bangkok, they decided to take a side-trip to Cambodia. Joanne emailed her mum and Vincent replied. 'Think again,' he urged his stepdaughter. 'It could be dangerous. What about all those landmines? Why not spend a bit more time in Thailand instead? Cambodia sounds too risky.'

But Peter and Joanne were eager to see some of the ancient temples, stunning remnants of the mighty Khmer Empire which once ruled much of what is now Vietnam, Laos and Thailand. The elegant French capital, the empty beaches and untouched forests were also major attractions and they'd heard from other backpackers that Cambodia was not to be missed. Besides, flights were cheap from Bangkok, and they bought a return ticket to Phnom Penh and set off, thrilled that they were now beginning to have the confidence to move more off the beaten track.

Once in Phnom Penh, however, they struck problems. Although they'd been warned about the city's street crime, they were still very much innocents abroad, and easy pickings for a skilled thief. On their second day there, it was with a sick thud in the stomach that they realised their money, travellers' cheques and return air tickets to Bangkok had all been stolen.

They went along to the British Embassy to ask for help, and were told the only assistance the authorities could provide would be to send them back to the UK, and charge them for the full-priced tickets. They advised them instead to report the crime to the police for insurance purposes and then to arrange for their travellers' cheques and tickets to be replaced. The cash, sadly, would be long gone. The easiest place to sort this all out was Bangkok, home to the headquarters of all the major banks, and far more English-speaking people. Another traveller they met lent them the money for a single plane ticket back to Bangkok, and they hastily returned to Thailand to sort themselves out. Shaken by the experience, they briefly considered going home.

'But we've lost all our money and survived,' Peter reasoned. 'It'd be such a shame to give up now when we've already come so far.' They agreed that on the morning of 16 January 2001, they would bid a bitter-sweet farewell to Asia and set off on a flight to Sydney. 'We might as well continue,' said Peter. 'We're over the worst that can happen.'

# CHAPTER SIX

# A Shot in the Dark

THE SHOT RIPPED THROUGH THE flickering darkness, smashing the rear window of Joe Ross's car, tearing through the headrest of the front passenger seat and slamming into the dashboard. Just seconds before, Ross's girlfriend had been sitting in that seat, laughing at something he'd said. But a shout from outside the car had attracted her attention and, leaning forward, she'd seen it was a friend with her newborn baby. She'd wound down her window and was just craning sideways to speak to her when the bullet whistled past, grazing her shoulder, and ripping through the leather rest where her head had just been. She screamed and Ross jumped. At first he'd thought it was a stray firecracker from the bonfire up ahead but, as he sniffed the pungent odour of the gunpowder, he realised it wasn't. 'Get down!' he yelled, pushing his girlfriend towards the floor of the car. 'Someone's shooting at us!'

The pair crouched down as two more bullets whistled past their heads. Ross scrambled from the car and raced to where the revellers were gathered, listening to the band on the old bridge over the dry riverbed at Fitzroy Crossing in WA's remote Kimberley region. He screamed at the people dancing by the bonfire to get down, but no-one could hear him over the music, so he climbed up onto the makeshift stage and shouted at the band to stop, trying to warn them that they were all being used as some lunatic's target practice.

When the lead musician with the Fitzroy Xpress realised it was Ross and understood what he was saying, they all stopped playing, threw down their instruments and leapt from the stage. In the sudden lull, Ross yelled at everyone else to get away from the light of the fire and into the darkness. It was bedlam.

The group had been celebrating the historic second grand final footy win in a row of the local Aboriginal Bunuba Magpies AFL team. It was the middle of winter, 20 August 1995, and the mighty Fitzroy River on whose banks the town lay had dried to a trickle. In the wet, water regularly surged over the old bridge, but in the dry, the river shrank, exposing the sandy riverbed. That winter had been particularly dry, and the 500-strong Aboriginal community had arranged a party to celebrate their grand final game – win or lose. They'd been planning it for days, and everyone in town knew the old bridge and riverbed would be busy that evening, particularly when the news filtered through that the Magpies had won. A bonfire had been lit to provide light, a BBQ was underway, the local band Fitzroy Xpress had been called in to play, and between 200 and 300 people had gathered as the sun went down to toast their team's great victory.

There had only been one puzzling incident earlier that evening. A visiting backpacker had raced down to the gathering, clearly distressed, waving his hands about and shouting in Russian. No-one could understand him, so they merely offered him a drink and gestured to a warm place by the fire. Frustrated he couldn't make himself understood, the backpacker raced back off. No-one thought any more about it at the time, and the party began in earnest soon after.

No celebration, however, would have been complete without Joe Ross, the lanky, good-looking, thirty-four-year-old who was one of the most respected members of the local Bunuba people. With a natural charm, easy-going manner and great mediator skills, he'd successfully bridged the divide between white and black and had won the respect and loyalty of all. On that dark night in 1995, when someone started shooting at his car, Ross kept his head, and his girlfriend, a child protection officer, ducked down in the car, as the shots kept coming. After about ten rounds had been fired, Ross turned the car around to shine the headlights onto the bank where they could see the red flashes of light. As yet another shot tore through the bullbar and into the headlight, Ross dived from the vehicle and shouted to four of the other men to join him to scramble up the bank under cover of darkness. As they reached the crest, they heard the sound of someone blundering away through the bushes, and saw a parked car. Ross recognised it immediately. It belonged to Bradley Murdoch.

BY 1994, MURDOCH'S PASSION FOR guns had landed him in trouble again, with two more firearms offences, and he felt he was ready for a change. While driving trucks, he'd met a couple of people who'd been working at a large cattle station, Brooking Springs, 18 kilometres outside Fitzroy Crossing, 400 kilometres inland from Broome on the far north-west coast of Australia. It was a massive property – just under a million acres with 10,000 head of cattle – and there was a demand for good mechanics and stationhands. Murdoch decided to give it a go. He enjoyed the work, being outside, and spending long hours on his own.

'We employed him as a mechanic and a grader driver, maintaining the station roads between the bores,' says Vera Fielder, the then owner of Brooking Springs with her husband Brian. 'I had no problems with him. I got him to do a few jobs around the house, too. He was pretty handy. He didn't say much.'

When Murdoch did want company, he generally mixed with the other stationhands. He also had a few friends in town but it didn't take him long to realise that Fitzroy Crossing wasn't his kind of place: whites were in the minority, and the Aboriginal community owned many of the businesses. Local Joy Motter, who works at the hospital, says the whites that live there are mostly transient. 'Unless you're into fishing, and more fishing, there's nothing to do here,' she says. 'People move here to experience something different, but most people move on fairly quickly. What he [Bradley Murdoch] did was a pretty awful thing. You don't do that with a crowd of people and kids there.'

Murdoch would go into town at night, drinking with mates, before sleeping at a friend's place, an old shed by a diesel garage at the new bridge built across the river in 1974. Sometimes he'd call into a local pub, the Crossing Inn, which until recently still segregated blacks and whites, despite being owned by the Aboriginal community for years. But Murdoch preferred the more upmarket Fitzroy Lodge, which the Aboriginal community also owns but rarely frequents, perhaps because of the pub's ban on both thongs and bare feet in a ruling that's seen by some to be deliberately aimed at black customers. Indeed, The Lodge has become somewhat of a focal point for strained race relations. In January 2003, after a seventeen-year-old Aboriginal boy fell to his death from the back of a police van, a group of mourners gathered at the Lodge to drink. Someone at the pub panicked at the sight of so many black faces, tried to close the bar and the police waded in. Following that, the Lodge was attacked, resulting in a great deal of damage.

Even in Murdoch's time, it was rumoured that the Lodge was frequented by local whites with Ku Klux Klan connections. No-one said to be involved will confirm or deny the existence of the KKK in the area, but Joe Ross is adamant there were active members. When police stopped a group of whites with KKK hoods on who insisted they were on their way to a fancy dress party, their leniency was roundly criticised. 'By not doing anything to stop them, these people thought they had protection,' says Ross. 'It was almost as if they condoned it. It felt like they were looking after each other rather than looking after issues in the community.'

While no-one can say for sure whether Murdoch had links with those people, he undoubtedly possessed a strong streak of racism against the Aboriginal community. On his left upper arm he had tattooed a picture of an Aboriginal man hanging from a noose by his neck above the flames of a fire, as well as the initials KKK. But, extreme as they were, his attitudes didn't single him out from any number of the people he mixed with in an area known for its casual racism.

'You get sick of all the Aborigine shit,' says one local. 'People in the eastern states, they say we're all equal, but some of us are more equal than others. I'm sick of everyone being told it's our fault. It's ridiculous. The cops can't touch them [Aboriginals]. It's stupid ... I know what those black-loving, do-gooder, politically-orientated people think. All the money the government's giving them, it's phenomenal! But the white person's being run down into the ground.'

Tim Brookner, the publican at the Fitzroy Lodge, says there's certainly racism around, although regarding allegations of KKK membership, he's more circumspect. 'I don't know anything about it,' he says. 'People don't gossip. They keep themselves to themselves. But I think drink and drugs are involved.' Brookner is another newcomer keen to move on. 'I'll do my time here in the next year, then get out. Let's say, the things you see on TV in the cities about black–white relations doesn't bear any relation to life up here. Here, the benefits they can get are incredible. We're the ones who don't get a fair deal. But you give them more money and it seems to keep them quiet.'

Bradley Murdoch certainly shunned the local Aboriginal population. But there was one man he couldn't seem to avoid: Joe Ross.

JOE ROSS'S MOTHER WAS A revered Bunuba Aboriginal leader, and his English father a hardy Liverpudlian orphan shipped to Australia as part of the post-WWII operation to clear out Britain's over-crowded children's homes and help populate the former colony, ironically, with fresh white stock. Despite promises that the 10,000 children were going to loving adoptive homes, only five did. Like most of the boys, Peter Ross, at the age of five, was sent to the Christian Brothers' Boys' Town, Bindoon, 100 kilometres north of Perth, and set to back-breaking work as an unpaid farm labourer from sunrise to sunset. The place later became reknown for its cruelty and, in 1993, responding to a lawsuit, officially apologised to its charges and paid reparations of $2.5 million to some of the children.

Growing up with a father who'd endured such a grim childhood and a mother with a proud Aboriginal heritage, Ross became a fiercely independent and strong-willed young man with a burning sense of natural justice. He was brought up on tales of Jandamarra, a former leader of the Bunuba from the nearby Windjana Gorge, and was fond of re-telling his story, both for the pride he felt for his clan, and as a way of awarding him his rightful place in the panoply of Australian heroes. Jandamarra was a native tracker nicknamed Pigeon and used by the white police force to hunt down local Aboriginals stealing the Europeans' sheep. But in 1894, Jandamarra rebelled, releasing a group of Aboriginal prisoners and permitting them to shoot the police constable holding them. From that point on, he became the country's most notorious outlaw, waging guerilla warfare against the European incursion into the Bunuba's traditional homelands and their bid to take them over for sheep, cattle and mining. Hiding by day in the limestone catacombs around the

Windjana Gorge, he won numerous battles against the ever-increasing number of troopers sent out to find him, until being eventually shot and killed by a black tracker three years later.

To most Aboriginals – and many white Australians today – Jandamarra is considered a hero and is often compared to Ned Kelly. 'He was very much like Geronimo, the North American Indian leader who tried to stop people taking over their country,' says Ross. 'Whether you'd call him a bushranger like Ned Kelly, I don't know, but to us, like Ned Kelly, he's a hero, an Australian hero.' With such a man as his idol, Ross grew up a rebel himself in a town with a black majority, yet with white Australians retaining most of the power and wealth. His parents provided solid examples of independent thinking; his mother presiding over disputes and often achieving consensus by saying very little, and his father one of only three Catholics in town who still managed to convince the bishop to build a church and convent in Fitzroy Crossing.

Sent to boarding school in Darwin as a kid, Joe Ross had emerged educated, confident and with absolutely no time for prejudice. He demanded that he be treated fairly, and usually was. Trained as an electrical fitter and working as a well-paid mines supervisor for BHP, he returned to Fitzroy Crossing in 1993 when his mother fell ill, to set up Bunuba Inc with the community to improve health, education, and job opportunities in an area notorious for its poor literacy, alcohol problems and lack of work. In the two years since he'd been back in town, he'd built the company into a major landowner. His 600-strong group had acquired nearly two million acres of pastoral lease, and successfully ran 10,000 cattle at Leopold Downs. Other Bunuba Inc operations included a Community Development Employment Program, eco-tourism and town-based investments. With every new enterprise, there was always a struggle between those who were keen to maintain their tribal culture in isolation, and those, like Ross, who wanted to play a role in mainstream Australia. Negotiating carefully in his softly-spoken voice, Ross was quickly stepping into his mother's shoes as a leader of his people, and most whites in the town regarded him with admiration and respect.

In such a town, newcomers had a clear choice: either muck in and become a part of the wider community – or stay apart. Whites like Joe Ross's dad, and most of the government workers, mucked in. People like

Bradley Murdoch stayed well apart. 'We tend to get lots of Murdoch's type here,' says Ross. 'They're misfits who're not accepted in their own community. They can come here and go missing, and be left alone. You can be the most racist bastard in the world, but here, nobody gives a shit. Murdoch went around in black leathers pretending to be a member of the Gypsy Jokers. But he was an outcast to them too.' Ross tended to ignore such people. He had enough work on his plate without them. Many of the Aboriginal inhabitants of Fitzroy Crossing had, over the past sixty years, been working on pastoral properties in the rich cattle country out of town, but their wages were extremely low, partly because station managers were paid by the government for their 'maintenance', as Aboriginals were still classed as government dependants. That changed in the late 1960s after the Australian Workers Union took up cudgels on their behalf, demanding equal wages for all. When the Arbitration Commission upheld their bid on 1 December 1968, many station managers refused to pay their Aboriginal workers equal wages, and instead simply forced them off the land that had been their home for generations. They flooded into town, angry, dispossessed and without the skills needed to survive away from the stations. Many of them soon turned to drink.

In addition, there had been recent trouble over claims by Aboriginal people to their native lands. From the time of British settlement, Australian law had considered the land *terra nullius* – literally 'land belonging to no-one' – entitling the British Crown to everything. However, the High Court in its historic 1992 'Mabo' decision, rejected this doctrine and held that Australia's indigenous inhabitants were entitled to a form of native title over their traditional lands. In many parts of the country, particularly in WA, this decision was greeted with horror. The West Australian government acted quickly and passed its own native title legislation before the Commonwealth's Act could be approved, effectively extinguishing native title and challenging the Federal law, and a number of large 'dummy' freehold leases were issued to head off any indigenous title claims. The High Court eventually found against the West Australian government.

The affair increased confusion and bitterness about Aboriginal land claims, and Joe Ross had firsthand experience of this. A little piece of land on the main highway, marked with a red mound, was part of the Aboriginal landholding in the area, but Bradley Murdoch thought he'd develop it for a petrol station. With one of the dummy freehold leases, he'd even borrowed money from the bank to build his new enterprise. When it was pointed out to him that it was Aboriginal land and his lease wasn't worth the paper it was printed on, he was furious.

He was broke again, and he needed someone to blame. His eyes alighted on Joe Ross, the charismatic man two years younger, almost to the day. The contrast was striking: Although physically, they were both tall, lean and strong, Ross was a man taking control of his life, leading his community against the odds to a hopeful new beginning. Murdoch, on the other hand, was becoming increasingly embittered, and believed his entitlements were constantly being snatched away. He focussed all his pent-up rage on to the Aboriginal man who was going from strength to strength in both his career and his personal standing, and who seemed never able to put a foot wrong.

THE COURT CASE, HELD ON 10 November 1995 in Perth, didn't last long. Murdoch pleaded guilty to all charges and admitted receiving stolen guns, having them, loaded, in his possession, while drunk and unlicensed, and being armed in public in such a manner as to cause terror to people. The charges outraged the Aboriginal community, however. They felt attempted murder should have been on the charge sheet. Prosecution lawyer Katherine Hitchins told the court that Murdoch had been drinking all evening at the Fitzroy River Lodge and had been driving home towards the Brooking Spring Cattle Station when he came upon the Aboriginal group celebrating their win at the river crossing. Murdoch claimed they had blocked the crossing and sworn at him, forcing him to drive the alternative route, 5 to 10 kilometres longer, back to the station. There, in an alcohol-fuelled rage, he grabbed two rifles, drove the 18 kilometres back and fired at the group, aiming at the cars. He'd then hidden until the following afternoon. When police mounted a hunt for him, he eventually gave himself up, saying he hadn't intended to shoot anyone, just to frighten them. He claimed he didn't know any particular person there, but was 'fed-up with Aborigines in general'. The two rifles, a .22 Magnum calibre Winchester lever action rifle fitted with a telescopic sight and a .308 calibre bolt action rifle, were both stolen, one during a burglary in Derby.

A report from psychiatrist Ross Smith said that Murdoch was of a 'fairly rigid character structure' while his defence lawyer, Claire Rossi, admitted her client harboured a degree of prejudice towards Aboriginals. She also revealed that, when his long-suffering mother, Nancy, heard about what he'd done, she'd soon after suffered a severe stroke. But the prosecution claimed Murdoch had been involved in the worst-case scenario for an offence of this kind. 'Somebody could have died; several people could have died or been seriously injured,' Hitchins said.

The judge, the Honorable David Charters, ticked off Murdoch for his 'long-standing hatred of Aborigines', told him violence was no way to solve problems, and passed a sentence of fifteen months' prison.

It was only later that Joe Ross bumped into the Russian backpacker. It turned out he'd been drinking with Murdoch the previous night and said he'd been told not to go down to the river after 9 p.m. because it could be dangerous. That evening, seeing the party preparations, the tourist had realised precisely what Murdoch had been talking about, and had tried to warn the Aboriginal community. The attack had evidently been premeditated, and Murdoch was lucky he hadn't faced a charge of attempted murder or murder. 'If I'd have been sitting properly, I could have been killed,' says Ross. 'But the police didn't really push it hard. He was showing off to his mates.'

It was to be Murdoch's first taste of life inside jail, but by no means his last.

# CHAPTER SEVEN

# Sex in the City

SYDNEY: SASSY, SEXY AND ONE of the most exciting cities in the world. For many British backpackers, it's a place of almost constant sunshine, spectacular golden beaches, fabulous nightlife and endless opportunity – whether it be jobs to earn cash, the myriad sights or simply the cheap booze, constant partying and casual sex. It's a beautiful city of four million people set around a spectacular harbour, and for new visitors like Peter Falconio and Joanne Lees, it was mesmerising. After the incessant rain of Britain and the hassles they'd faced in Asia, summer in Sydney was truly a slice of heaven.

There was such a buzz in the air at that time too: January 2001 was a record month in a record year for overseas tourists visiting Australia. A combination of 'The Best Olympic Games Ever', an aggressive marketing campaign by the Australian Tourism Commission, and bargain airfares had made Sydney one of the hottest tickets around. That month, more than 426,000 international tourists arrived, some 18 per cent up on the previous year. And the British had responded to the call even more than most. Joanne and Peter were among 58,200 visitors from the UK in January, 25 per cent more again than in 2000.

The pair checked into one of the numerous hostels that line the tourist precincts but immediately set about looking for somewhere more permanent to live. They planned to stay three to four months in Sydney before travelling around the rest of the country for another three to four, and wanted a good base from which they could work, explore the city and sample all the delicacies on offer. Peter asked around about good places to live and the answer was unequivocal. For backpackers, especially sun-starved travellers from Britain, there was nowhere more seductive than Sydney's landmark Bondi Beach, just a twenty-minute bus ride from the city centre and a million miles from Huddersfield.

On any given day in summer, Bondi glistens with hundreds of well-oiled bodies worshipping the sun, joggers pounding the golden sands, walkers meandering along the promenade, skateboarders flicking somersaults off ramps, bronzed, broad-shouldered lifeguards patrolling the surf and any number of locals and tourists there simply to people-watch. On a good day, sun-seekers arrive with the first rays of the dawn. Later, as the sunset ripens and long shadows of the buildings on the main beachside drag, Campbell Parade, creep across the sand, couples move to the numerous restaurants, bars and cafés along the strip.

Peter and Joanne were entranced from the moment they set eyes on the place and visited the real estate agents just up from the beach. They'd already decided against the eight big backpacker hostels, and they avoided the many dirt-cheap and illegal shared backpacker apartments where as many as twenty would doss on mattresses on the floor. They were travelling cheaply, but not *that* cheaply. They'd come to have a good time, but they needed to live sensibly too. If they were both to find jobs and stay for a period, they'd have to rent somewhere they could come back to and relax. After a few days, they found exactly what they were looking for: a flat share in a small apartment block in North Bondi with a thirty-five-year-old Dutchman and his five-year-old daughter. It was nothing flash, in the middle of a row of similar scruffy, rundown blocks with cars crowding the road outside, but it was affordable and clean, and only a few minutes' walk to the beach.

Peter began calling round the firms he'd heard employed travellers, and was soon in luck, finding work fitting office furniture and equipment for a company called January Design. Joanne took a little longer. She canvassed the shops along the city's main shopping street, George Street, with copies of her résumé, asking for work. One day, she dropped into the Dymocks bookstore by Martin Place. 'I just wondered if you might have any work going for a few months?' Joanne asked the owner, Gary Sullivan. 'Not at the moment,' he smiled back at her apologetically, 'but leave a copy of that here, and I'll keep you in mind in case anything crops up.' As she walked disconsolately up the front steps to the street outside, one of the other workers in the shop caught Sullivan's eye and shook his head. 'Give her a go!' he urged. 'She's a real looker ...'

Joanne phoned every couple of days to check if anything had cropped up and, when finally a vacancy arose in late February, Sullivan relented. 'She was fairly persistent,' he says. 'I don't think she particularly wanted to work in a bookshop but I think someone gave her a bit of encouragement when she rang one time, so she thought she was in with a chance. We get a lot of backpackers coming in here asking for work. On their visa, they can only work for three months at a time in one place, so we seem to be on the circuit. But Joanne worked out well. She was a lovely girl, a nice, fairly innocent kind of girl who, once you'd got to know her, had a very outgoing personality. But generally, she was quiet and soft. Peter came round a couple of times to pick her up, and he seemed a lovely guy too, also very quiet and gentle. He actually came and helped us a couple of nights with our stocktake too. They seemed well-matched. He looked after all the tax and banking for them both.'

Joanne worked hard to fit in. When Sullivan told her he was planning a trip to the UK for the annual bookfair in March, and was going down to Brighton to visit his niece, Joanne insisted he call into the travel agent where she'd worked to say 'hi' to her old boss. In between marvelling that the beach was simply a pile of pebbles and trying to keep warm in the spring temperature of five degrees, he did. For the rest of the bookstore staff, Joanne regularly volunteered to go on coffee runs during working hours to the little stall around the back of the shop. As she grew in confidence, she also took it upon herself to organise staff social nights. 'They'd go and dance and play pool and often drink too much,' says Sullivan. 'They were mostly young girls and they all got on very well so it was a natural thing to do.'

Joanne revelled in her new life, and saw it as the perfect opportunity to reinvent herself. At home, she'd often been seen as shy and retiring; here, she took a deep breath, smiled and spoke to everyone she could, and soon became known as a bit of a live-wire. It was a role she'd never played before, and she loved it. 'She was different to the other travellers who work at the store,' says one of her ex-colleagues, Paul Jones. 'They know they're not going to be there for long, so they don't care much about staff relations.

But Joanne was different. She formed strong friendships with so many people at the shop.' Among them, she became particularly close to another young woman of about the same age, Amanda Wealleans, and together they'd go to St Patrick's Tavern around the corner on King Street on a Friday night, to listen to live music. On Thursday nights, a group of them would go to a pub in Newtown, a more raffishly colourful suburb a few kilometres away filled with second-hand clothing shops, cafés and live music venues. There they'd drink at the noisy, grungy-looking Cooper's Arms, which offered cheap backpacker accommodation and meals and, with a pool table out back, often served as a meeting place for young travellers rather than inner city clubbers. After an evening out there, Joanne would often sleep the night at a friend of a friend's place and go straight to work the next morning. Occasionally, they'd visit a smarter nightclub in Kings Cross, like the popular EP1, hidden away in a backstreet. One memorable night, Joanne was even persuaded to take half an ecstasy tablet there, her first taste of a feelgood drug being used so widely in the city clubs.

With so much excitement, it wasn't long before Joanne suggested to Peter that they stay in Sydney a little longer. 'Sydney had exceeded all my expectations,' she says. 'I fell in love with it straightaway, more so than Pete, I think. I would have happily stayed there longer.' She was having so much fun, she really wanted to delay the rest of their trip by a couple of months. They were in no mad hurry, and besides, she had another reason she wanted to stay on. A secret reason.

AS SOON AS THE COUPLE had seen all the main sights of Sydney, Peter's mind had clicked straight into gear about the next part of their trip. This was the adventure that most interested him: the long drive around the southern coast of Australia, up through its remote centre to Darwin, its most northerly city, and over to Queensland on the north-east coast. His job was going well, but wasn't particularly stimulating, and after five months of being away, the twenty-eight-year-old was getting restless to hit the road. 'He had itchy feet,' says Joanne, now twenty-seven. 'I was really settled in Sydney and I didn't want to leave, but Pete was pushing to go.'

He began scouring the travellers' ads posted up in all the backpacker haunts for a campervan to make the long trip up north. Peter was handy around cars – one of his brothers, Paul, has his own auto electrical business – and he knew exactly what he was looking for: something big enough to allow them to be self-contained, but cheap and reliable. One Saturday morning, he went to the Kings Cross Car Market, a popular sale yard held in an underground car park where travellers are permitted to sell their vehicles. Chatting to the owners lounging on camping chairs or snoozing on the front seats while waiting for buyers, Peter spotted an old orange VW Kombi pop-top van on sale for $3000. It had seen better days but it came complete with a fridge, a fitted gas cooker and sink, a CD player, curtains on the back windows, and a full service history. The owners, a young couple who had just finished their own tour of Australia and were due to fly back to Europe in a few weeks, swore that the van was a beautiful runner, and that they'd had no trouble with it at all. It had recently had a new paint job in bright orange with a white go-faster stripe along the body, and bore Tasmanian plates. It also had 85,000 miles on the clock, but 185,000 could well have been closer to the mark. The couple was keen to sell, but Peter wouldn't be hurried. He took it out for a test drive, then left, saying he'd think about it. He went back the next day and asked if they'd cut their price. He noted that it was due to run out of registration in the middle of July, so he'd have to re-register. By the end of the week, on May 24, he bought the van for $1200.

When Joanne saw it, she wasn't quite as thrilled. They were planning to drive vast distances, and the van's top speed was around 80 kilometres per hour. It could go faster – the speedometer went up to 60 miles, or 96 kilometres, per hour – but the vehicle shuddered and strained so much that it didn't seem safe. The gears were clunky and often hard to find and she worried it might break down in the middle of nowhere. Peter's spirits, however, wouldn't be dampened. 'He loved that old van,' says a friend he met in Sydney, Michael Hardacre. 'He loved everything about it. He couldn't wait to get out into the outback in it. He spent every spare minute tinkering with it.' Peter installed a lamp in the back to read by and a shelf under the dashboard for things like cans of drink, his Ventolin inhaler and his cigarettes. Then he hooked up two spotlights to the rear of the van, and installed a safety deposit box for their documents and money.

Joanne's lack of enthusiasm wasn't based solely on the state of the Kombi. She was having too much of a good time in Sydney to leave just yet, and had made great friends. She, Amanda and another work friend,

Alison, had even earned the nickname 'The Angels' after the TV icons *Charlie's Angels,* because they were always together. In addition, Joanne loved everything about Sydney: the easy lifestyle, the beach and the nightlife. Peter went along with Joanne and her friends a couple of times, but he felt a little left out. Joanne, however, didn't mind all that much that he didn't join them more often.

Because she'd met another man.

HE WAS A BRITISH BACKPACKER called Nick Ellis Reilly who'd been working as an IT specialist at a city firm near the bookstore and who often came to the same stall where Joanne went on her daily coffee runs. It had started innocently enough. Nick was twenty-seven, a Reading University graduate, and had been in Sydney for eight months, mid-way through his trip around the world. He was good-looking with dark hair and eyes, just like Peter, but with more chiselled features. His personality, however, was markedly different. While Peter was earnest and intense, Nick seemed to take nothing seriously. He loved drinking and partying hard with the boys, and finishing off the night with a good-looking girl. Sipping coffee at the stall, he enjoyed bantering with any attractive women who passed by. He could be flirtatious, a real ladies' man but, in truth, he was simply a young lad having the time of his life in a new city on the other side of the world, determined to make the most of every opportunity before going back home, finding a steady job, and re-entering the drudgery of normal life.

He noticed Joanne immediately. With her pale skin now tanned and her glossy dark hair always worn down to brush her shoulders, she looked more beautiful than ever. She was shy at first, and Nick loved to tease her and watch her blush. He was friendly with Tim Ford, one of the staff members at the bookshop, and suggested a group of them go out drinking one Thursday night at a good pub he knew close to the house he shared with a number of other backpackers in Brown Street, Newtown. Joanne went along, and one thing led to another ...

She wasn't proud of what happened, but she couldn't stop herself. She loved Peter, but Nick offered her something quite different. It was the excitement of the forbidden, the danger of the unknown and the thrill of the unexpected, with a man who was hell-bent on having a good time.

Beside Nick, Peter seemed plodding, dependable and all too familiar. Joanne fully expected Peter to propose to her on their way home from Australia via New Zealand, Fiji and Hawaii, and knew she'd say yes without hesitation. But she and Peter had grown up in the same tiny corner of England and knew exactly what each other was thinking, and what their future would undoubtedly hold. Nick, on the other hand, was an unknown quantity, an adventure. For the new Joanne, the outgoing, sociable party girl Joanne, this could well be her last chance to have a fling. She was smitten.

One of the women with whom Nick shared the large Gothic Newtown house said that Joanne certainly wasn't the only woman he brought home, but that he seemed to like her a lot. 'She had become quite important to him,' she said. 'He calmed down considerably. But he was a bit of a dark horse in that he played his cards close to his chest.'

Another of the group who went drinking on a Thursday night noticed how close Joanne and Nick were growing, despite her relationship with Peter, but chose to say nothing. 'I wouldn't say they were all over each other but they certainly seemed comfortable in each other's company, and she always stayed the night in an upstairs bedroom at the front of the house,' he said. 'There were probably four people staying there at any time, so no-one really noticed.' Often the pair would have coffee together the morning after at the Satellite Café on the corner before catching the train into town, and work. At one point, Joanne even briefly considered leaving Peter for Nick, one of her Sydney girlfriends later told the police. The idea was only mentioned once, in an idle 'what if' conversation.

For Nick and Joanne both knew, really, that their relationship was always likely to remain no more than a brief encounter. Nick was due to leave around the end of June for a Contiki tour to the US. Peter too was growing restless and wanted to make tracks. As the deadline for both their departures approached, Joanne and Nick's Thursday nights together grew in intensity.

ON JOANNE'S LAST FRIDAY AT Dymocks, the staff presented her with a going away gift of a pendant and organised a farewell dinner at the Blackbird Café, a funky restaurant with loud music and flamboyant wait staff at Cockle Bay. Employing so many backpackers, Gary Sullivan had been to numerous farewell dinners before. 'We all thought what a great couple they were,' he says, unaware of Joanne's clandestine romance on the side. 'Everyone was sad to see them go.' After the restaurant, some of the group went back to the EP1 nightclub to dance the night away. After Joanne had left, there was a raid by police and sniffer dogs to look for drugs. It was a lucky escape: Joanne, Peter and their friends were by no means innocents in that regard but no-one left there that night had any on them.

Joanne and Nick also managed to fit in a private farewell, and agreed to keep in touch via email in the future. Nick even set up a Hotmail account with the name 'Steph', so that if Peter caught her emailing him, she could say she was contacting a girlfriend. Joanne was torn between the two men. Time with Nick was exciting, although she knew the thrills were heightened by the fear of discovery, not to mention the fact that he liked to play the field. But she also knew Peter represented a more caring, and steady, future. She made the right choice: before she'd even left Sydney, Nick had gone off with another woman to New Zealand.

As Peter and Joanne finally set out from Sydney on the morning of 25 June 2001, their friends urged them to take care. Just a few months before, yet another British tourist, David Eason, had gone missing. He'd gone for a walk on the heritage-listed Fraser Island, the largest sand island in the world just north of Brisbane, and no-one had seen him again. The newspapers were full of the mystery, and revived it again a few weeks later, just before Peter and Joanne's departure, when two of the dingoes running wild on the island killed a nine-year-old boy and savaged his younger brother. The speculation was intense: had David Eason been attacked by those same dingoes; had he faked his own disappearance; had he drowned after swimming in the rough surf; had he just become lost on the way back to the tour bus; or had he met an even more sinister end?

But such dangers couldn't have been further from the couple's minds. They were intent on the journey ahead, travelling west through the Blue Mountains two hours away en route for Canberra, Melbourne and then Adelaide before taking the long road north to Alice Springs and Darwin. Peter was overjoyed finally to be on the road in his beloved Kombi, heading for adventure, while Joanne was quiet, thinking of the adventure she was leaving behind.

# CHAPTER EIGHT

# Fast Cars, Drugs and Guns

SOON AFTER BRADLEY MURDOCH GAINED early release for good behaviour, he turned to a new moneymaking enterprise: drug-running. It seemed a sensible career choice, combining as it did many of his passions – easy money, long-distance driving, guns and, increasingly, drugs. When he stepped back into society in August 1996, he felt better equipped for the job than ever. With West Australian jails holding countless bikie criminals, many of the gangs actively used the institutions for recruitment. Time behind bars is often employed wisely too, to sharpen skills and nurture the necessary contacts for a flourishing outlaw life afterwards. Murdoch was thirty-eight, tall, broad-shouldered and weighed 108 kilograms. With a lantern jaw, high forehead, lips curled into a disdainful sneer, his top front teeth missing and tattoos over his arms and legs, he was an intimidating figure.

'He was a prickly son of a bitch at the best of times,' says one of his old mates, Gary Jones. 'He could get really moody. Then you knew to watch yourself. But when he was in a good mood, he could be all right. You have a few beers with him and a laugh. He could turn his hand to anything and make a fist of it as well. Cars … trucks … Brad was fucking great at fixing anything and making stuff. He was always messing around with his tools. And he knew his way around the place like the back of his hand.'

His years as a truck driver had taught Murdoch everything he'd ever need to know about Australia's highways, byways and backroads. He knew the fastest route from A to B, the best road for heavy loads and just which way you could travel to be sure of not meeting a soul. He knew the seasons you could cross the desert, and precisely when the heavy rains would turn mud roads into treacherous bogs. From his time as a grader driver he was also familiar with all the little-known, unmapped pathways criss-crossing the outback, and which way the drain gullies ran and where even the faintest of tracks would lead you.

For many, the vast wilderness of the Kimberley can seem threatening. To Murdoch, it felt like home. At 423 square kilometres, the Kimberley covers an area about three times the size of England, yet with 1500 times fewer people. Indeed, the Kimberley is one of the most sparsely populated places on earth. In 100 square kilometres of England, there's an average of around 38,000 people. In the same area of the Kimberley, there's an average of about eight. It's a rugged, tough landscape with spectacular gorges, mighty rivers, arid desert areas and, occasionally, thick rainforest. It's home to predatory saltwater crocodiles, white-bellied sea eagles, kangaroos and rough, hard towns reminiscent of the American Wild West. Much of its coastline is so isolated it has yet to be surveyed. It was exactly the kind of remote, untamed place Murdoch liked.

At first, Murdoch set up home in Derby, 250 kilometres north-west of Fitzroy Crossing. With its imposing jetty built high to survive the occasional 11-metre king tides while the area's wool and pearl shell exports are being shipped, it's also the home of the Royal Flying Doctor Service. The place suited Murdoch, at first. The town's so spread out, it appears almost empty, and he enjoyed the lonely, eerie atmosphere of somewhere that feels like it's perpetually waiting for something, anything, to happen. The massive Boab trees with their spindly branches looking more like their roots, and the blood red earth only added to the air of desolation. As a roadtrain driver in a remote area where nearly every necessity has to be trucked in and everything of value – beef, diamonds, uranium, black granite – has to be trucked out, it was easy to find work. Murdoch did some time fixing crab pots, but mostly he took the wheel of heavy trucks, driving for a number of different companies, including the world's biggest single producer of diamonds, the Argyle Diamond Mine, 900 kilometres east of Derby. His prison contacts proved useful as well and he'd already been recruited by a bikie gang to ferry marijuana and speed – the two bikie favourites – around the country as he drove.

It was good work for him. If you can stand the loneliness and cope with the long hours motoring across featureless vast distances, and then put up with temperatures outside the cab soaring over 40 degrees Celsius in the wet season from October to March, it's not bad at all. It helps too if you can sort out the problems if anything goes wrong, and Murdoch was nothing if not handy with a spanner. Better still, out there on the road you're completely your own boss, with no-one standing over you. The toughest part was trying to stay awake for hour after monotonous hour, and keep going without breaks, in order to collect the big wages. Many drivers need a little help with that, and the use of stimulants like speed is so common in the Australian trucking industry that random drug tests are about to be introduced. For those drivers badly affected by long-term amphetamine use, cannabis can be smoked to help them sleep after shifts that can last more than sixteen hours a day.

Murdoch was a regular caller at many of the towns on his route. 'Yeah, I know Brad,' says one drinker in Derby's Spinifex Hotel. 'Top bloke. Staunch. He often had a drink here on his turnarounds. Didn't say much.' Murdoch had a few girlfriends along his route too. One was secretary Lana Powell whose car he'd always fix if she needed a hand. 'He was a gentle giant,' she says. 'He would always come round and see me when he was in town.' Another was a woman called Jodie, with whom he briefly set up house, and later lovers included Beverley Allan and Jan Pittman. He was never short of a girlfriend and, it was rumoured, often had more than one on the go at the same time.

BY EARLY 1998, MURDOCH WAS growing restive again, and decided on yet another change of scene, moving out to the busier Kimberley coastal town of Broome. He hadn't lived in a proper town for years but soon took a liking to Broome's laidback lifestyle and rough, knockabout charm. The tropical climate is kind, the living is easy, and the characters are colourful. It's the kind of place people drift into from all over the world. Nearly everyone is from somewhere else, either escaping from – or looking for – something or someone. No-one asks questions and if they do, they rarely expect to be told the truth. The old pearling town is now fashionable and multicultural, attracting an increasing number of tourists every year to its white beaches, turquoise waters, red sandstone cliffs and exotic history. But scratch the surface, and beneath lies a battlers' town. Real men in blue, sweat-soaked singlets, frayed shorts and workboots eat pies in the bakery and drink in the Roebuck, eyeing the bikini-clad barmaids pouring schooners from a raised platform, all the better to see them when they lean over to hand you your drink. Their women buy cut-price groceries in the big supermarket just outside town, leaving the bijou boutiques, cappuccinos and pearl stores in the centre for the tourists. Families are able to live on much less than in any other major conurbation in Australia, but many still struggle.

An old truck-driving mate of Murdoch's brother Gary, Brett Duthie, had set up a trucking company, West Kimberley Diesel, and Murdoch picked up part-time work. Happily, he was paid in cash, and was also allowed to live in a caravan in the ramshackle yard of the workshop. He moved in around August 1998, with his pet dog, a Boxer. 'He was a great bloke,' says Duthie. 'I have good instincts about people, and I'd always liked him. The only difference between Brad and myself is that I've got a ticket basically. He was casual, depending on the work. It was convenience for myself mainly. If I was too busy, Brad would help.' Murdoch also worked at a couple of other trucking companies in Broome's sprawling industrial area outside the town, Sandfire Transport and Broome Contracting among them. Because he had the stamina for driving long distances, as well as the mechanical know-how, he found he could pick up and drop jobs whenever he liked. 'He had a good reputation as a hard worker,' says Tony Norton, owner of Sandfire Transport. 'He didn't mess about on a job. You wanted workers like that.'

Murdoch would work for a while for one or other of the companies around town, then disappear for weeks at a time. He rarely explained where he'd been or what he'd done during those long absences, and no-one wanted to ask. 'He didn't work on a continuous basis,' says Edward Egerton-Warburton, who worked alongside Murdoch as a mechanic for his brother-in-law, Duthie. 'Several times he left to go away or work elsewhere and then would come back and work for a little while.' Even his girlfriends were unsure where he went. 'At times I knew he'd be going away on a trip because he told me,' says Beverley Allan, at the time thirty-

*bove*: Peter Falconio and Joanne Lees at his graduation ceremony in Brighton in 2000.
(*Newspix/News Ltd*)

*elow*: Peter's quiet green village of Hepworth, nestling in the hills of the West Yorkshire
ɔuntryside. (*Sue Williams*)

*Above*: Nick Reilly, the fellow backpacker with whom Joanne had an affair in Sydney. She says they remained friends afterwards. *(Fairfa.*

*Below*: Joanne with her friend Amanda Wealleans at her farewell party at Dymocks booksellers in Sydney before leaving on her ill-fated trip around Australia.

*(Friends of Joanne Lee*

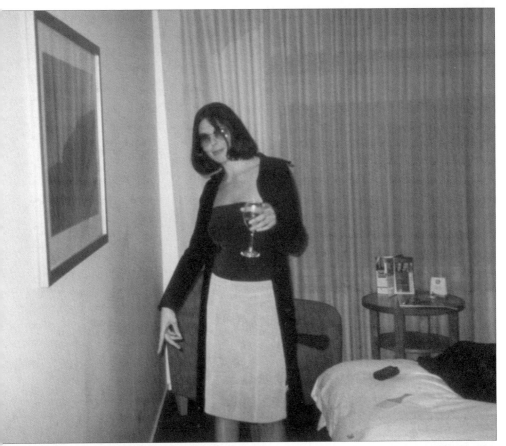

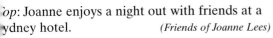
*Top:* Joanne enjoys a night out with friends at a Sydney hotel.   *(Friends of Joanne Lees)*

*Middle left:* Joanne and Peter in the earlier days of their dream trip around the world.
   *(Newspix/News Ltd)*

*Middle right:* Peter on top of the world at the Blue Mountains.

*Right:* Peter in the red heart of Australia.

*Above*: Joanne and Peter's beloved Kombi. Peter spent many evenings fixing it up for th
couple's trip around Australia.

*(NT Police*

*Below*: A self-portrait in the Kombi – full of excitement about the adventure that
lay ahead.

*(Newspix/News Ltd*

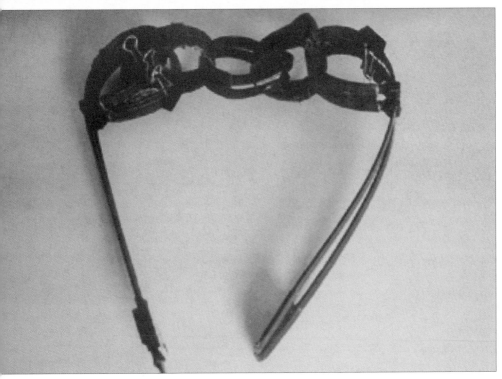

*above*: The lonely outback road north of Barrow Creek where Peter was lured out of the vehicle, never to be seen again. *(Sue Williams)*

*below*: The electrical cable ties skilfully knotted together to form homemade handcuffs from which Joanne struggled so hard to escape. *(NT Police)*

*Above*: The Bull's Transport road train, driven by Vince Millar, which carried Joanne to safety.

*(NT Police*

*Below*: Les Pilton, the owner of the Barrow Creek Roadhouse, pictured behind his 'colourful' bar – and the unlikely refuge for Joanne.

*(Sue William*

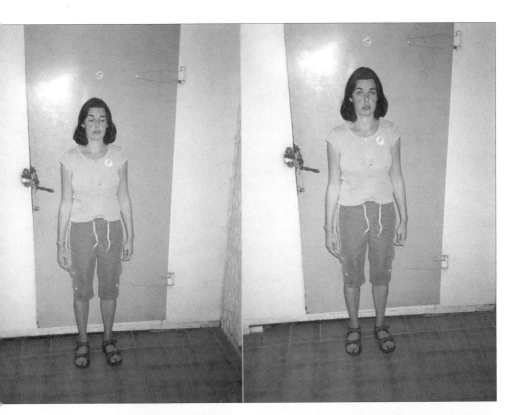

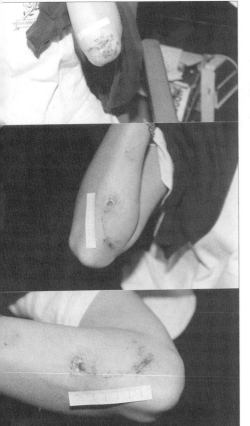

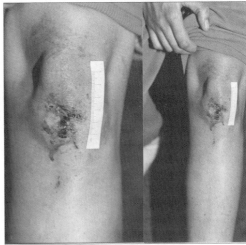

*Top*: A distraught and devastated Joanne, photographed by police at the Barrow Creek Roadhouse shortly after the attack. Her blue T-shirt is marked with the blood of another man.

*(NT Police)*

*Below*: Joanne's injuries to her elbows and knees, sustained in her fight with her attacker and subsequent escape, recorded by police at Barrow Creek.

*(NT Police)*

*Above*: The mystery white 4WD ute pictured in the Shell Truckstop video.

*(NT Police*

*Below left*: The shadowy figure in the grainy Shell Truckstop video. Was it Bradley Murdoch?

*(NT Police*

*Below right*: Famed Aboriginal tracker Teddy Egan crouches down to examine the area stained by Peter's blood, and marked by police.

*(Sue William*

eight, who worked at Broome Diesel and Hydraulics Service where Murdoch was an occasional customer. The pair had started going out in October 2000. 'He'd be gone sometimes for a week at a time, sometimes up to three weeks. I [only] knew where he was going a few of the times.'

When Murdoch did stay in Broome and work, however, he was constantly fiddling with his own vehicles. He changed the configuration and the style of them often, but never seemed to be satisfied with any of them. 'He always seemed to be working on his own vehicles,' says Egerton-Warburton. 'He was always tinkering. That would be his hobby: maintaining and working on his vehicles.' For his personal use, he favoured Toyota Landcruisers as they were rugged enough for every kind of terrain, powerful enough to be driven long distances at speed, and spacious enough to carry all manner of goods and equipment. You could even live in them if you ever needed to. Murdoch enjoyed adding extra features, taking away others and adapting his vehicles to every kind of job. At one stage, he installed oversized fuel tanks capable of carrying an extra 200 litres of diesel, which would enable him to drive more than 1800 kilometres without refuelling. And at another, he'd change the open back tray, or mix and match his vehicles, buying old cars and newer secondhand vehicles, and cannibalising parts and sections. He'd tell anyone who asked that it was just an interest, but the police would say later it was for a far more sinister purpose. For those long, unexplained absences, he'd designed a series of vehicles that were perfect for transporting large quantities of drugs around the country, they would claim, and he changed the look of the vehicles frequently so people wouldn't start recognising one single car, and becoming suspicious.

LIFE WAS GOING WELL, BUT Murdoch decided the caravan wasn't the ideal base for his activities, and he rented a unit near the corner of Forrest Street and Guy Street, 2 kilometres from the heart of town. It was nice and private, in a little double-rowed complex protected by thickets of brilliant bougainvillea and gum trees. It was convenient too. Close by was Fong's Store, a mini-mart that sold almost everything, and Murdoch quickly befriended the owners.

'He used to come here for a yack,' says Graham Fong. 'He was a nice bloke.' His wife Meg agrees. 'He was moody at first, then when you got to know him, he was all right. We don't live in each other's pockets here, you know? People don't like to know each other's business. We all keep separate. But I make everyone talk to me. No-one gets away.'

Two blocks away through the soft orange dust was Murdoch's favourite drinking hole, the Beer and Satay Hut at the Palms Resort on Hopton Street. Just by the little swimming pool along from the blocks of low-priced rooms is the outdoor bar beneath a novelty thatched roof, covered with corrugated iron to protect it from the storms, with stools or white plastic tables and chairs for the more discerning drinkers. Beyond is a pool table with the pool competition results chalked up on a board, and the small barbecue hut that gives the place its name, serving hearty steaks, pumpkin, peas and chips. Marge, who's been cooking there for years, says Murdoch was a regular.

'He used to come and sit at the bar,' she says. 'I used to say hello as he was there so often. But he never used to talk. It was mostly locals drinking there, especially in the off season. It's the people who live nearby who like it most, so they can stagger home afterwards. A lot of them come at 5 p.m. for Happy Hour, go home for a shower, then come back again for the rest of the evening. For a lot of them, it's every night, too.'

Even when relaxing, Murdoch didn't like leaving his guns behind – by this stage, a Magnum 357 handgun and a .22 revolver. At home, he'd hide them under the bed in the spare room or tape them with heavy masking tape to the underside of the kitchen table. When he was driving, he'd stash them in a hidden compartment of the side panel on the driver's side door, or tuck them down beside the seat. But generally he much preferred to keep one on him at all times, tucked into a leather shoulder holster that he could wear beneath his shirt, so the gun sat hidden under the left armpit. At times, he exuded an air of quiet menace; at others he looked comparatively harmless among some of the other characters who frequented the bar. It wasn't long before he started talking to one of them, a gruff, dark-skinned, broad-shouldered Maori called James Hepi.

Nine years younger than Murdoch, Hepi was a muscular labourer who'd drifted into Broome in 1998 to work as a pearl diver. The work was extremely hard, however, and Hepi had quickly moved on to other things. He drove taxis for a few years and took on grass-cutting contracts. He'd also bought a cheap property in South Australia, a rundown house on an isolated 75-acre back block of the Riverland, deep in the mallee country at Sedan. He was a well-known figure around Broome, a casual knockabout kind of guy, thickset with unruly black hair and a deep, husky growl, who'd do pretty much any little job for cash. The pair got on well and, after a while, Hepi moved into Murdoch's unit to share the place with him. They also took a trip to SA to view Hepi's property. The mallee attracts few visitors, with its long stretches of uninhabited country, broken up with fields of barley, durum wheat and lucern. The only real plant to thrive there these days is the spindly, squat tree-like eucalyptus shrub that gives the area its name. In earlier times, the soil was rich and dark, and vast tracts of fertile farmland were owned by single families, passing them down proudly through the generations. But with the fall in produce prices and successive harsh droughts, many of the older families abandoned the area and subdivided their plots. As a result, nowadays it attracts a different sort of settler. Land is cheap and housing even cheaper, with 80-acre blocks of land sold for as little as $16,000, two-bedroom stone-built homes on sizeable acreages for a bargain $73,000, and nothing much to do but shoot animals, camp, fish and hide out. 'Too many ferals these days,' publican David Pearce remarks as he stands behind the bar of the Sedan Hotel. 'They've moved in because the places are dirt cheap. The blocks are all remote and hidden away, and the police don't bother with them, so they grow drugs. You never know what goes on around here. Often, you don't want to know.'

Hepi had bought his secluded property in 1998 for $34,000, and divided his time between Sedan and Broome. In Sedan, he'd established a business sourcing cannabis and amphetamines, parcelling them up with the help of an older male friend, and then driving them to Broome to sell. In around 1999, when Hepi returned to New Zealand to see family, he invited Murdoch to join him. He also introduced him to his friend who, together with his wife and young daughter, seemed to warm instantly to Murdoch. On one visit, the wife even gave him a puppy to replace his late, beloved Boxer. It was a Dalmatian cross, which he named Jack.

From that time on, Murdoch and Hepi took turns to make the 4300-kilometre run from Sedan to Broome. They'd get organised in Hepi's shed, load crates for their cargo and a spare fuel tank into Murdoch's ute, then lay plywood sheets, carpet and a mattress over the top. While that made the back sit slightly higher than the tray sides, it was level so it was fine if either of them needed to unfurl a swag. Murdoch would stock up with food and drink, usually beer and iced coffee which was kind to a gnawing hiatus hernia, and fill his extra tanks with diesel. They'd use one of several mobile phones they had to coordinate their activities, and then usually throw it away to avoid being traced. Then they'd head north past the vast inhospitable Simpson Desert, and take a left across the Tanami Track, the long, mostly dirt road that's a monotonous 1050-kilometre short-cut through the Tanami Desert to Halls Creek in the far north-west. The advantage of this route was that there were never any troublesome inspections aimed at stopping the dangerous pest, the fruit fly, from being spread. They'd then continue through the northern rim of the Great Sandy Desert, and back again. Turnaround time for the 8600-kilometre return trip would be about a week. It was a lucrative business: half a kilogram (a pound) of good cannabis could be bought from local hydroponic growers in SA for around $2700 and on-sold in WA for between $15,000 and $20,000.

For those long drives, Murdoch even had a special cushion made for his new pup, Jack, who by now was accompanying him everywhere. Often he also took a cat he'd adopted in Broome too. 'The dog was a bit loopy as pups are till they're two, but he was faithful,' says a close mate of 15 years, Peter Jamieson. 'It just liked to run.' Which meant Murdoch sometimes couldn't let the dog out of the cab unless he knew he'd be able to catch him again, something that would occasionally prove a real problem.

# CHAPTER NINE

# The City of Corpses

TO LOCALS, ADELAIDE IS KNOWN as the City of Churches. Others know the genteel capital of SA by a more sinister title: the City of Corpses. For while Adelaide did indeed once have more churches per capita than any other Australian city, it also lays claim to the grisly record of having been home to far more bizarre mass murders than any other. Author Salman Rushdie once visited Adelaide in the 1980s and described it as a perfect setting for a Stephen King novel or horror movie. Hearing of the gruesome toll of serial killings, bodies found horrifically mutilated and the mysterious disappearance of young children, he said ominously, 'Sleepy conservative towns are where those things happen.'

Adelaide's macabre subtext is not, however, immediately apparent to casual visitors. Arriving in Adelaide after the long drive from Canberra and Melbourne, both Peter Falconio and Joanne Lees felt their spirits soar as they rattled over the green Mount Lofty Ranges to the east of the city, and then through the leafy parklands that ring it. The day was sunny and warm, and Adelaide sparkled as Joanne pored over the map. After the chaotic sprawl of Sydney, and the complex tangle of motorways on the approach to Melbourne, Adelaide came as a pleasant surprise. The town centre is a compact, well-planned grid, criss-crossed by a series of wide, tree-lined boulevards which makes it easy to navigate and very beautiful. In stark contrast to the bigger cities, it also has a mellow, laidback pace, coupled with an easy-going liberalism residents claim dates back to the days when it was the only Australian city to be founded by free settlers.

South Australia, after all, was the first to give women the vote and the first to decriminalise homosexuality under the flamboyant, pink-shorted Premier Don Dunstan in 1975.

Locals are proud of its cosmopolitan air, and are astounded that the city of just over a million people isn't able to attract as many visitors as it so obviously deserves. It has countless attractions: excellent restaurants of every ethnicity; the sprawling undercover food market on Rundle Street; and even free buses around the city centre. Close by are the pine-fringed beachfront at Glenelg, and the picturesque wineries of the Barossa Valley, responsible for a quarter of Australia's total wine production, as well as the Adelaide Hills. In addition, SA is known as 'The Festival State', and Adelaide prides itself on the 500-odd festivals it holds every year, ranging from international arts and theatrical festivals to small regional events.

Outsiders, however, are under no illusion why visitors, particularly from overseas, so frequently ignore Adelaide. For a start, it feels in the middle of nowhere, jutting up against the sea to its west and with its northern outer suburbs petering out into the great featureless central deserts. Then there's the climate: filthy hot and buzzing with flies and mosquitoes in summer, and temperatures that dip towards freezing in winter. And, finally, all those chilling crimes ...

THE JURY'S OUT ON JUST why Adelaide has been the scene of so many gruesome events. South Australian police chiefs claim it's mere coincidence, and allegations that their state is the murder capital of Australia and according to one notable later British documentary, *of the world*, are way off the mark. But by the same token, it's true that the sheer scale of some of those crimes in Adelaide monster those of elsewhere. Backpacker visitors, in particular, love to dwell on the city's morbid history. 'We like to frighten each other with scary stories about life – and death – here,' says Bridie O'Loughlin, an Irish backpacker working casual shifts in one of the city's hostels. 'It makes us all feel braver. It's part of the experience of crossing Australia. It's a rite of passage.' Peter and Joanne were no exception. Like many tourists, they weren't spending long in Adelaide, just time enough for a quick sprint around the main sights. Staying a night in the Windsor Gardens Caravan Park on the eastern outskirts of the city, they also picked up another six months worth of registration for the Kombi, with new South Australian plates, W01 597. The long road north was their focus, their first venture into the vast sunburnt outback they'd heard so much about. To two young Britons, raised in small green villages outside Huddersfield, the outback was a new experience, a taste of the *real* Australia, a glimpse of the unfathomable vastness of the continent, and an adventure in the truest sense of the word.

But the horror stories nagged. Dropping into the seaside suburb of Glenelg for a stroll along the sandy beach, for instance, it was hard to dismiss thoughts of the mystery that has plagued Australia since 1966, the abduction of the three Beaumont children, Jane, nine, Arnna, seven, and four-year-old Grant. They failed to return from a lone Australia Day outing with Jane in charge, and the biggest search ever mounted in Australia found nothing. Five years later, just south of Adelaide, a man went berserk and shot dead ten of his relatives, including his wife, their new baby and seven of their other children. The Bartholomew murders were, at the time, SA's worst. Two years on, another two children, Joanne Ratcliffe, eleven, and Kirsty Gordon, four, disappeared from the Adelaide Oval while watching a football match and, in a case that brought painful memories flooding back of the Beaumont siblings, they were never seen again.

But there was worse to come. In the Truro area, which Peter and Joanne drove through for a flying visit to Adelaide's stunningly beautiful wine-producing district of the Barossa Valley, Australia's deadliest pair of serial killers were once active. The bodies of seven young women, aged between fifteen and twenty-six, were variously found shot and stabbed to death over seven weeks from December 1976. James Miller was later sentenced to life imprisonment while his accomplice and lover, Christopher Worrell, was killed in a car accident two days after the pair's last victim disappeared. Even as that case was winding up, however, another series of murders was alarming the authorities. In what were to become known as 'The Family Murders' in the four years from 1979, five males, one aged just fourteen, were abducted, held prisoner, drugged, sexually assaulted, horrifically mutilated and murdered. Their bodies were all found, one diced in garbage bags, on the outskirts of Adelaide. Local accountant Bevan Spencer von Einem was convicted of the murder of one fifteen-year-old and charged with the murders of two other teenagers, but the charges were dropped by the Director of Public Prosecutions when vital evidence was ruled inadmissible. He was jailed for thirty-six years.

PETER AND JOANNE HAD BEEN looking forward to their trip to the wine-producing Barossa Valley and they set out early the next day. It was the beginning of July 2001 and the middle of winter, and the mornings were chill with a light frost snapping on the grass as they walked over the verge to their Kombi which was parked by the main road. Joanne pulled her fleece tighter around her. As soon as the sun came up, she knew it would be warmer, but she was still keenly anticipating heading north into the stronger sunshine. This would be the pair's last sightseeing side trip before taking the long highway to the Northern Territory and, although they were impatient to begin their epic journey, they knew it could be many years before they returned to Australia and they were determined not to miss a thing.

The B10 road northeast towards the Barossa drilled a straight line through flat, featureless suburbs of single-storey homes with pretty wooden verandahs, charcoal chicken outlets and churches imploring their congregations on giant billboards to 'Come To God!' Just to the north was Elizabeth, a 1950s township built primarily for the 'ten-pound Poms', the Britons offered cheap fares to migrate to Australia. Plagued with social problems, just like many of Britain's New Towns, Elizabeth is nevertheless notable for producing members of three of Australia's most famous bands – AC/DC, Men At Work and Cold Chisel.

As the housing estates petered out, the Torrens Valley slowly unfolded, the rolling hills a brilliant emerald green, dotted with grey ghost gums, creeks snaking through their folds and the odd lone farm building glowing in honeyed sandstone. The Kombi rattled through villages selling antiques, and past front gardens fiercely pruned, stripped of all native vegetation and planted with roses and peonies in order to look like English country gardens. An elderly man cutting back his hedge with shears stopped to wave, and the pair laughed at the signs advertising 'Pony Poo $2 a kilo', and the sight of llamas amid the cows and sheep on the hillsides. At the picturesque Barossa town of Angaston, its avenues lined with huge fig trees, there is a crossroads, and Peter and Joanne debated briefly which way to turn. To their left, lay the main road north towards Alice Springs and Darwin; to their right, the more irregular, lumbering hills and rougher stony outcrops of the desolate mallee country off towards Sedan and Swan Reach.

They agreed they'd had enough of the Barossa, and decided to turn left. If they'd turned right, they might have driven through increasingly bleak and inhospitable countryside, out to Sedan. There they might even have passed Bradley Murdoch en route to or from his southern hideaway on a drug deal and waved innocently to him as their vehicles passed. But their wave may not have been returned – Murdoch had as little time for tourists as he had for blackfellas. And the long road trips and the uppers and downers that fuelled them were starting to play tricks with his mind.

# CHAPTER TEN

# The Perfect Gentleman

SHE WAS PRETTY, SHE WAS twenty-two and she was driving the 2700 kilometres from Perth to Adelaide alone when she encountered Bradley Murdoch. It was a dark night on Tuesday 19 June 2001, and as the young woman's Suzuki Vitara was overtaken by a white traytop Toyota Landcruiser, she waved, then tucked in behind to follow the light its large spotlights were throwing on the dark road ahead. By that time, the softly-spoken brunette had drunk a couple of six-packs of beer, and was feeling sociable. When she stopped for petrol at the start of the Nullarbor desert, near Caiguna, 350 kilometres before the WA–SA border, and found the other driver had also pulled up, she suggested they do the rest of the journey together. He readily agreed, and they introduced themselves.

Murdoch was now sporting a grey Mexican-style moustache that came down over the sides of his mouth, and he suggested they meet up at the next truck stop for a beer. They were both on one of longest, straightest stretches of road in the world, and while following someone else's tail lights at night might be boring, it was still better than driving alone in a place where the greatest hazards come from kangaroos, wallabies and feral camels, or worse, other drivers falling asleep at the wheel. The woman, Julie McPhail was tall and slim with long hair curling down past her shoulders, framing an attractive heart-shaped face. She seemed sweet and innocent, but in fact was worldly beyond her years. She had been working as a barmaid in a bikies club in Broome run by the infamous Coffin Cheaters gang and she and Murdoch knew many of the same people. They also both liked to drink and take drugs as they drove.

BUSINESS HAD BEEN GOING WELL and Bradley Murdoch was feeling happy and relaxed. He didn't mind the long journeys of his business with James Hepi, and loved to feel the power of his well-equipped vehicle beneath him. His friend and part-time employer Brett Duthie knew it too. 'Basically, Brad's car or vehicle was his home, he had everything in it,' he says. 'If he was required to go camping for work, he had everything on him.' He even had a pair of clippers, so he could cut his own hair and moustache when necessary. Occasionally, though, company on the road was welcome. Once, he'd taken his friend Darryl 'Dags' Cragan along for the ride, an old childhood friend from Northampton who'd been badly burnt as a kid when he fell in a fire, and who sometimes had trouble finding work. Cragan regularly helped out with odd jobs, but Murdoch sacked him in Broome in September 2000 when they argued about Cragan's habit of injecting himself with speed. Murdoch gave him $3000 and told him to get out. A more regular travelling companion was Brian 'The Sheriff' Johnston who says he was recruited to help through an ad in the newspaper. Johnston did three trips with him, and helped him out with various tasks, including buying a red fire extinguisher and fixing it onto the back post of his Landcruiser by the passenger seat with cable ties. Johnston knew Murdoch carried a .38 revolver in his ute, inside a panel in the driver's door, but it didn't seem to bother him; he'd stayed at the Broome flat for a couple of months and said he'd seen James Hepi playing with Murdoch's Magnum 357 in the lounge. Johnston also knew Murdoch bought a prepaid sim card in Adelaide for his mobile phone so he wouldn't have a phone bill in his name, but he was still surprised to see Murdoch take it out of the phone on long trips. 'He reckoned you could track a mobile if it had a sim card in it,' says Johnston. The long-term use of amphetamines, of course, is known to make people paranoid.

Another time, Hepi's girlfriend, Rachel Maxwell, accompanied Murdoch on one of his trips. She liked him. 'He talked slow, not dumb slow, but like he was thinking,' she says. His ute was comfortable too.

He and Hepi had fixed up a hose for a shower with cable ties and black tape. One day at their place, she walked in to see Murdoch and Hepi at the table with a gun with a wooden handle and a silver barrel. 'Like an old gun,' she says 'that John Wayne would have used.'

IN LATE JUNE 2001, MURDOCH had been driving on his own, however, so he welcomed the chance to pull in to have a drink and a chat with the woman who'd been driving behind him. On one stop, he even gave McPhail a line of speed and may have given her a joint – she can't quite remember – before the pair set off again. At each of their stops, they'd drink more beer, do another line of speed, sometimes some cannabis, and chat for a while longer. When they took to the road, she was careful to ride behind him and not beside him on the double-lane highway. That would have been dangerous, she would later blithely tell a court in Darwin, apparently not realising that drinking vast quantities of alcohol, consuming speed and smoking cannabis might also be viewed by some as more than a little hazardous when driving long distances. At one point, McPhail mentioned she needed a rest. Murdoch recommended they stop for a few hours at the Head of Bight, 200 kilometres past the border along the 65-metre high Bunda Cliffs, a popular whale-watching spot. When they arrived, they parked their cars together to provide room between to sleep. She unrolled her swag and laid it out on a flat rock; Murdoch went to sleep on the mattress in the back of his ute, his dog Jack by his side.

Just before dawn, McPhail was woken by Murdoch offering her coffee, and the pair soon set off again. They stopped at a roadhouse for a shower but, far more often, they stopped to drink and take more drugs. When the woman stopped to withdraw $180 and check her bank balance at Ceduna, on the shores of Murat Bay and the first sign of civilisation since the long drive across the Nullarbor, Murdoch waited for her further up the road. Earlier, she'd remarked that she was on the lookout for a small ladies' revolver, a nice one, preferably with a mother-of-pearl handle. Now, Murdoch took a small revolver out of his car and asked if she'd be interested in buying it. He also offered to let her fire it. His behaviour was impeccable: he'd given her beer, cannabis, speed and now a gun. 'He was a complete gentleman,' McPhail says today without a trace of irony.

Nevertheless, she declined to try out the gun and, instead, Murdoch fired a round of bullets into the bush.

MURDOCH WAS, OF COURSE, A dab hand with guns, having been fascinated with them since those childhood rabbiting expeditions. Now, he had at least two besides the one he'd brought out to show the woman. James Hepi says Murdoch owned a big revolver, a Magnum 357, as well as a lighter, smaller revolver, a .22. Hepi had fired the 357 on a fishing trip up at the Fitzroy River, and the .22 on his block at Sedan, shooting at cans arranged on a fence. Murdoch usually wore a gun in his dark-coloured, leather body holster, or kept one in his car.

His demonstration of one of his guns on the lonely highway, however, spooked McPhail and she began feeling uneasy. 'I didn't feel very comfortable there at all,' she says. 'I kind of wanted to get back in my car. We parted ways at Port Augusta … He told me he was heading off to the Riverland. I said, "If you come into Adelaide, give me a call." I gave him my number.'

She did, however, leave him with another parting shot. 'If you go back through the centre, you must stop at Barrow Creek. I spent some time there and know the publican there, Les Pilton.' She told him it was a great place.

He looked at her thoughtfully. 'I might do that,' he replied.

# CHAPTER ELEVEN

# The Long Road North

WHEN PETER FALCONIO AND JOANNE LEES finally hit the long road north, they breathed sighs of relief. They were on the last leg of their long journey around Australia, with perhaps its greatest wonders just over the horizon. The 3000 kilometre Stuart Highway was, up until 1980, mainly a dirt surface which could be washed away by the heavy rains that struck at certain times of the year. Today, it's a sealed two-lane highway stretching from Adelaide to Darwin. Named after the Scot John McDouall Stuart, who was the first person to cross the continent from north to south in the early 1860s in preparation for the Overland Telegraph Line, the road passes through Alice Springs and the sacred Aboriginal site of Uluru, or Ayers Rock. At its start, it heads north between Gulf St Vincent and Spencer Gulf and, just 142 kilometres out of Adelaide, swerves past the pretty little town of Snowtown nestling in the flat farmland, with its wide roads, neat stores, chocolate-box houses and population of just 520. It had always been considered a peaceful rural backwater but, at the time that Peter and Joanne passed through, it had become the centre of intense worldwide interest.

In May 1999, police investigating a routine missing persons case had forced their way into the disused local branch of the State Bank of SA, an unassuming single-storey redbrick building on the main street, and found six barrels behind the thick steel doors of the vault containing hydrochloric acid and human body parts, including fifteen feet from eight different people. Further searches closer to Adelaide unearthed three more victims.

Subsequently, four men were arrested and, during their 'bodies-in-a-barrel' trials, police alleged John Bunting and Robert Wagner had launched a cold-blooded campaign to kill suspected homosexuals and paedophiles, cutting their bodies into pieces and keeping them as rotting trophies. 'The stench was unbearable,' said Detective Steve McCoy, one of the chief witnesses in the trial. 'It was putrid. It permeated your hair, clothing, everything. It was horrific.' Bunting was found guilty of eleven murders and Wagner seven, making them the worst serial killers in Australia's history.

From Snowtown, the road passes through Port Pirie and its lead smelter, and then past the oceans of dusty green spinifex up to the large sprawling port city of Port Augusta. To the east, the great granite folds of the Flinders Ranges tower up from the flat plains and to the west, dry salt lakes sprawl and the long, long road across the Nullarbor starts its journey to WA, while north lie the great scrubby plains of the desert. Many travellers use the town, particularly the giant Woolworths supermarket at its centre, to stock up before the long drives north or west. Bradley Murdoch knew it well.

Peter and Joanne, however, were eager to push on. The Kombi seemed slow and lumbering against the vast distances between the places of interest along the road. To kill time, they played music and chatted. Peter smoked as he drove, and both drank Coke to keep alert. It was all too easy, particularly when driving into the sun, feeling warm and drowsy with the rhythm of the never-ending road, to let your eyes close.

THE NEXT BIG AREA, WOOMERA, was a familiar name to anyone who'd spent any time in Australia. Britain had needed a large remote area to test new weapons systems after World War II, and had chosen the vast empty spaces out from Woomera, in conjunction with Australia, to use as a rocket range and missile testing program during the 1950s, 1960s and 1970s. Further to the west lies Maralinga, the sacred lands of the Tjarutja Aboriginal people which were confiscated by the British Government, again with the support of Australia, to carry out nuclear testing between 1952 and 1963. A number of military personnel there were used in callous radiation experiments to test the effects of fall-out, and many of the Aboriginal people who remained in the testing range, unaware of the risks, were badly affected.

But at the time Peter and Joanne passed through, Woomera was better known as the home of the most notorious, and largest, detention camp for asylum-seekers in Australia. In stark contrast with the pleasant green town itself, the camp on its outskirts was desolate. Surrounded by double steel fences with two layers of razor wire, it had been the site of riots, hunger strikes, suicide attempts and escapes since its opening in 1999. Asylum-seekers from Iraq and Afghanistan, most of whom were declared by Amnesty International to be genuine refugees, were housed in old military barracks with few facilities and minimal access to legal representation. Protests included inmates sewing their own lips together as a symbol of how they felt ignored, and unheard, by the outside world.

It wasn't a nice place at all, and Peter and Joanne continued quickly north, stopping off at the odd town along the way to buy provisions and mostly sleeping in the Kombi at night. Occasionally they'd go to a proper campground where they could get a good shower and mains electricity and would then either cook at the van, or find somewhere to eat nearby. There were long periods of nothing between stops, and they'd take turns to lie in the back and read. Often they'd discover that they'd driven through places marked on the map, before realising that a few broken-down old cars parked on wasteground and a huddle of houses with corrugated metal roofs and fences were actually called towns.

COOBER PEDY, 848 KILOMETRES NORTH of Adelaide, was yet another shock. A well-known centre for opal mining, the pair expected an established town with the usual range of facilities. Instead, it turned out to be in the middle of some of the most desolate and harsh countryside they'd ever seen and, with all the piles of grey dusty diggings from each of the thousands of little mines standing in peaks forlornly beside them, it looked like some kind of bizarre moonscape. There were warning signs everywhere telling visitors to be wary of uncovered mineshafts – many with tunnels as deep as 30 metres – where it's rumoured that numerous bodies lie at the bottom of long-forgotten shafts as a result of the fierce competition between miners over their opal finds. And when people go missing there, the alarm is rarely raised. In fact, the whole place is populated by 'missing persons', people taking time out from regular lives to buy a share in a cheap, partly exhausted mine, and then spending their days and most of their nights digging, hoping for that elusive pocket of cloudy colour that could make their fortune.

The Aboriginal phrase 'Coober Pedy' means, literally, 'whitefella's hole in the ground', an apt description since many of the locals live in underground homes which offer them some protection from the searing summer heat and the freezing winter nights. There is little vegetation in the area and most supplies, including water, have to be trucked into the town. There's rusting machinery and old sheets of corrugated iron lying everywhere, dogs howl late into the night, and bored local hoons roar around town in the evenings in their utes, with heavy rock music at full volume, kicking up clouds of dust in their wake. The police station has been bombed twice since 1987, the courthouse once and the area's most successful restaurant was taken out by a blast, while two police cars were also blown up. Dining out inevitably involves large amounts of reheated frozen food and bars sell vast oceans of beer. Like many visitors, Peter and Joanne weren't at all surprised to learn the area was used to portray the post-Apocalypse world of the Mel Gibson movie *Mad Max III*.

Yet the 2700 locals, drawn from some forty different nationalities, are friendly to outsiders and most visitors find a visit to the town an unforgettable experience. 'The nuisance is that you're not allowed to dig for opal in the town, only outside,' says one old-timer. 'But you are allowed to make renovations to underground homes, so what's the difference? If you happen to find opal while you're doing it, who's going to take it away from you?'

Peter and Joanne stayed at the Backpackers' Inn at Radeker's Downunder Motel, in an underground double room with shared facilities and did the usual round of museums, mines and opal shops. They were both stunned that humanity could thrive in such a grey, barren place that felt so much like the ends of the earth. Physically and psychologically, it couldn't be further from the tame green hills and valleys of Huddersfield.

AFTER A COUPLE OF DAYS, they set off again. Joanne had sent a postcard in her childish capital lettering to her mum, stepdad Vincent, brother Sam and even dog Jess, saying how much the pair were now looking forward to some warmer weather after the cold, crisp temperatures of South Australia. They still had a long way to go, however, and this time there was even less to see: just the never ending desert country mottled with hummocks of spinifex grass and the occasional splash of colour of hardy wildflowers.

There were plenty of roadtrains to watch out for though; the monster vehicles comprising a cab with a powerful engine pulling a series of trailers behind, which can weigh up to 115-tonnes and stretch back as long as 50 metres. The first was imported into Australia in 1934 as an experiment in carrying heavy loads through isolated areas. Since then, they've become a regular feature of the landscape. For drivers of smaller vehicles, like Peter and Joanne, they can represent a real hazard. When they overtake, it's like being slammed by a gale-force wind. When overtaking them, the road ahead on a two-way highway like the Stuart Highway has to be seen to be clear for many kilometres as it's often impossible to tell quite how long they are until you're almost past. There's nothing quite like the heart-stopping adrenalin rush of being half-way up a roadtrain's length in the lane of oncoming traffic, and seeing another roadtrain bearing down on you.

Next stop was the small township of Marla which marks the turn-off to the Oodnadatta Track, the old dirt road leading into the heart of the Simpson Desert. From there, it was only 170 kilometres further to the SA–Northern Territory border. Just before the border is the old Sundown Station where the bodies of a murdered woman, her fourteen-year-old daughter and a family friend were found in their car after they'd set out to do the reverse of Peter and Joanne's journey in 1957. When they'd failed to arrive in Adelaide, the search for them, at that time the most widespread in Australian history, had covered all tracks leading east and west of the road without trace of the missing vehicle or its occupants. Their killer was later hanged.

Crossing the border after such a long journey was a distinct anti-climax. The Northern Territory comprises nearly a sixth of Australia's landmass, six times the size of Great Britain and two and a half times the size of Texas, but has fewer than 200,000 people. Yet there's precious little on the road to demarcate it besides a road sign telling travellers how much further everything else is, and another sign announcing that the Territory has no speed limit. While this delights many drivers, Peter and Joanne exchanged a rueful look. Their old Kombi couldn't even reach the South

Australian limit of 110 kilometres per hour. Still, they felt the excitement rise in them, and they pushed onwards. They knew that only around 100 kilometres ahead lay the turn-off for Uluru, the vast russet monolith that rears up suddenly out of the desert plains that, together with the Opera House and Sydney Harbour Bridge, is one of the country's best-known and most-loved icons.

By the time they finally left the Stuart Highway to drive the last 250 kilometres to Uluru, or Ayers Rock as it used to be called by whites, the soil had become a deep, blood red. This was old country, inhabited for the past 30,000 years or more by Aboriginal people, and full of sites sacred to the custodians of 'the rock', the local Anangu people. Their major challenge over the years has proved to be discouraging visitors from climbing Uluru which they see as a violation of 'tjukurpa' – their system of law and culture which is inextricably entwined with the landscape and its spirituality.

These days, most tourists know it's highly culturally insensitive to climb the rock and while the Anangu have agreed not to ban people from doing so, there is a sign posted at the base asking visitors to respect their culture and leave well alone. As well as being offensive, the climb is also said to bring years of bad luck to anyone who ignores their pleas. Guides say they regularly receive small pieces of the rock back through the post from tourists who climbed, souvenired a stone, took it home with them and have susequently endured a run of bad fortune. 'We do not wish it on them at all,' says one guide. 'But you would be amazed how often this happens.'

Peter and Joanne had come prepared. They'd brought their climbing boots.

# PART TWO

# THE BLOOD RED HEART
# OF AUSTRALIA

# CHAPTER TWELVE

# TO GO A'STALKING

ELEVEN HUNDRED KILOMETRES ACROSS THE desert as the crow flies, two female backpackers sat in the front seat of a beaten-up old white Kombi. They'd been trundling through the outback for hours, and they were tired and bored. The road stretched out endlessly before them, empty and hazy. With the sun beating down on the black bitumen, at times it looked as though it might even be melting under the fierce heat.

Suddenly, the woman driving saw something out of the corner of her eye in her rear-view mirror. At last! A sign of life! They'd just passed through the tiny cattle town of Hughenden, deep in the Queensland outback, heading for Julia Creek, Mount Isa and the Northern Territory border. There was nothing to look forward to for kilometres and kilometres ahead on the Flinders Highway. Instead, she watched as, slowly, slowly, she was able to make out the shape of a big white four-wheel-drive. It was really moving. It was gaining on them quickly.

Their Kombi had known much better days. It was only travelling at around 85 kilometres per hour, not far below its top speed. It was carrying plenty of weight too: surfboards on the roof, a backpack propped against the back door, and clothes draped over a makeshift clothesline inside. All over the body were various stickers proudly proclaiming the towns the Kombi had survived. On the back there was a big smiley face.

The four-wheel-drive was fast approaching. 'Look at this bloke,' said the driver. 'He's right up my arse. I wish he'd bloody hurry up and overtake me.' The woman beside her twisted round in her seat to get a better look. She could only just make out the driver. 'Oh well,' she said. 'He's probably lonely.' They giggled.

At last, the man in the four-wheel-drive revved the engine and pulled out to overtake. As he drew level, he glanced into the front of the Kombi. The two women were both young and good looking. The woman driving half-lifted her hand in a casual wave but, when the four-wheel-drive didn't appear in front of her, she glanced to her right for a look at who had been tailgating them. He seemed to take that as his signal to gun the engine, and he roared off in front.

'DID YOU SEE THAT?' SAID the woman behind the wheel to her friend. She stared at the road ahead, at the green canvas canopy of the white ute now speeding off ahead. 'Get a good look, did you? Filthy perve!'

Her friend nodded her agreement. 'Creepy,' she muttered.

'He'd been right on my arse. A couple of times I thought he might hit us,' she said. 'Wanker!'

TEN MINUTES ON, THE WOMEN were smoking cigarettes as they drove. They'd put music on the cassette player, but the sound was crackly and indistinct. As they creaked up a hill and got to the top, they both jumped. There was a white four-wheel-drive with a green canopy parked up by the side of the road, and the driver was sitting inside with his door half-open, smoking a cigarette. They could see him looking at them as the old white Kombi lumbered past.

AS SOON AS THEY WERE gone, the man turned the key in his ignition and pulled smoothly away. He was in no rush. He gained steadily on the Kombi and again drew up close behind. The driver was now looking in her mirror every couple of seconds. Her friend swivelled in her seat twice to look at him, to see if he was still there. He pulled out and sped up slightly to draw level once again. Then the two women both looked towards the back of the Kombi, and the man followed their eyes. A young man's face appeared at one of the windows looking straight at him. They were not alone. The other driver touched the accelerator lightly so he was level with the women, smiled at them, then put two fingers to his head like a gun, and jerked them as if he'd fired. He revved the engine, then sped off past them into the distance.

THE WOMEN FELT UNNERVED BY the man, and scrabbled to find a pen and paper to write down the vehicle's registration number. They decided to call the police as soon as they reached civilisation. There was a maniac on the road out there, and someone should stop him. But it would not be them. In the event, by the time they arrived in the next town, they'd pushed it to the back of their minds. They didn't call the police until a few weeks afterwards.

# CHAPTER THIRTEEN

# The Dead Centre

THE FIRST SIGHT OF ULURU strikes awe into everyone, and Peter Falconio and Joanne Lees were no different. They were amazed by its size, its stark presence in the midst of the low-lying desert, its sheer magnificence. It was just as they'd imagined it, but *more*, somehow. Tomorrow, first thing, they'd climb. The sun was close to setting and they went straight to Yulara, the accommodation centre for the national park, and checked into the campsite. There were plenty of people around, and a buzz in the air. At 3.6 kilometres long, a towering 348 metres high, with a base that's 10 kilometres in diameter, and extending 2.5 kilometres below the surface, Uluru is the second largest monolith in the world after WA's Mount Augustus. Peter and Joanne knew that climbing it would be arduous and that each year several people died trying, some as a result of heart attacks, some because of heat exhaustion and others because of falls. They agreed to do the climb early in the morning to avoid the worst of the heat, wear hats and take plenty of water. They were young and fit, and felt sure they'd be okay.

It was hard for anyone to stay at the area's campsite, however, without hearing the name 'Lindy Chamberlain'. Twenty-one years earlier, at around the same time of year, Lindy and her family had camped near the base of Uluru. She'd been making tea for her children when her son Aidan thought he'd heard his nine-and-a-half-week-old sister, Azaria, crying. Lindy raced over and her next words were to be forever imprinted on Australia's psyche: 'The dingo's got my baby!'

The child's body was never found, and Lindy and her husband Michael went to hell and back while the nation debated whether or not a dingo really was capable of carrying off, and killing, a baby. Lindy was convicted of murder in one of the most publicised trials in Australian history after forensic scientist Joy Kuhl testified she'd examined the family's car and found traces of foetal blood, which later turned out to be sound-deadening compound. Lindy served three-and-a-half years in jail until the conviction was quashed. The couple was later paid $1.3 million in compensation by the Northern Territory government.

At the time, many people still believed Chamberlain had killed Azaria, but less than a month before Peter and Joanne left Sydney, a nine-year-old boy, Clinton Gage, had been savaged and killed by a dingo on Fraser Island. The dingo then attacked his seven-year-old brother Dylan. After that, many people wrote to Chamberlain, apologising for having doubted her. She said the little boy's death gave her no satisfaction. 'The big heartache is that it was avoidable,' she said. 'I predicted this, but I hoped with all my heart it would never happen. I've been saying for twenty years that dingoes will kill again. And now it's happened, and this won't be the last time. If they'd listened in the first place, Clinton would still be alive.'

THE NEXT DAY DAWNED WARM and clear, and Peter and Joanne watched the sun rise over Uluru, admiring the quality of its changing colour as the light struck the sandstone. The infusion of minerals like feldspar gives the rock its red glow at sunrise and sunset, while oxidation gives it the colour of deep rust. The pair set off on their climb, took a photo on the summit, and then wandered back down to look at the caves and paintings at its base. At sunset, they sat on the sandy scrub a short distance away, and watched as, yet again, the rock gradually changed hue to a fierce blood red.

They relished the chance to stop and experience the spectacle, and were relieved to be off the endless highway and among other travellers, even though they generally tended to keep to themselves. Travelling as a couple can be tough at the best of times, but for Peter and Joanne, on a limited budget and covering vast distances through sparsely populated desert, there were definite strains. In addition, Joanne felt guilty about cheating on Peter with Nick Reilly. Peter may have sensed that something was wrong, but couldn't pinpoint why.

Around Uluru, however, there was plenty to do. Just 30 kilometres away are the Olgas, or Kata Tjuta, a collection of more rounded rock formations, with the tallest standing at a mighty 546 metres above sea level. The hiking trails, particularly through the Valley of the Winds, are astonishingly beautiful. Peter and Joanne spent a few days there and then set off around July 6, heading back towards the Stuart Highway. Just outside Uluru, they noticed another young couple hitchhiking, Canadian backpackers Mark Hladun and Izabelle Jette. Peter pulled over, asked them where they were headed, and when they said they were on their way to King's Canyon, en route to Alice Springs, the young Britons agreed to give them a ride. One hundred kilometres before the Stuart Highway, the foursome turned left towards King's Canyon.

The road winds 160 kilometres past the massive meteorite craters thought to have punctured the earth's crust 5000 years ago, before reaching the Watarrka National Park, featuring the sandstone gorge with its spectacular rock formations, lush palms grouped around waterholes and a walk up to the rim for breathtaking views. The group spent a couple of days there, before retracing their route back to the highway, and turning north once more for the final 200 kilometres to 'the Alice'. Their anticipation mounted as they neared the town in the very centre of Australia. At the 60 kilometres mark, they came across a rest stop with two picnic tables, packed with four-wheel-drives, and Peter slowed down and stopped, saying the Kombi was pulling oddly to one side. Joanne and Izabelle wandered around, peering over the wire at an area fenced off to give its plant life the chance to regenerate, while Peter and Mark checked the steering. There was a definite problem, and Mark devised a temporary solution, using cable ties to hold the steering rod in place. They set off again and 10 kilometres before Alice Springs billboards started appearing for accommodation. The first was for the Stuart Caravan Park, with its proud boast: 'Closer To Town'. 'That'd probably be worth checking out,' Peter said to Joanne. She nodded.

With the blue and green of the MacDonnell Ranges in the distance, and a welcoming avenue of gums as they reached the outskirts of town, Joanne directed Peter to the backpackers' lodge where the Canadians planned to stay. The four hugged and said their goodbyes, and Peter and Joanne drove back out of town to a mechanic's they hoped would be able to fix the Kombi. Peter wanted to get the steering checked before they went any further, but the mechanic said he couldn't fit them in that day; they could drop it in on the Friday morning if they liked. That night, Wednesday July 11, they parked the Kombi on a road in a residential area and slept in the back. This was to be their last major stop before Darwin, where they planned to double back and then head east towards Cairns in Queensland's far north, before finishing their epic journey around Australia in Brisbane, on the coast further south. There they intended to sell the Kombi and fly across the Tasman to New Zealand in time to celebrate Peter's birthday. Their next stop would be Fiji for Joanne's birthday, then it would be the US and home.

After so long in Australia's vast dusty interior, they were both looking forward to seeing the sea again. This journey had been the experience of a lifetime, they knew. But neither realised how short that lifetime, for one of them, might prove.

# CHAPTER FOURTEEN

# A Maniac with a Gun

ON 9 JULY 2001, a man with straggly brown hair, a greying moustache, a sallow complexion and sunken eyes approached a local magistrate in the West Australian town of Derby to ask if he would lend him his gun. JP 'Jacky' Dann refused, and the next day Geoffrey Nicholls returned to ask again. 'I want to go camping at Udialla Station to go pig shooting with my girlfriend and her two kids,' he pleaded. 'I need a gun.'

Dann eventually agreed to lend him his .22 Magnum rifle bolt action repeater, telling him he'd keep the freezer clean in case he returned with some pigs. But Nicholls, aged forty-one, didn't go pig hunting. Instead, he loaded the gun and two shots were heard from behind the local police station. Then he set off with his girlfriend Judy Rose and her two children, Lance, eight, and two-year-old Marcus, to drive south to Sydney in his white car, on a route that would, a few days later, cross Peter Falconio and Joanne Lees' path.

Nicholls wasn't a well man. He'd endured a wretched childhood and was having an even more heartbreaking time as an adult. He was born the youngest child of nine to an Aboriginal mother and a white Australian father, neither of whom cared much about their kids. When their twin boys were taken to hospital to be treated for malnutrition, the mother vanished – and only returned when the police found her and forcibly drove her back to collect them. In the end, the children were separated and taken into care, in both government-run institutions and various foster placements.

'But all of us ended up being badly treated,' says Shane Nicholls,

Geoffrey's elder brother. 'Geoff and I were both abused, physically, mentally and emotionally. Geoff took it particularly hard. I never asked him too much about his childhood. It was all too painful.' The younger Nicholls battled for years with mental illness, and spent lengthy periods in psychiatric hospitals as well as in jails in WA, SA and NSW. He had a criminal record in every state bar Tasmania and the ACT. He often didn't take his medication to calm his behaviour and suffered from paranoia, anger problems and depression. In April 1992, he'd sliced 4 centimetres into his left arm in a foiled suicide bid, and in October 1996, he drove away from a service station in Broome without paying for fuel. When he was stopped by police who snatched his key from the ignition, he retaliated by emptying a 20-litre jerry can of petrol over himself and his twelve-year-old son Troy sitting on the front seat. Then he took out a box of matches and threatened to set fire to them both.

'Give me the fucking key, or I'll kill us,' he yelled to the police officer. 'I'm fucking mad. You just ask the cops in SA.' The constable, Bruce Wyborn, held the key out but, as Nicholls went to grab it, he took hold of his forearm and hand holding the match. The two men then wrestled through the open driver's window until the box of matches eventually fell between the seat and the console. At that point, Nicholls seized the police officer's holstered gun and tried to pull it free. As Wyborn felt the securing lip snap open and the revolver start to come out of the holster, he realised he was now fighting for his life.

'I punched Nicholls as hard as I could to the face to make him let go,' he said in his statement later. 'Nicholls released his grip and fell over on his side to the passenger seat. I re-secured my revolver and tried to open the driver's door. But the door wouldn't open and Nicholls started to fight again. I reached in and grabbed him by the scruff of neck and pulled his head out of the window. I then held him in a headlock until back-up police arrived one to two minutes later.'

Nicholls was charged with two counts of attempted murder – one on Wyborn and one on his son – in court, but a guilty plea to lesser charges was eventually accepted.

SHANE NICHOLLS HADN'T HEARD FROM his younger brother in years, but in 1998 he received a call from him saying he had nowhere to live, so offered him his caravan in his backyard in Sydney. Tragedy dogged the younger Nicholls however. His son Troy died from petrol-sniffing the following year. His behaviour after that became steadily more suicidal and, in March 2001, he was admitted to hospital in Ceduna, SA, following a car chase which ended when he tried to set his vehicle, and himself, alight with a cigarette lighter. He told staff in the mental health unit at the State's Glenside Hospital that he had received hallucinatory commands to steal and burn the car the day before.

So when Nicholls set off in his car with his girlfriend, her kids and a loaded gun in July 2001, trouble was never going to be far away. 'Along the way, Geoff shot a cow at the side of the road,' Rose told police later. 'It didn't die immediately so he and Lance chased it for an hour, so Geoff could continue to shoot it. It finally died when Geoff struck it over the head with the butt of his rifle, with such force that it broke the rifle butt off.'

Later, the rifle accidentally discharged into the floor near the accelerator pedal while the whole family were in the car. Later still, he threatened Rose with the rifle, then jumped out of the car and put the barrel against his chin, saying he was going to shoot. He had spent most of the journey drinking heavily and taking large amounts of medication, and Rose feared the worst.

Others too waited with dread for news of the trip. Meanwhile, Peter Falconio and Joanne Lees were driving straight towards him.

# A Town Like Alice

ALICE SPRINGS IS ALMOST AT the dead geographic centre of Australia; remote, rugged and with the kind of frontier town raucousness that comes from being 1500 kilometres away from the nearest city. Its physical setting is spectacular. The town of around 22,000 people is set in what feels like an amphitheatre, with the mighty red sandstone walls of the MacDonnell Ranges to the south and its spurs to the north and east. The Todd River flows through the centre with its bridesmaids of tall red river gums and is either a swirling brown torrent of water in the wet season, or a modest trickle of red in the dry, often disappearing completely into the parched river bed of sand. As the traditional home of the Arrernte Aboriginal people, Alice has a large black community. With its formal foundation in the 1870s as a staging post for the overland telegraph line which connected to the submarine line from Darwin to Java, it also has a large white community. The rest are drawn from a wide mix of people who stumble into the town every year: tourists, transients and a swathe of CIA operatives from nearby Pine Gap, the US–Australian joint space research project.

Peter Falconio and Joanne Lees liked the town from the moment they arrived. With plenty of accommodation, shops, cafés, internet offices, bars and art galleries, it was a true oasis in the desert. Being in the middle of so much nothingness, with Darwin 1540 kilometres to the north and Adelaide 1660 kilometres to the south, the place has the air of a community battling to survive together against the elements, so people are generally extremely friendly. Like many remote outposts, the Alice is also home to plenty of larger-than-life characters, including crocodile hunter and stockman turned singer-songwriter, author, filmmaker and raconteur Ted Egan. He's one of those big, bluff, heart-of-gold blokes who seems to personify the outback town so well, it's a shock to learn he's actually from the city of Melbourne. He left there, however, at the age of sixteen and has been in the bush ever since. The archetypal Aussie larrikin, he was the bloke who introduced Rolf Harris to the song *Two Little Boys*, and recently received the Northern Territory's highest honour, being sworn in as its Administrator – the Queen's representative – in November 2003.

He loves Alice, and says it's a wonderful place. 'Yes, it's got its faults and its shortcomings and problems, but it's a magic place to live, and people from all over the world come here to see it,' he says. 'It's frontier territory, it's the end of the line and it's filled with end-of-the-road people. It still has a very transient population, with people who come here for twelve months for whatever reason, and then they're gone.'

As a perfect illustration of the enormous mix of people who have made Alice Springs their home, Egan's Aboriginal namesake, a former employee who took his name as a gesture of respect to him and is now known as Teddy Egan Tjangala, also lives there part of the time. One of the most sought-after black trackers in Australia, he was born around 1925 into the traditional Aboriginal way of life, hunting for food and living off the land. He was initiated early after the great Walpiri tribe of the Central desert lands annointed him a rainmaker from his birth. He would grow up great, strong and powerful, they said; a born leader. At seventeen, he was still wearing only a loincloth when he met, face-to-face, his first white man.

Now, when he's outback, he still walks incredible distances to hunt and commune with the land, hold talks with his people, paint, play music and perform traditional dances. When he's in Alice, he sleeps in a little humpy he's constructed of sheets of plastic in the back garden of his granddaughter's house in one of the main streets. 'It's a very good place,' he says, stroking his snow-white beard. 'The country is my home, but this is also home.'

Then there are the travellers, tourists, casual workers and lost souls who have settled in town. White Egan says they fit right in. 'It's a no-names, no-packdrill kind of place,' he says. 'A lot of people come here to get as far away as possible from everything else. Lots of bizarre things happen here as a result.' When a man was refused a drink at an Uluru bar in 1983, for instance, he drove his massive road train into the bar, killing five people. And, strangely enough, Alice Springs was the site of Australia's first attempted air hijack. As an Ansett Airlines flight from Adelaide was approaching the town in 1972, a man emerged from the toilet with a gun and demanded, not a flight to Paris or Tripoli, but a parachute and a jumpsuit and to be flown 1000 kilometres into the desert. On the ground, he kept an air hostess and six passengers hostage until a police officer, disguised as the navigator of the Cessna that was supposedly going to take him into the outback, jumped him. The hijacker, after injuring the officer, eventually shot himself.

The Northern Territory also has the dubious distinction of having the highest rate per capita of violent crime in Australia, together, in 1999, with the highest murder rate of 3.63 victims for every 100,000 people. More usually, however, the threats come from nature, accidents or mistakes: travelling without water, a first-aid kit, or supplies; treading on snakes; becoming lost in the desert; running out of fuel and leaving the vehicle to walk for help; fishing from mudflats close to saltwater crocodiles; or sharing their waterholes for a swim.

But the area's dangers were furthest from the mind of Peter Falconio as he collected the Kombi from the mechanic, noting how much more smoothly it was now running, and went into town. He called into the tax office, hoping to pick up a refund on the tax he'd paid while working in Sydney. He was disappointed. 'They said he owed them money, when he was expecting a tax return,' explains Joanne. Accountant Maureen Laracy had examined his group certificate and realised he'd been taxed as a resident instead of as someone on a working visa. She asked him if he'd like to fill in a tax return to pay the difference. 'He declined,' she reported, later. Their other chores were carried out more successfully. They both emailed friends and family at the internet office next door to the Melanka Lodge to tell them they were having a great time, but were looking forward to getting back to the east coast of Australia, and then to New Zealand afterwards. They dropped into a travel agency nearby to ask how much it would cost to make a side-trip from Brisbane to Papua New Guinea as Peter had been talking to a friend back in Sydney about taking a week's walking holiday there. Joanne didn't like the look of it at all, and said if he wanted to do that, she'd return to Sydney to spend a few extra days there with the friend's girlfriend while they were off doing 'guy stuff', and then they'd meet back in Brisbane. They took away the brochures and a quote for prices, saying they'd think about it. Joanne wrote her mum a postcard to say she was missing home, but enjoying her trip. Peter phoned home and spoke to both his mum and his dad to tell everyone he was having the time of his life.

ALICE SPRINGS GAVE THE YOUNG couple a chance to relax. They wandered through the mall with its blind busker escorted by a different, sighted friend every day, and wondered at the town having a pedestrian mall when there were so few cars. They took a walk around the grassy parks where Aboriginal families come to sit and enjoy the sunshine with their kids playing nearby. They sipped coffee in some of the trendy cafés which felt as though they'd been transplanted from Sydney's eastern suburbs or Melbourne's St Kilda. And they scuffed through the dry riverbed, where groups of people congregate each evening to talk, to sing and to drink. The town was full of live music, most of it country Australian and much of it for the benefit of tourists. But its cheerful amateurism could be charming. Peter and Joanne ate one day in the cheesy Bojangles Saloon and Restaurant, guarded by a full-size replica of Ned Kelly, while another night they dined at the Overlander Steakhouse, with its choices of kangaroo, snake, crocodile and emu. With sing-songs, corrugated tin roofing and a complete wall of cricket memorabilia, it's not a place for the pretentious. 'What's the house wine?' one diner was heard to ask the waitress. She didn't hesitate for a second before replying, 'Cask.'

The Stuart Caravan Park was a pleasant enough place to stay, too. They parked the Kombi under a shady gum, had long, hot showers, and cleaned the Kombi inside and out. Peter bought some material to try to make new seat covers to replace the torn ones, hoping they'd then get a better price for the Kombi when they came to sell it. 'That was ambitious,' smiles Joanne later. They abandoned the attempt soon after.

They also took some time to unwind. 'They seemed a nice couple,' says owner Leonie Marshall. 'We were very busy at the time, but I still remember them. She was very quiet, but he was more talkative.'

It was peak season when they'd arrived and the Camel Cup – a series of bizarre camel races with an assortment of riders, prizes and events – was due to take place on the Saturday. It was one of the highlights of the year in a community that loves nothing more than to have fun, and the louder and *odder*, the better. On the Friday evening, 13 July 2001, Peter and Joanne got chatting to a couple who were camping nearby. 'Are you going to the Camel Races tomorrow?' the woman asked them. 'You should go. It's a hoot!' That night, lying on the back seat of the Kombi, they discussed going. If so many people made the trip all the way to Alice Springs especially for the event, it must be worth seeing. They could set off that afternoon, after they'd seen some of it, on the long road north to Darwin.

It'd be a fun way to say farewell, they agreed as they fell asleep that night, Friday the 13th. After all, it would be many, many years before they'd be back in Alice again, they mused sleepily – if ever.

# CHAPTER SIXTEEN

# Dangerous Delusions

ANDREW HEFFERNAN'S PROBLEMS first began in 1994 when, as a twenty-year-old, he punched a man who'd been abusing his friends. He ended up coming off worse, far worse, from the fight. He was stabbed in the back and spent a long period in hospital undergoing delicate lung and abdominal surgery. But the real damage couldn't be seen. Heffernan, from the dairy centre of Moruya just south of Batemans Bay on NSW's south coast, suffered post-traumatic stress disorder which, in turn, led to a long bout of psychiatric illness.

No-one realised quite how bad it was until four years later when he attacked, without provocation, the ex-boyfriend of a female friend. He leapt from a car, knocked the man down with a flying kick, struck him in the head and, when he was crawling on his hands and knees trying to get away, punched him in the head and back. The man sustained a fractured jaw and spent eight days in intensive care. A psychiatric report written the next year, in 1999, said that immediately prior to the assault, Heffernan had been talking to himself, wandering aimlessly, sharpening knives and fashioning daggers. There'd also been incidents where he'd slashed his own abdomen and foot. He was assessed as being mentally ill with severe paranoid schizophrenia, and was admitted to a high dependency mental health unit where he responded well to medication.

When Heffernan was released, he continued to drift. He'd left school during Year Eleven to start a carpentry course but had subsequently been turned down for apprenticeships. For a while he worked on his stepfather's farm – he and his mother had separated – then a supermarket, before again leaving town to travel Australia and work in a series of short-term, dead-end jobs. By July 2001, he was in the South Australian Riverland, looking for work. When he couldn't find any, he decided to drive north to Alice Springs to seek employment there. He set out in his old car, leaving his medication behind. As the distance between him and Peter Falconio and Joanne Lees narrowed, his paranoid schizophrenia again began to take hold. He was a ticking time bomb.

# CHAPTER SEVENTEEN

# The Camel Cup

IT LOOKED CRAZY: DOZENS OF people running around Alice Springs in strange costumes and face paint. There was a carnival atmosphere sweeping the whole of the town. 'Come and watch the camels!' called a man on a tannoy. 'You can even eat them afterwards!' The annual Alice Springs Camel Cup attracts a huge crowd of locals and tourists every year, as one of those strangely surreal events for which Alice has become renowned. Ever since local Noel Fullerton suggested settling a feud with his mate Keith Mooney Smith with the challenge of a race on camels along the dry Todd River bed in 1970, it's become one of the most celebrated dates on the Northern Territory calendar. For Australia is today the only country in the world where wild camels roam free. First imported from India in 1840 to help explorers cross the vast desert interior, they proved to be the perfect creatures in desert conditions, capable of travelling around 40 kilometres a day carrying loads of up to 600 kilograms. In 1866, a few escaped from a team of 260 transporting goods from Adelaide to Perth, and turned wild. On the advent of the railroad from Adelaide to Alice, and then of trucks on the road to Darwin, others were turned loose. Now Australia has so many wild camels, it even exports breeding stock into the Arab world.

For the Camel Cup, domesticated animals are brought in from all over the country, and jockeys flock to take part. It's a hard ride, and only the toughest cope. 'Once a camel starts galloping,' explains one jockey, 'it kind of feels like being strapped to a poorly functioning washing machine.' At a gallop, they can race for short distances at speeds of up to 60 kilometres per hour, but the problem lies usually in trying to keep them on course, or stopping them.. 'I was in front, I was screaming, I was happy,' recalls another jockey. 'And then the camel stopped like a shopping cart and turned left ... but at 35 miles an hour, I just kept going ...'

Peter Falconio and Joanne Lees had spent the morning at the accountant's, visiting the library and dropping into a café for breakfast, but arrived at Blatherskite Park just outside town in time for the 12.30 p.m. opening ceremony for the 32nd charity fundraising Camel Cup. They paid their entrance fee and were each given a smiley sticker to prove it: 'Try Hugs Not Drugs – The Australian Lions Drug Awareness Foundation'. It felt like the whole of the Northern Territory was there. Indeed, Bradley Murdoch was thought to be in the midst of it too.

Peter and Joanne milled about, enjoying the atmosphere and laughing at the contestants who'd dressed in fancy costume for the novelty races. 'I really liked it,' says Joanne. 'It reminded me of the local galas and family fetes we used to have in our village.' Passers-by smiled to see the two young tourists, so far from home, obviously having a wonderful time.

THE RACE HAD JUST STARTED when Peter and Joanne took their positions two back from the wire fence that runs around the park. The camels were thundering down the track, their leathery pads sending clouds of dust into the air. The jockeys strained to control their mounts – and to hang on for dear life. The commentator was getting more excited as the camels came closer to the finish line, with a $100 first prize at stake for the winner, and the glory of the title. Some camels were jostling others but the race caller gave a running commentary on how the rules of the race can change all the time, depending on the mood of the judges. The only steadfast rule was for spectators not to approach the camels directly; their teeth are notoriously sharp, and they can spit over a distance of more than 3 metres.

The race finished in a wave of cheering from those who'd placed winning bets, and boos from those who'd lost their money. Spectators were reminded that the Rickshaw Race would be coming up soon, so why not volunteer you and your mates? The only other event for the public to take part in was the Miss Camel Cup. 'Come on, ladies,' he chided. 'Don't be shy!' Peter looked at Joanne and she smiled.

'No way!' she laughed, shaking her head. She felt thirsty and her lips were dry, so she slicked them with a stick of strawberry-flavoured lip balm she had in her shorts pocket and then wandered off, alone, to find a stall selling cold drinks. A group of men standing near the beer tent made a lewd comment as the dark haired woman in a pale blue, tight-fitting French Connection T-shirt, green board shorts and sports sandals ordered her drink in a distinctive English accent. Joanne ignored them. She could see they were the worse for alcohol and she'd become used to men leering at her in outback Australia. She didn't notice, however, a tall, rangy man standing alone, off to one side, eyeing her hungrily.

AS JOANNE RETURNED TO PETER with the drinks, she had the uncanny feeling she was being watched. She looked around and noticed a man with a video camera panning across the crowd; an innocent enough activity. She paid him little heed. After the last heat of the Rickshaw Race, the pair agreed they'd had enough, and decided to head off. They had originally planned to leave earlier, but had gotten carried away with the fun of the big day out. With a start they realised it was nearly 4 p.m.

They both climbed into the Kombi and raced back to the caravan park to have a final shower before they left. Then they drove to the chicken fast food chain Red Rooster on the Whittaker Street ring road for a last meal. Peter bought pizza and Joanne picked at his leftovers.

NEITHER OF THEM NOTICED the auto parts store Repco on the other side of the road, opposite. There, a man standing alone noticed Joanne climb back into the driving seat of the Kombi. He darted off to pick up his own white four-wheel-drive ute. He started the engine and checked his gun was still in the vehicle. He then watched the Kombi as it turned out into the road. He hung back to see which direction the van would take after going through town. He saw it turn north, and then pulled over on to the side of the road.

He had plenty of time. He would catch her up later.

# CHAPTER EIGHTEEN

# And Then
# The Darkness

JOANNE LEES DROVE AWAY FROM the showgrounds, with Peter Falconio bowed down beside her over the map, feeling slightly irritated that they were leaving for Darwin so late. Next stop would be the giant granite boulders, the Devil's Marbles, south of Tennant Creek. The guidebooks recommended seeing the Marbles – known in Aboriginal legend as the eggs of the Rainbow Serpent – at sunrise, but nobody advised driving after dark. At the snail's pace of the Kombi, it'd take them five to six hours. Joanne hated driving at night in the outback; not just because of the threat of wildlife wandering across the road, but because the tales of strange murders and mysterious disappearances had begun to eat at her.

BRADLEY MURDOCH WAS IN THE area, halfway along the long drug-run from Sedan in SA to Broome in the north-west, armed to the teeth and, his brain fried by booze, speed and lack of sleep, looking for trouble. Geoffrey Nicholls was driving south, still drinking heavily and playing with his rifle every now and again, as he made his way from Derby in the Kimberley. Andrew Heffernan was driving into Alice Springs just as his medication ran out and his paranoid schizophrenia kicked in. And God only knew who else was out there ...

JOANNE SHIVERED EVEN THOUGH THE afternoon was a warm 23 degrees Celsius. She was still just in her T-shirt and boardshorts, with her denim jacket hanging off the back of the seat, and had tied her hair back with a black elasticated Lady Jane hair band with a gold-coloured clasp and twist pattern. She'd offered to drive the first shift, so Peter could take over when it got dark.

As the scattered houses of Alice Springs gave way to car yards and forlorn industrial sites, a large, brightly-lit Shell Truckstop, the last chance to refuel before the long road north, came into view. But Joanne didn't stop. The sun was already hanging low in the bleached sky, and they were behind schedule. By the time the Kombi rattled past the turn-off to the Tanami Track, Bradley Murdoch's preferred route between SA and Broome, the sun was casting its last soft golden rays over the acres of parched spinifex back in the middle of nowhere.

Peter was reading his book, *The Catcher In The Rye*, and Joanne had put on a CD of the Scottish rock band Texas to keep herself awake. After a while, she noticed his head was drooping, and she suggested he climb over the seats to lie down on the bench in the back to read. He clambered over, and settled down. The next time she turned round to look at him, he was fast asleep.

THE TALL MAN FROM Alice Springs easily caught up with the orange Kombi and hung back, keeping his distance. He didn't want to attract attention. Through the back window, he could see the English girl's dark head alone in the front of the van. The passenger seat was empty; she was obviously alone. He gunned the engine, overtook the vehicle and roared off along the road ahead, to get ready.

JOANNE DIDN'T NOTICE THE OTHER vehicle overtaking. She'd been watching the sunset and marvelling at how beautiful the light was. Far ahead she saw a wedge-tailed eagle diving towards the road, presumably picking at roadkill. By the time she drew level with the Ti Tree Roadhouse she guessed they were about halfway to the Devil's Marbles, and she needed a break. She made a sudden decision and came down hard on the brake, veering left into a layby on the opposite side of the road to the Roadhouse and service station. At that, Peter woke up and asked what was happening.

They both wanted to stretch their legs, and climbed out of the Kombi. Joanne had a drink while Peter rolled a joint with some dope a friend had given him in Sydney, and they watched the show before them in silence.

Peter would drive the next stretch, so Joanne could relax. There were hardly any other vehicles on the road, but it was only around twenty minutes after they'd set off following a stop to get petrol and snacks and use the toilet when they saw two small fires in the scrub. Peter went to pull up 50 metres on, suggesting they go back and investigate. Joanne, however, felt strangely spooked by the way they were both burning so brightly – obviously only just having started and when there seemed to be no-one else around – and implored him to keep going.

Further down the road, there were two more similar fires, but the pair continued on. They were now making good headway. The mechanic they'd seen in Alice Springs had said the van should take them wherever they were going, as long as they didn't thrash it too hard.

The night was darkening as they passed through Barrow Creek, 89 kilometres north of Ti Tree, and a place avoided by many Aboriginals. 'It has bad spirit,' says black tracker Teddy Egan. 'It's a place where bad, bad things happen.' The bad blood began in 1874, when two white men were killed during an attack by the Kaitej people on the Telegraph station, built two years earlier too close to a local waterhole. In retribution, up to sixty local Aboriginals were trapped at Skull Creek, back towards Ti Tree, and then massacred. In 1928, the reputation of the area became even darker. When Aboriginals killed an old dingo trapper on neighbouring Coniston Station, the chief of police and, coincidentally, Chief Protector of Aborigines, led a posse which killed seventy black men, women and children in a bloody series of reprisals.

The Barrow Creek Roadhouse was lit up as Peter and Joanne passed it at around 7.30 p.m., but neither of them particularly noticed. Joanne had changed the CD to one of Peter's favourite bands, The Stone Roses, and was feeding Peter sweets as they drove. Every time she saw the shadowy shape of a kangaroo bounding near the road, she warned him to be careful. Ten kilometres further on, Peter saw headlights coming up fast behind and slowed to let the vehicle overtake. But the vehicle remained on his tail. 'I wish this bloke would hurry up and pass me,' he said to Joanne. 'He's blinding me.'

Joanne twisted in her seat to look back and screwed her eyes up against the other vehicle's headlights. 'Tosser,' she said.

At that, the other vehicle took its cue, and pulled out behind them. But when it drew level, the driver slowed down to the same speed.

THE MAN GLANCED UNHURRIEDLY ACROSS at the window of the Kombi lumbering along beside him, and was taken aback to see the face of a young, clean-shaven man. The girl was now sitting beside him, in the passenger seat. The man hadn't realised she wasn't alone.

But he had everything he needed with him: a gun, cable ties twisted into home-made handcuffs, rolls of heavy-duty black duct tape, and a sack in the back. This stretch of road was dead straight, so he'd be able to see anything coming well in advance. Just up ahead was a little dirt track off to the left he'd scoped out earlier. No, he had plans for that girl, and he wasn't about to give them up easily.

PETER LOOKED OVER TO THE man driving the vehicle and waved. The man reached over, wound down his window and gestured urgently towards the back of the Kombi. Peter could just make out the words, 'Sparks!' and 'Exhaust!' Joanne leaned over to look at the man too, and didn't like what she saw. In the reflected light, she could see he was white, around forty to forty-five, with a droopy, grey moustache. He was wearing a black baseball cap over his dark, straight hair and a dark-coloured T-shirt with a black-and-white check shirt. His dog was sitting up in the passenger seat beside him. She felt Peter slow down and suddenly had a premonition that something bad was about to happen. 'Don't stop, Pete, don't stop!' she urged. 'I don't like it.' But Peter continued to brake. He loved his Kombi and there'd been faults on it before. 'We have to see what it is,' he replied. 'It'll only take a minute.' He pulled up on the gravel shoulder and the white vehicle pulled up behind. Then Peter smiled at Joanne, opened his door and stepped out. 'You wait there,' he said, reassuringly. 'It's cold out here.' He left the door slightly ajar when he got out so the interior light stayed on as he walked around to the back. Joanne shuffled over to the driver's seat from where she could get a better view of what the two men were doing. She was looking in the mirror and hanging out of the driver's door looking back, and could see

Peter bending down as if to look at the exhaust. She strained her ears to try to catch what they were saying.

'I saw sparks coming out your exhaust,' the man was telling Peter. 'It's been happening for a while. You've got a problem there.'

She heard Peter's voice. 'Cheers, mate,' he said. 'Thanks for stopping.' Joanne chided herself for being so suspicious. He seemed like a nice man, she thought to herself. It was nice of him to stop and help.

Peter stood up and walked back to Joanne. 'Could you rev the engine?' he asked her, as he reached to the shelf under the dashboard for his cigarettes. 'We'll see how bad it is.' He walked back to the rear of the Kombi, and then the darkness enveloped him. Joanne glanced in the rear-view mirror and caught the other man looking at her. For a few seconds, he held her gaze until she looked away. She couldn't help it, but she suddenly felt nervous again. Uncomfortable.

She put her foot on the accelerator and revved the engine, all the while trying to see if Peter was signalling any further instructions. She listened hard over the rattle of the engine, in case he was shouting at her to stop. But instead, a sudden, loud crack split the cool night air, like the sound of a vehicle backfiring – or a gunshot. She swivelled round in her seat and saw the man standing there, right beside her at the driver's door window, alone and with a gun. And then Joanne felt her blood turn to ice.

# CHAPTER NINETEEN

# Taken Prisoner

JOANNE LEES SAT STARING IN horror at the man holding the gun in his right hand. With a start, she suddenly realised he was now pointing it at her. He reached out to the driver's door, wrenched it open wider, and then started climbing in. 'Pete!' she screamed. 'Pete!' But the man kept on coming.

'Turn off the engine,' he ordered roughly. Still stunned, Joanne reached for the key, but her hands were shaking so violently, she couldn't grasp it. Impatiently, he shoved Joanne aside, grabbed it himself and turned it off. He pushed her into the passenger seat, sat himself heavily behind the wheel and leaned over to grab her. 'He was to the side of me, behind me, he seemed to be all over me and around me,' says Joanne. She was terrified, but she still thought that, at any moment, Peter would turn up to save her. 'Pete!' she screamed again. But Peter didn't come.

Instead, there was only the man, now calmly instructing her to put her head down and her hands behind her back. Joanne, still stunned, went to do as he'd commanded but then suddenly seemed to wake from the reverie. 'No!' she gasped, as she struggled against his big hands trying to force her into the position. She lifted her feet up on to the shelf Peter had built under the dash hoping to get enough leverage to swing herself round and get out through the passenger door. But the man seemed to realise what she was doing. 'Put your head between your legs, I said,' he barked. 'And put your fucking hands behind your back!' He pushed the muzzle of the revolver against her head. Joanne, terrified, finally did as she was told. The man pulled out some black electrical ties, looped them around her wrists, and pulled them tight.

The next few minutes were a blur. It seemed to her that she could still feel the steel against her forehead, but she'd also been bundled out the passenger door of the Kombi and thrown face down onto the ground. Her bare knees were throbbing from the impact, she could taste blood in her mouth and she could feel the gravel against her chest through her T-shirt. She could also feel the man straddling her, bending down and trying to tie her ankles together. Joanne realised that this man meant business. She cried out again for Peter, but her voice sounded thin and weak in the blackness and the only noise back was the crunching of the gravel under the man's feet and his heavy breathing and cursing as he fiddled with the tape. She couldn't see Peter anywhere in the darkness. He could be out there injured or even … dead. She suddenly felt engulfed by a sense of emptiness. She was staring into a void, and there was only one way out. She decided to fight for her life. 'I got so angry,' she says, 'I just kicked and kicked and kicked.' She twisted her body and tried to kick upwards aiming at where she imagined the man's crotch must be. Her hands were still tied together behind her back, but the 10 centimetres or so of the electrical cord between her hands gave her some room to manoeuvre. She tried to push her arms up and away from her body to punch him between the legs.

'Fucking keep still!' the man shouted in exasperation as he struggled to avoid her hands and feet and keep her ankles still enough to tie them with electrical tape. 'You bitch!'

Joanne could feel the pressure suddenly released from her ankles. He'd given up trying to tie them together. But then she realised he'd walked around to stand beside her head. He leaned down towards her and punched her hard against the right temple. The force of the blow took her by surprise and she felt waves of blackness shudder through her. The next thing she knew, he'd hauled her to her feet and was pushing her, one hand at the nape of her neck, the other on her shoulder, towards his vehicle.

THIS WAS ALL PROVING MUCH harder than the man had thought. The girl was a fighter all right. He'd give her that. He'd wanted to tie her ankles together to make it easier for him. But he couldn't keep struggling with her. Every second they were still on the road there was the danger someone might pass and see what was happening. He couldn't risk that. He had to get out of there quick-smart. There was still the body to get rid of before he could take away the girl and have his fun.

STUNNED BY THE BLOW TO her head, Joanne was pushed towards the back of the man's ute. She felt him try to put tape on her mouth but he couldn't seem to get his fingers to work properly and she kept twisting and squirming away from him. The tape got stuck in her hair instead, and then he couldn't wrench it free back over her mouth. He gave that up too, and instead reached over to the back of his ute, lifted the loose collar of the canopy, pushed his hand inside and pulled out a canvas sack. He wheeled her around, and yanked it over her head. The man then pushed Joanne to the front of the vehicle. The sudden darkness of the sack shocked her into finding her voice again. 'Help!' she screamed. 'Pete! Pete! Where are you?'

The man shook her. 'Fucking shut up!' he yelled. He yanked open the passenger door and pushed her in. As she twisted round, the bag came off her head and she saw the dog sitting patiently in the driver's seat. It was a medium-sized, broad-shouldered dog, that looked brown and white in the gloom of the night. It took no notice of her at all and didn't make a sound. Joanne edged towards the driver's door thinking she might be able to escape that way, but the dog remained in the way, blocking her exit. Then she started screaming again and shouting for help. At that, the man climbed into the cab and pushed her somehow – maybe through an opening – into the back of the ute. She landed on something warm and soft, something that felt like a mattress, and which seemed higher than the front of the vehicle. She lay sprawled there for a moment on her stomach, with her legs towards the back of the vehicle and her head nearest the cab. She rolled over onto her back and tried to sit up. She could see little but, as her eyes adjusted, she noticed a patch of faint light at the rear of the ute and wondered if that might be the tailgate. She could hear the man at the side of the ute, the crunch of his feet on the gravel and a strange scraping sound. Joanne was still yelling. 'What do you want with me?' she shouted. 'Is it money? What do you want? Where's Pete? What have you done with Pete?'

She heard more footsteps in the gravel. 'Be quiet,' he said. 'If you don't, I'll fucking shoot you.'

Joanne was quiet for a moment, and then took a breath. 'Are you going to rape me?' she asked. There was a silence, and Joanne realised with a start that she was more afraid of being raped than of being shot and killed. She took a deep breath and summoned up all her courage to keep confronting the man. 'Have you shot Pete? Have you shot my boyfriend?' she asked. There was silence and the realisation suddenly hit her that he may well have shot Peter. It seemed like an age before he answered.

'No,' he finally replied.

Joanne then heard the sound of something – or someone – being dragged away through the gravel. She didn't want to think about it, but she couldn't stop an image of Peter flashing through her mind as she'd last seen him – smiling, telling her to rev the engine, so trusting of everyone. He'd even thanked the man for bothering to stop. The anger then started to rise again. And with that came the need for action. She guessed the man was preoccupied with his task, and that this was her one opportunity. She might not get another. 'I kept thinking, "Oh my God, I'm going to die",' she says. 'I was thinking, "Where's Pete? This is over. This is the end of my life".' Slowly, quietly, she began sliding from the front of the ute towards the tailgate, her hands still tied behind her back. When she'd finally inched her way down, she hung her legs over the tray. 'I thought, "This is it, this is my chance to get out",' she says. She looked around for a second, couldn't see anything, and then jumped. As she landed, the crunch of the gravel, to her ears, was deafening. But she didn't wait to find out if it had alerted the man. She ran for her life.

# CHAPTER TWENTY

# The Hunter and His Prey

JOANNE LEES RAN AS FAST as she could into the scrub on the western side of the highway. It was difficult to run with her hands still tied behind her back, crashing through the spinifex and mulga bushes in the pitch black of a moonless night. Twice, she tripped over and thudded to the ground. Twice, she scrambled back up and kept on running. Eventually she sank to the ground and crawled under a bush to hide. It felt like she'd run a long, long way from the road. In truth, she'd managed to cover just 40 metres.

To her ears, the noise she'd made had been thunderous, and she could still hear the echoes roaring through the still night air. She curled up into a ball under the prickly fingers of a metre-tall mulga bush and tried to control her breathing. She'd been gasping with the effort of running, and fear, and she needed to stay as quiet as she could. 'I didn't have any energy left to keep running,' she says. 'And it was so quiet out there, that every noise I'd made running over branches and trees sounded so loud. My heart was making such a loud noise. I knew I had to be as quiet as I could.' Her life could depend on it.

WHEN THE MAN HEARD A sudden crunch of gravel, he wheeled round to see what it was. He couldn't see anything in the inky black behind his ute but he immediately strode over to the canopy and ripped it aside.

Empty. He could now hear the girl blundering through the grasses on the side of the road, and he cursed bitterly to himself. He should have been more careful. He should have hit her harder, then tied her ankles like he'd planned. Now he'd have to go after her.

But it wouldn't take long to catch her. She couldn't get far with her hands tied like that. But it'd be a pain if she injured herself. That'd make everything more awkward. And, besides, he planned on doing the hurting.

He raced around to the front of his cab, opened the door and reached inside the dash for a torch. 'Good boy,' he said to his dog, still patiently sitting there. 'Stay!'

This was a hell of a nuisance but then again, a little chase made it all the more exciting. He was the hunter, she was his prey. He'd show her who was in charge.

LYING UNDER THE BUSH, HER heart pounding with terror, Joanne tried to curl up even smaller and put her head on her knees and covered the white of her legs with her hair. She could hear the man's footsteps crunching through the gravel, then thudding through the undergrowth, getting nearer each second. The dried grass smashed under his weight, and branches cracked and fractured. But she couldn't run any more. Her legs were shaking too much. She'd just have to stay where she was, and hope, and pray. She could see the light from his torch, sweeping the tops of the long grassy clumps. She closed her eyes. He couldn't fail to find her.

The man edged closer and Joanne could hear his muttered curses. She tried not to breathe. He must be looking right at her. She tensed, waiting for him to spot her and the blow to fall, but he appeared to be looking the other way. The torch light was near, but not directly on her. He walked right past her another three times – he could have reached out and touched her he was that close – but then he turned and walked away, back towards the highway. Joanne felt her body turn to jelly. But she mustn't relax now. He might be back. And he might bring his dog next time.

WHERE THE HELL WAS SHE? The man was getting increasingly frustrated, trying to peer through the scrub to find his quarry. She couldn't be far, but he couldn't see a thing. He couldn't believe his bad luck. If only he'd tied her legs. None of this was going to plan. He was worried too about the body and the two vehicles still back on the road. If anyone drove past, they might get suspicious and stop to see what was going on. He'd then have them to deal with too.

The whole thing was lurching more and more out of control. By now, the girl's van should have been hidden and he should have been driving far away, with her tied up in the back of the ute. Instead, he was rummaging through the scrub and having to get rid of a body he hadn't bargained for. He made a sudden decision: he'd better see to the body first. She could wait. After all, she was in handcuffs; she wouldn't get far. He'd do the business, and then he'd find her. No-one would think there was anything odd about a single vehicle on the side of the road. She would be the easy part.

JOANNE REMAINED HUDDLED IN A ball, too scared to move. What was the man going to do now? Would he come back with his dog? If he came back and found her next time, she wondered if she'd have the strength to keep on fighting. Now the fear had seized her, she felt absolutely wiped out. The odds seemed so overwhelming in his favour. What hope would she have? The tears were starting to come now, too. She could feel them well up in her eyes. She blinked and tried to control them. She couldn't let go now. Once she'd started, she might not be able to stop. She made herself concentrate on the only other human presence in this lonely landscape. Where was the man now, and what was he doing?

She heard a vehicle door slam, and an engine start. Maybe he'd given up. She heard the gravel crunching again as the vehicle pulled off, but then saw the powerful headlights of the ute flash over the scrub and blind her where she was lying. Oh my God, had he seen her? What chance did she stand now, if he was going to use his spotlights to light up the bush?

But then, just as suddenly as the headlights had come, they swerved away and she realised, to her astonishment, that the man was driving off. But still she didn't dare move.

THE MAN HAD BEGUN TO panic. He had been planning to leave the girl tied up in the ute while he dumped her Kombi in a little hidden turn-off he'd scouted out earlier further north along the road. But now he had to get rid of the body as soon as he could. He finished heaving it into the back of the ute but then realised he didn't want to get caught with a dead body in his truck. He'd get the ute off the road then run back to get the Kombi.

While he was climbing into the ute, he had another idea too. He fired the engine, switched on his powerful spotlights, then reversed back into the road. Suddenly, the scrub was lit up like a stage. He reversed a little more and swung to the right, so the lights danced over the scrub where the girl had disappeared. He peered into the light. But it was no good. The bushes and clumps of spinifex dotted over the ground were like a solid wall when you looked straight into them, and the light reflected off them made it impossible to see anything beyond.

Then, off to the right, a long way north up the road, he saw the first flash of distant headlights. He cursed silently to himself, and glanced quickly into the floodlit scrub again. But as the other car's lights got closer, he swung back on the road, and pulled away.

Now he was going to have to do something with that body. And then he'd think about the girl.

JASPER JIMBAJIMBA HAINES AND HIS wife Pamela Nabangardi Brown were driving south along the Stuart Highway, going home after a pleasant day spent visiting family in their home town of Ali Curung, 80 kilometres north of Barrow Creek. The Aboriginal couple didn't get the chance to visit very often, since they had to rely on other people for a lift, so it felt like a rare treat.

Now, however, they were feeling flustered. Having driven there with their niece, a friend, their thirteen-year-old daughter and a nine-year-old girl, plus three grandchildren under the age of ten, they'd intended to leave straight after an Aussie Rules football game between two local sides had finished on the radio. But they'd taken too long saying their goodbyes. Then, at Taylors Crossing, half-an-hour into their journey, their Holden Commodore stationwagon had a flat. They didn't have a jack, so they approached a group of tourists camping near the creek and asked them for help. The tourists were happy to oblige, and Haines changed the tyre. By the time they set off again for their twenty-strong Nturiya community, west of Ti Tree, night had fallen.

They were driving slowly, around 80 kilometres per hour, to avoid another flat. There was hardly any traffic on the road, but about 30 to 40 kilometres south of Taylors Crossing, they saw another car. That seemed odd. It didn't look like a tourist vehicle, and country people don't generally drive in the dark unless they really have to. 'I saw this car come on to the bitumen road on the right-hand side in front of us,' says Brown, 'just a glimpse of it. It was white, a high vehicle. It sort of looked like a tray top.' Haines added, 'It had a canopy on the back.'

A little farther on, they noticed an even more unusual sight – parked up by the side of the road, was an old orange Kombi van with a white roof.

THAT CAR APPEARING OUT OF the dark really unnerved the man. It felt like an extremely close call. What were all those Aboriginal people doing out here packed in a car like that anyway? And why were they driving so slowly? Were they suspicious? What did they see? Did they see his face? He wasn't concentrating. He hadn't even thought to pull his cap low over his eyes.

If they'd driven by just a few minutes earlier, they would have seen everything: the boy lying dead on the ground, him lifting the body up into the ute. His hands were shaking. He had the beginnings of a headache. He wondered if they'd noticed the Kombi on the side of the road, and somehow connected him with it.

Things were going from bad to worse. He'd better hurry up in case they'd thought something strange was going on, and came back for a second look. That'd be all he needed. A little way up the road, when he saw the lights in his rear view mirror had safely gone, he pulled over on to the verge again. He then jumped out of the ute, locked the doors, and half-ran back up the tracks, then down the highway, back to the Kombi, and the girl.

JOANNE WAITED TO HEAR THE rumble of the vehicle coming back, but it didn't come. This was a chance for her. The electrical cable was biting into her flesh, so she twisted her wrists. She then had an idea: with the two cuffs tied with 10 centimetres of cable between them, she wondered if she'd be able to move her hands to the front. That would make it easier. Still lying on the ground with her knees up to her chest, she brought her wrists down her back and then under her backside. She passed first one leg through, then the other. That felt much better, and she chided herself silently for not thinking of it sooner.

She tried to pick at the ties, but they were fastened too tightly to budge. She raised them to her mouth and chewed at the tape, but only managed to bite off a corner, and spat it out on the ground. That wouldn't work.

Her hair kept falling in her eyes, and she realised her hairband must've fallen off at some point, maybe when the canvas bag had come off her head in the front seat of the man's ute, or when she'd been thrown into the back. She tried to push her hair back out of her face with her tied hands, and felt tape still in her hair. That could wait. The most important thing now was to free her hands. She tried to ease her wrists from the cuffs, but she couldn't quite get them over her hands. Think, think. How could she do this? It was then that Joanne remembered the stick of lip balm in her shorts' pocket and she moved both hands towards the pocket and pushed it up through the material. As it popped out, she grabbed it with her right hand, lifted it to her mouth and pulled off the cap with her teeth. She then spat it out on to the ground, and wiped the stick over the ties and on the skin of her left hand, hoping she'd be able to slide her wrist from the cuff. No, it was still too tight. She swapped the balm between hands and tried to grease her right wrist and the ties. She was almost weeping with frustration by the time she realised they weren't going to budge.

But then she heard footsteps on the gravel. He must have come back on foot to try to find her. She felt her body start trembling again. 'I thought, "He's going to be so mad when he finds me, and he's going to be really determined to find me this time",' she says. She could hear him clearly on the hard shoulder, making that same dragging noise again, pulling something or digging something into the gravel.

Then, just as abruptly, the noises stopped and a car door slammed.

THE MAN LOOKED OUT INTO the scrub where he knew the girl must be hiding. He itched to get his gun and go back out there again after her. But he knew he couldn't risk it. He'd been seen and now he had to get out as fast as he could.

He finished covering the pool of blood with dirt and stones to hide it, and got into the Kombi and started it up, sneering at the distinctive clatter. He then drove back up the highway, past his ute. Eighty metres along the road, he turned left up the dirt track he'd checked out earlier and stopped another 100 metres in, by a large white gate to his secret little road. He then pulled into the bush a way, just so the van wasn't too easy to find.

He slammed the door behind him, and trudged back down the track to the road. When he got there, he looked back. Yeah, you could barely see the van from the road and that was even if you knew what you were looking for. It'd be a long time before anyone found that. He turned right into the scrub near the road and half-ran towards his vehicle. He clambered in, gunned the engine, did a three-point turn and drove back to the girl. He slowed a little when he drew level with where she must be hiding, felt a pang of regret that he didn't have more time, and then roared off. Still, she'd never survive, a silly little English girl out there on her own.

JOANNE LAY SOBBING QUIETLY. SHE heard a vehicle return before thundering off south down the highway. She felt confused. Had the man really gone? Or was it a trick to get her to come out of her hiding place? If only Pete were here, he'd know what to do.

'I really wanted to come out but I didn't know what to do,' she says. 'I thought I'd better stay there. I was hidden so well. I felt safe in my little hiding place.' So she stayed exactly where she was, awaiting the man's return.

# I Have To Be Brave

JOANNE LEES LAY MOTIONLESS UNDER the mulga bush for hours. She had no idea how long she lay there. She was just waiting for the man to drive back to her, to resume the hunt. She didn't dare risk believing he might have gone. He could be laying a trap and had parked up the road, and walked softly back. He could now be out there somewhere, waiting silently for her to emerge from the safety of her hiding place. And then he'd pounce. As she lay there quietly, however, hearing only the odd scuffle of a bush animal in the scrub, the cry of a bird and the rustle of the grasses, she realised she'd have to move sometime. She'd actually been in the same spot for over four hours and it was cold, with the temperature plummeting to 11 degrees. While earlier she must have been sweating with the fear, now she felt chilled to the bone. More than that, though, she felt anxious about Peter. If he was still alive, she'd have to fetch help quickly. 'I was too scared to get out of the bush I was hiding under,' she says. 'I didn't think it was safe. But I thought I would have to be brave and get some help for Pete.' It was a superhuman effort.

She uncurled her body slowly, careful not to make much noise, and stretched out her legs, and then her arms. She sat up gingerly and then, putting her hands face down on the ground, crawled a few metres back towards the road. It was painfully slow, and the sharp spinifex kept whipping her face, and the spindly branches of mulga catching in her hair. This was crazy. They could have her eye out if she didn't get up. Tentatively, she got up to her feet and stood stock still, waiting to see if anything would happen. The black night with its faint smattering of stars and no moon at all remained as quiet as a graveyard.

Slowly, very slowly, she walked towards the road. When she reached it, she looked nervously both ways. It was a long straight stretch of road and there was absolutely nothing, and no-one, in sight. Where she was standing, though, there was no cover. She felt exposed and vulnerable.

She noticed long grass on the other side and she darted across and lay down. From this position, she could see any approaching vehicles, but they wouldn't be able to see her. After lying there a short time, she saw headlights dancing in the south, and realised a car was approaching. She decided not to try to stop it. It could be the man again. Maybe it would be better to stop a big truck. At least she would know that wasn't him, and the driver would be out at night for a legitimate reason. A while later, she heard the unmistakable roar of a road train approaching from the north. She took a deep breath, stood up and got ready to run alongside it. When it was about 30 metres away, she took a couple of steps onto the road so the driver would be able to see her, and held her handcuffed hands in front of her so he'd see them too, and realise she needed help. 'I was next to the road train,' she says. 'As close to it as I could possibly be without being run over. I was trying to get in the view of the lights.'

The road train thundered past in a blast of warm air and, for a moment, Joanne thought he wasn't going to stop. But then she heard the howl of the air brakes being applied. She jogged down the road and as she reached the road train, the driver was already out of the cab and calling to her. Joanne felt relief flood through her body.

BULLS TRANSPORT ROAD TRAIN DRIVER Vince Millar was bringing a three-trailer, 90-tonne load down from Darwin and had been driving since just outside Tennant Creek, when he'd swapped over with his co-driver Rodney Adams. Adams had gone to lie down on the bunk behind the seats after his stint, so Millar was alone in the front. It was 12.35 a.m. and he was travelling at a steady 90 kilometres per hour, looking forward to Barrow Creek, when it would be his turn to rest up for the long journey ahead to Adelaide. Then, out of nowhere, looming up in his headlights, he saw the ghostly figure of a woman holding her arms outstretched towards him.

'She just jumped out from the spinifex on the side of the road,' he says. 'I swerved to miss her but I thought she probably would have gone under the second or third trailer, because I didn't think they would have moved out of the way as quick as the cab … I swore. I was just thinking maybe she might be stuck under the axle at the back. I was a bit worried.'

Adams woke up when Millar cursed and asked what was wrong. Millar told him everything was okay, he was just going to do a tyre check, and Adams lay down and went back to sleep. When the road train finally came to a stop about a kilometre up the road, Millar rummaged for a torch and couldn't find one, so walked back down the length of his vehicle instead, peering under and in between the trailers. 'I was looking for a body,' he says. 'Whether it be an arm or a leg, or her clothes.' When he reached the second trailer, he heard footsteps and a woman's voice shouting for help. He bent down and saw a woman, pale and wide-eyed but most definitely alive, on the other side of the truck. He told her to calm down and duck under the coupling to the second trailer to get to him. When Joanne emerged, she launched herself at him, sobbing. Millar was caught off guard, then prised himself free and pushed her away from him to get a better look.

'She was sort of saying, "Help me, look I'm tied up",' says Millar. 'I was trying to sort of see, and she was showing me her hands.' Then he saw the cable ties around her wrists, the duct tape on one of her legs, and the tape in her hair and around her neck. 'Geez, hang on a minute, stay here!' he told her before calling out to Adams in the cab: 'I got some sheila out here all tied up! Come out and give us a hand!'

Adams climbed down from the cab to see Millar with a woman in handcuffs with duct tape hanging off her. 'She was almost hysterical,' he says. 'She had ties around her wrist, and I sort of looked and thought: "There's something wrong here".'

Joanne was crying and talking at the same time, trying to explain what had happened, and telling them about someone called Peter Falconio. 'My boyfriend's gone, I can't find my boyfriend,' she kept saying, over and over, between sobs. 'I can't find my car.'

Millar tried to assess the situation. 'You could see she was shocked and, I suppose, disturbed,' he says. He yelled at Adams to get some cutters from the toolbox and removed the cable ties, keeping them to give to the police. He then pulled off the duct tape on her leg, and started on the tape in her hair. In the end, it was far too painful having two men pulling at her hair so she took that out herself. The pair put her into the cab, sitting in the middle between them on the engine which was the warmest place. It was now 12.45 a.m. 'Don't worry,' Millar told her gently. 'You're safe now. Everything's going to be all right.'

AT EXACTLY THE SAME MOMENT, a man stopped for fuel at the Shell Truckstop – the large service station Joanne and Peter had driven past on their way north from Alice Springs. He had dark straight hair, a droopy moustache and a baseball cap, and was driving a white ute with a green canopy. He parked beside a bowser, pumped 120 litres of diesel – about 26 gallons or twice the capacity of a standard family saloon car – and then strode to the door of the shop. Andrew Head, the console operator, hadn't noticed the man drive up. It was a quiet night, and he'd been busy restocking one of the fridges.

The man took his time, picking up two bags of ice, two large bottles of Mount Franklin mineral water and a carton of iced coffee. He paid the bill of $136.65 in cash, with three $50 notes. Head assumed the man had long-range diesel tanks fitted to his ute, to buy that amount of fuel. 'I can't recall whether he spoke or not,' he says.

The entire transaction was captured on the closed circuit security cameras.

RODNEY ADAMS TENDED TO THE injuries on Joanne's knees, elbow and arm, all the while discussing with Vince Millar what to do next. They considered taking her to the police station at Alice Springs, then wondered if there'd be police at the station at Ti Tree. They felt sure Barrow Creek would be closed at this time of night.

But Joanne kept insisting she wanted to find Peter, and Millar eventually relented and said they'd have a look around. He moved the truck to the side of the road, disconnected the trailers, and turned the cab back to drive slowly north, looking along the sides of the road. At one stage, they noticed a small pyramid of dirt, around 15 to 20 centimetres high, at the edge of the bitumen, but their cab headlights were too patchy to be of much help. Only later were they to discover it was a pool of blood over which gravel had been hurriedly kicked. They also saw fresh tyre marks in a dirt track leading off the Stuart Highway 80 metres further north, but after following them for a short way, they doubled back for fear of getting bogged.

Joanne had begun recounting what had happened. 'We couldn't work out who Peter was,' says Adams. 'She said, "my boyfriend", but through the sobbing it was hard to decipher a complete sentence.' When she got to the part, however, where the man pulled out his gun, Millar blanched. He and Adams exchanged looks over her head.

'How do you know he had a gun?' Millar asked Joanne.

'Cos he held it against my head when he tied me up,' she replied.

Millar looked at her aghast. 'So what the bloody hell are we doing out here looking around in the bush for a bloke that's got a gun?' he said. 'It's too dark, we're not going to see anything.' He drove back to the trailers, hooked them up again and headed south, the same direction the man had driven, towards Barrow Creek.

# CHAPTER TWENTY-TWO

# A Blow-in at Barrow Creek

AT 1.30 A.M. ON SUNDAY 15 JULY 2001, the roadhouse at Barrow Creek was in full swing. Since it was the middle of the Australian winter, popular, if eccentric, publican Les Pilton had held his mock Christmas party the weekend before, and this was now the dregs of his annual New Year's Eve party. Around fifteen diehard friends, family members and tourists were propping up the bar. Pilton had visited Barrow Creek from Alice Springs and liked it so much, he stayed … for the next thirty-four years. In 1988, he'd taken over the roadhouse, combining fuel pumps, the bar and various basic forms of accommodation.

Pilton, fifty-one, is a genial host. Two hundred thousand people a year drive up and down the Stuart Highway, he says, so if he meets only half of them, he's got a pretty good social life. It wasn't always so good, however. Five years after he and his wife of fifteen years moved to Barrow Creek, she went off with someone who'd also been passing through. Pilton tried to commit suicide, but failed. Since then, he feels he makes a contribution by chatting to everyone who comes through, even talking through their problems with them. 'I think that's part of the reason I'm here,' he says. 'I talk to people who have hard circumstances and understand how they feel. It's a sort of ministry in a way. You help people.' In 1999, Pilton had got together with an old friend the same age, Helen Jones, who'd also split up with her husband, and who'd returned to Alice Springs after a time away to nurse someone dying of cancer. She came up to live with him at Barrow Creek in early 2001.

The couple were proud of the place. Pilton serves cheerily behind the bar nearly every day, yarning with customers with unfailing good humour. 'It's a lifestyle kind of thing, I think,' he says, of Barrow Creek, population eleven – all of whom work for him. 'Some days are absolutely great here. And others are fucking fantastic!'

The dusty, stained walls of the bar are adorned with countless postcards and mementoes, including an old pair of panties, bra and various other items of underwear. Tattered army memorabilia takes up another space, as well as a decrepit Australian flag, crude jokes, and old cigarette packets beneath a shroud of spiders' webs. There's graffiti scrawled over the bar, and an old broken clock with the message that any time is 'Beer O'Clock'. Behind the bar is a display of thousands of moth-eaten banknotes. Tradition has it that anyone passing through leaves one on the wall so, if they ever return, they'll always have enough cash to buy another beer. Most Aboriginals still drink outside, buying their grog through a hatch in the wall. Some visitors see the roadhouse as an eccentric slice of old Australia; others as a filthy, decrepit hole in the middle of nowhere they only visit because there's no alternative.

TRUCKIES VINCE MILLAR AND RODNEY ADAMS were sure the Barrow Creek Roadhouse would be shut, but all the lights were still blazing when they pulled up. Millar jumped out, but Joanne Lees refused to budge. 'She wouldn't move at that stage,' says Adams. 'She was terrified.' The reason was obvious: she was petrified that the man might be inside. In the end, Millar said he'd go in alone to check the coast was clear. Adams stayed with Joanne. Inside, Millar found Les Pilton behind the bar and briefly explained what had happened.

'Yeah, right mate!' said Pilton, disbelievingly.

'No mate,' replied Millar. 'It's fair dinkum.'

Pilton looked at Millar's eyes, and could see the adrenalin pumping. He nodded, and rang the nearest police station at Ti Tree, but only reached their answering machine. He then dialled Alice Springs, gave a precis of what he'd been told to the senior auxiliary on duty, Tony Stafford, and then passed the phone to Millar. Stafford told Millar he'd have to speak to someone higher up. 'That fella doesn't believe me,' Millar told Pilton after their conversation had finished, 'but he says he'll ring back.' Pilton then went out to the truck with Millar to try help persuade Joanne to come in. She was sitting with her head on her knees. 'I know you've had a hard time up the road,' Pilton told her, 'but this place is safe and we'll look after you.' Eventually Joanne agreed. She sat on a bar stool but refused offers of a stiff drink; instead, she agreed to a cup of tea.

Adams was pleased. 'I thought: "cup of tea, half a teaspoon of sugar for shock, ideal",' he says.

For it was clear that she was still in shock. She was barely speaking, just nodding or shaking her head mutely. 'She had calmed down from actually being out there,' says Millar. 'But she was just shocked. You could see there was some sort of shock there. She got upset … She was worrying about Peter all the time, that was her main concern. I think if Peter had been there with her, it wouldn't have been so bad. But because Peter was gone …'

Pilton noticed the same thing. 'When she was being asked about some of the events, she was welling up and started to have tears,' he says. 'Then she made herself not actually break down and fully cry.'

STAFFORD ALSO TRIED TO CONTACT the Ti Tree police, but got the answering machine as well. He called the watch commander, Senior Sergeant Geoff Sullivan, who called Barrow Creek and spoke to Joanne personally. When she'd put the phone down, the others noticed she was shivering. Millar went back to the truck to fetch her a jumper, while Pilton lit a fire in the grate. Millar suggested she might like some female company, and went out to wake up one of the bar staff, Cathy Curley, who'd gone to bed in one of the sheds 50 metres away from the main building about an hour before.

Curley came in ten minutes later, and introduced herself to Joanne. Her eyes took in everything: the grazes on her knees, elbows and arm, and the marks around her wrists from the cable ties. 'She seemed a bit shaken up, so I offered to take her down to wash her face,' says Curley. '[Her face was] a bit like, scrubby, dirty.' There wasn't a towel in the bathroom, so Curley took Joanne to the laundry to find one. At the sound of her voice, her eight-month-old Blue Heeler cross puppy Tex ran in. Joanne asked her what breed of dog Tex was. 'A Blue Heeler,' replied Curley. Joanne nodded. 'I recognised it as the same breed of dog as the one that the man had,' she says. The colours, however, were different – the man's dog was black and brown, whereas Tex was more blue.

When the women returned to the bar, Pilton thought Joanne might want a nap as it would be a couple of hours before the police arrived. He took her to one of the rooms just off the bar area to lie down but she agreed to go in only if he left the light on and the door open, but even then she lay down for no more than a few minutes. She was far too wound up to sleep and was anxious for the police to arrive so they could start searching for Peter.

BRADLEY MURDOCH WAS THOUGHT TO be in the area at around the time, driving north from Alice Springs and then taking a left to thunder, in his white four-wheel-drive Landcruiser, across the dirt Tanami Track to Broome.

THE POLICE ARRIVED AT ABOUT 4.20 a.m. and took a statement from Joanne. Detective Sergeant Ian Kesby photographed her standing next to the cool room, took pictures of her injuries and asked his colleague, a female officer from Tennant Creek, Senior Constable Erica Sims, to examine her clothing. Sims found a hair that looked as if it might be from a dog. Then Kesby took Joanne outside and showed her a ute with a green canvas canopy, asking if that was similar to the vehicle her attacker had driven. 'She said the canvas on the other ute was a darker colour,' says Kesby. 'You could go from the front to the back of the ute she was in, and there was bedding in the back. She was obviously in shock. She was shivering from time to time and was very upset.'

In the meantime, Helen Jones, Les Pilton's Dublin-born girlfriend, who moved from London to Australia at the age of twenty with her then husband, had been woken up by all the commotion, and had come into the front bar to see what was going on. Jones saw Joanne sitting huddled by the fire. 'She was very distressed and yet, in a strange way, calm,' she says. 'She just kept asking if anyone knew where Peter was.'

The police were glad to see Jones there, and asked her to give Joanne some fresh clothes and help her to shower. They needed her clothes as evidence. Jones led her to the bathrooms, and chatted to her to try to put the frightened girl – the same age as her youngest son – at her ease.

Hearing her accent, Joanne relaxed a little. At least that was something familiar in this strange place, where everything else felt so foreign.

'I felt so desperately sorry for her,' says Jones. 'She kept saying how much she missed everyone at home. But she was frightened that if she went home she would somehow be abandoning Peter.' Jones asked her if she'd like to call England from the roadhouse, to tell her mum and stepfather what had happened. Joanne shook her head mutely. She knew she wouldn't be able to find the words.

Outside, the police asked Millar to draw a rough map of the area where he'd found Joanne and to accompany them back out to the spot. He found the dark pile of gravel on the roadside again without any difficulty, even though it had, by now, been run over many times by other vehicles. It was only later that he found out it was blood. Soon after, he gave up driving trucks. Friends say he had too many flashbacks of that terrible night, and lost his taste for it.

Millar at least thought he'd brought an end to Joanne's nightmare. But neither he nor she were to know another one was just beginning.

# CHAPTER TWENTY-THREE

# Where's My Peter?

ALICE SPRINGS CID SENIOR Constable Trent Abbott was on a rostered day off on Sunday July 15, so he was startled to hear his phone ringing at 3.30 a.m. He lifted the receiver blearily. Senior Sergeant Geoff Sullivan filled him in, and directed him to drive straight to Barrow Creek with two other officers to set up a cordon around the roadhouse. He set out immediately, and arrived at about 6.30 a.m. After cordoning off the area, he drove north with a group of officers and truck driver Vince Millar to the spot where he'd been told the attack had taken place. They stopped further up the road from the crime scene, 10.7 kilometres north of the roadhouse, positioned themselves on both sides of the road and walked slowly south, looking for anything suspicious. In the daylight, they could see exactly how rough the scrub was. With dull orange rocky dirt, and different tones of green from olive to sun-bleached grey-green, the area looked grim and inhospitable. Mulgas, the long-life variety of acacias in the area, were stunted by the lack of moisture, but still spread out prickly branches as far as they could reach. Tufts of tough, sharp spinifex, the local porcupine grass, broke up the ground with their hardy roots. And there were burnt patches of land everywhere, probably from the wild bushfires that struck in November 1999.

It wasn't long before Abbott spotted the orange Kombi van in the bush. The men spread out and slowly approached the vehicle, stopping around 50 metres away. 'Is there anyone there?' called Sullivan. 'Come out!' He repeated it a few times, with no result, so Abbott walked up to the van and peered through the windscreen. There was no sign of life. The officers sealed off the area for the forensics team. Abbott went back to the spot where Sullivan had by now found the stain. He was told to set up roadblocks 100 metres away in both directions. No traffic at all was going to be allowed through, just in case Peter Falconio was somewhere there, lying injured, waiting for help. In the circumstances, that felt the very best they could hope for.

SERGEANT GLEN MCPHEE, A MEMBER of the police support unit, the Territory Response Group (TRG), had arrived at 5.15 a.m. 'Our primary concern was locating a missing person who might be alive at that stage,' he explains. 'So I was urgently looking through the area close to the incident site.'

On the eastern side of the Stuart Highway a fence ran parallel to the road, some 20 metres away. On the western side, a fence ran at an angle at distances varying from 100 metres to 400 metres from the road. The team walked 2 kilometres in both directions. TRG Senior Constable Kevin Paice, who'd flown down to Ti Tree from Darwin, was part of the search lines, and as he walked he poked long sticks into all the drain gulleys. They swept the area, over and over again. McPhee was in charge of keeping a running sheet of everything of significance; sadly, there was little to report. They found footprints, later confirmed to be Joanne Lees'; they found a boot, but it was old and had been abandoned a number of years before; and they spotted a large flock of birds circling, and raced there only to discover it was merely the site of the local tip. Their sole real finds were some black duct tape and a small white plastic cap from a stick of lip balm, buried under leaves found in a depression where Joanne could have been lying.

TRG Sergeant Bruce Grant was part of another nine-strong team who were combing the spinifex with metal detectors over an area 300 metres north, 500 metres south and 300 metres west of the crime scene. For six days they searched for clues: a murder weapon, bullets, car keys or personal items that may have been dropped. All they found were screws, parts of trucks and old horseshoes. An alert had gone out for a white four-wheel-drive ute, but in a place like the Northern Territory, that description fitted just about every second vehicle. The highway was closed in both directions and people in Alice Springs were warned about travelling north. In spite of the measures taken, in all likelihood, the attacker would have been long gone.

One of the key officers involved was Senior Constable Ian Spilsbury, the crime scene examiner from Alice Springs. He went straight to the Barrow Creek Roadhouse and photographed and videoed Joanne and her injuries, and took DNA swabs and fingerprints. He then went on to the crime scene, where he examined and bagged items including a cigarette butt, two pieces of tape and the lid off Joanne's lip balm. He supervised the measurements of distances and areas, including the bloodstained section of gravel with its 58-centimetre diameter, and the taking of 300-plus photographs. He had a turn at operating a metal detector too, but only came up with old bottle tops and ringpulls. Spilsbury's priority was finding a spent firearm cartridge, but he knew it was a big ask. If the weapon was a revolver, there wouldn't be a cartridge at all and, depending on the calibre and projectile, the bullet may not even have exited the body.

Another crime scene specialist, Senior Constable Tim Sandry, videoed the area, at the same time as helping with the search 40 to 60 metres north and south of the bloodstain. By that stage, the officers were down on their hands and knees, minutely examining every square centimetre of the ground. A request was put in for Aboriginal trackers to come and help but they were unable to get there until the following Friday.

Later, that came to be regarded as a critical error.

JOANNE WAS ESCORTED BACK TO the crime scene and was asked to check the Kombi to see if anything was missing. Looking pale and exhausted, she did exactly as she was told. She didn't flinch at the sight of the vehicle. She would be one of the last people to see it in that spot. Soon after, Abbott returned with a tow-truck driver to take it back to Alice Springs.

Later that afternoon, the police suggested to Joanne that she accompany them to Alice. She looked scared. Everyone she knew was out there at Barrow Creek. She turned to Helen Jones. 'Please, please come with me!' she begged. Jones nodded. With four children of her own, she felt it was the very least she could do for this young girl, all alone in a foreign land. To try to reassure her, she told Joanne she could stay with her at Les Pilton's parents' house in Alice.

The pair was driven into town and Joanne's interviews recommenced at 7.20 p.m., this time with Senior Sergeant Helen Braam, a detective and qualified negotiator from Darwin, and Detective Senior Constable Isobel Cummins, who was trying to put together a photo-fit image of the attacker. Braam asked Joanne about everything that had happened, and Cummins showed her pictures of various features – mouths, noses, facial shapes, moustaches and hairstyles – asking which, if any, resembled those of her attacker.

'[Joanne] went through a whole range of emotions,' says Braam. 'She was tired, teary, angry. She was stressed.' But after short breaks, she always managed to rally again, to provide them with the information and descriptions they needed.

Braam used cognitive interviewing techniques, where she asked Joanne to go through the entire story from start to finish uninterrupted, then go back and focus on a particular area, and continue to the end, and then re-tell the story backwards. At the same time, Cummins was concentrating on a description of the attacker. Joanne claimed the man had a long or ovalish face, collar-length hair, sunken cheeks, deep-set eyes with dark circles underneath, black and grey streaky hair, a black-grey moustache down past his mouth, and a stocky build. He was at least forty-five years old. She added he had a 'cowboy-style' look, with a dark coloured T-shirt under an open-necked black and white check shirt, heavy trousers made of either denim or canvas and a black baseball cap with a shield motif, bordered with yellow. Gradually, they refined the photo-fit image of the man's face, even though Joanne found looking at her attacker's face over and over again so utterly harrowing, and she was dead tired and still extremely distressed. Outside, Abbott handed the orange Kombi over to forensics, and then went off duty. In the interview room, around midnight, Braam finally called it a day and said they'd pick up where they left off the following morning.

But still Joanne had to work. On the way to Piltons' parents' house – the police had been unsuccessful in their attempts to persuade Joanne to stay at a hotel – Braam drove past a number of car dealerships and car rental agencies to see whether or not Joanne could spot a vehicle similar to the canvas-backed four-wheel-drive ute. This exercise yielded little, however. Joanne didn't see anything she thought resembled the ute, and some places were so dark, neither of them could see anything at all.

THAT EVENING, TWO POLICE OFFICERS, Jason Hastie and Jonathan Beer, called into the Shell Truckstop on the northern outskirts of Alice Springs. They showed the man behind the till, Andrew Head, one of the rough photo-fit images and told him they were hunting this man for the possible murder of a tourist and the attempted abduction of his girlfriend. Head recognised the man in the picture immediately. 'When I was shown the picture, I recalled serving the guy,' he says. He was unable to access the closed circuit security system, however, so the police called Val Prior, the Shell area manager. She was used to it; the police were often looking for stolen vehicles that stopped for refuelling. But this was late on a Sunday night. 'Oh my God, what do you want this time of night?' she aked jovially, but when told, didn't make a fuss about coming in. She had a good relationship with the police and they often responded quickly when she called them about 'runners' driving away without paying. She unlocked the system and ran through the tape with the officers.

It was an awkward process. The cameras didn't tape direct to video, but onto a computer hard drive, which only enabled Prior to obtain still images and print them out individually, or to save them to a floppy disk instead, which would then need to be sent to a specialist to be transferred onto video. The police officers took away the stills prints and said they'd return for the disk.

THAT NIGHT, HELEN JONES MADE up the spare room for Joanne. But Joanne's face crumpled when she saw it. 'Please don't leave me alone,' she pleaded. 'I couldn't bear it.' Jones agreed to sleep in the same bed with her, and listened as Joanne recounted what had happened. She talked about how wonderful Peter was, and how they'd always done everything together. She talked about that last sunset, and their plans, one day, to marry. When, exhausted, she finally fell asleep, she dozed only fitfully, and Jones heard her weeping. She would wake up confused then, realising she hadn't simply had a nightmare, would break down again. 'She kept asking me over and over, "Where's Peter? Where's my Peter?"' says Jones. 'We both felt in our hearts he must be lying dead somewhere, but I just kept reassuring her he'd be all right. What else could I say?'

# CHAPTER TWENTY-FOUR

# Hoping For The Best, Fearing The Worst

BY EARLY NEXT MORNING, Monday July 16, the area was swarming with police, police auxiliaries and members of the TRG in their distinctive pale khaki uniforms. Roadblocks had been set up on all highways leading into SA, WA and Queensland, where heavily armed police were pulling over vehicles, checking the occupants and warning them about stopping for strangers. The 1.5 million square kilometres of the Northern Territory was virtually closed off to the outside world. Even the air space above had been closed to all aircraft other than eight planes, some of them privately-owned and lent by neighbouring cattle stations, sweeping the skies looking for any telltale clues.

With only one bitumen road travelling north to south, but hundreds of rough tracks and hidden trails that you could travel for days without seeing another soul, people get lost, disappear and die in that part of Australia. It's one of the most remote areas of the world and the size of the American mid-west … only without the people.

Everyone was hoping for the best, but feared the worst. 'As the days went, by the distance that could have been covered by any person involved turned into thousands of kilometres in a radius around the site,' says Sergeant Glen McPhee. 'Given our limited resources, we had to use what we had to best circumstances.'

AT 4 A.M. THAT DAY, Bradley Murdoch's drug-running partner James Hepi was in bed at the flat in Broome. His phone rang. Murdoch had just arrived back in town after the long drive from Sedan and was at the workshop of West Kimberley Diesel in the outer suburbs. Could Hepi pick him up?

Hepi was surprised: Murdoch usually rang from a roadhouse which had mobile reception about 30 kilometres out of town. Hepi would then know to open the gates, so Murdoch could drive straight in to unload his cargo. It was odd that he'd go directly to the workshop. But when Hepi saw him, he was even more taken aback. Murdoch had left a few days before with collar-length hair and a long handlebar moustache. Now, he was clean-shaven and had razored his hair to a smooth number one. Hepi didn't ask why. 'I wasn't really interested,' he said later. After all, men running drugs aren't the type either to ask, or answer, personal questions. In addition, Murdoch appeared 'scattered', says Hepi. He'd been on amphetamines for the past four or five days in order to stay awake on the long drug runs, and was wired.

During that day, news came through of the attack on two young backpackers just north of Barrow Creek. 'It wasn't me!' Murdoch immediately exclaimed. Hepi looked at him quizzically. He hadn't even asked. He did ask, though, why Murdoch had gone straight to the workshop instead of coming home first. 'The vehicle needed work,' Murdoch told him. It was something to do with the gearbox. Hepi saw the white four-wheel-drive Landcruiser was covered in red desert dirt.

The work seemed to take a long, long time and was bloody expensive too. 'Not sure quite how much, but quite a lot of money,' says Hepi. 'A whole aluminium canopy made, turbo, exhaust, $1000 alone for the exhaust.' What irked was the fact that Hepi was helping foot the bill. It was paid for from their drug proceeds, 'just from the money we'd been making'. By the time the work had been completed, the vehicle had been heavily modified and looked completely different to before. '[It'd had the] tray removed, the canopy removed, a complete new one made,' says Hepi. 'So the appearance of the vehicle changed dramatically.'

THAT MORNING, JOANNE LEES WAS picked up by Senior Sergeant Helen Braam, and the interview resumed. It continued for eight more hours and over two days, twelve one-hour tapes were recorded. Joanne also continued to help Cummins refine the photo-fit image of her attacker. By draft number nine, Joanne declared that was as good as it was going to get. A mouth swab was taken for DNA testing as well as her fingerprints and, at one stage, another officer came in to show her a selection of firearms in the hope she might recognise the features of the one she'd been threatened with. 'Nothing mirrored what she thought she'd seen,' says Braam. Braam also made a number of sketches of various things, and recorded a description of Joanne's injuries.

Senior Sergeant Jeanette Kerr, who'd come down from Darwin to coordinate the intelligence gathering, was pleased with progress. She felt, however, that Joanne needed to be allocated a female chaperone. 'Because Ms Lees was alone in Australia, we felt she was extremely vulnerable, frightened and traumatised,' says Kerr. 'She needed a support person with her at all times.' By the end of the day, it was felt Braam and Joanne had been through so much together, Braam would make the ideal candidate.

THE INCIDENT HAD HAPPENED IN possibly the worst place on perhaps the worst day. Barrow Creek was isolated, communication was difficult, and those long drives there and back all the time were proving exhausting for the police. It didn't help either when a few of them billeted at the roadhouse refused to stay there for more than a night. The rooms in the main block were oppressively dingy, with sweaty walls, sticky carpet and torn rags at the windows, and you could hear all the noise from the bar – or from the occupants of the other rooms – through the gaps between the walls and the ceiling. The toilets were outside, through a courtyard. The officers said they'd much prefer to stay in tents, outside, which meant a whole new camp had to be set up.

The timing was terrible, too. The Northern Territory Police's Assistant Commissioner John Daulby, the man who'd normally take charge of any big investigation, was in New Zealand visiting his kids who lived there with his ex; his relief officer, Superintendent Kate Vanderlaan, was in Perth for an operation on her shoulder; Southern Region Commander Bob Fields, in charge of the Alice Springs region, was in Darwin for a farewell; and the police's Darwin-based head of media,

Denise Hurley, who'd only been in the job six months, was in Brisbane at a conference. In addition, her one staff member operating out of the Alice Springs office, 1490 kilometres away from HQ in Darwin, had just left. Hurley flew to Darwin in time to greet her parents who were visiting her, and then headed straight back out to Alice Springs.

Complicating matters even further, Prime Minister John Howard was in Alice Springs attending a ceremony to turn the first clod of earth for the start of work extending the Adelaide-to-Alice Ghan railway line to Darwin with a horde of local and overseas journalists. The media circus was already in town when the news broke.

LATER ON MONDAY JULY 16, BRADLEY MURDOCH dropped by to visit his girlfriend Beverley Allan when she'd got home from work. She couldn't help noticing his changed appearance. When she'd last seen him, just over a week before, he'd had a bushy moustache going down the sides of his mouth, and his hair was quite long. Now he looked entirely different. 'He was cleanshaven with no moustache, and he'd shaved his head,' she says. 'It was really, really short, a number one, close-shaved.' His demeanour was also strange. He looked 'fairly wrung out'. Allan asked him how his trip had been. 'He told me it hadn't been a good trip,' she says. 'There'd been a few dramas.' She looked concerned. 'What sort of dramas?' she asked. His reply didn't leave her any the wiser. 'He believed someone was following him, and that he'd had to find out who was following him, and he'd had to deal with it.'

Murdoch said that he'd come through Fitzroy Crossing on his way back, where he'd called in to see his friend Peter Jamieson. Jamieson later said he remembered him dropping by. Murdoch had arrived at his service station at around sunset, just after he'd locked the bowsers for the day. He'd unlocked one for his mate, sold him around 50 litres of diesel that he'd paid for in cash, and then sat down and chatted to him about fishing while he ate a steak sandwich and drank a mug of coffee.

To Beverley Allan now, though, Murdoch mumbled something about using Jamieson as a back-up. 'He'd also had to come the long way home or had run into a roadblock,' says Allan. The roadblock was one of the police roadblocks aimed at finding the man who'd attacked Peter Falconio and Joanne Lees.

A FEW HOURS ON, ONE of the most experienced forensic scientists in the Northern Territory, Carmen Eckhoff, arrived in Alice Springs from Darwin. Fingerprint expert Sergeant Neil Hayes had just finished examining the Kombi van, so immediately Eckhoff set to work, donning a gown and gloves before searching the interior for documents, keys, passports, diaries, fuel receipts, email addresses, photographs ... anything at all that could prove significant. Everything that was taken out, including a camera, atlas, CD, plastic bag with a sewing kit inside, even cigarette butts from the ashtray, was carefully photographed. Eckhoff took Peter Falconio's Ventolin inhaler from the shelf under the dashboard to use for a sample of his DNA. A set of three keys were also swabbed for DNA. Then she sprayed Orthotolodine and Luminol, liquids that illuminate on the presence of blood, inside and outside the vehicle. The only blood she found was on the Kombi bumper. It belonged to a kangaroo.

By this stage it was getting late but Eckhoff, a woman with a reputation for being extremely strong-minded who doesn't take orders easily, wanted to visit the crime scene. She drove out and arrived around 11.30 p.m. Again, she sprayed Luminol and Orthotolodine on, and around, the stain on the road. It lit up straight away. When she moved a few stones and dirt, it lit up even more. The dark substance was definitely blood and, what's more, it was clear that someone had tried to hide it.

# CHAPTER TWENTY-FIVE

# You Never Know Who's Out There

WHEN THE NORTHERN TERRITORY POLICE finally broke the news to the outside world of what had befallen two British backpackers on a lonely road north of Alice Springs, they didn't pull any punches: Peter Falconio was missing and Joanne Lees was lucky to be alive. 'I don't entertain any doubt whose blood it is,' Southern Region Commander Bob Fields told the assembled media on Monday July 16. 'We're thinking the worst.' On the subject of Joanne, he came as close to sentimentality as any hardened copper on what must be one of the world's toughest, loneliest beats ever could. 'I just thank God that she didn't get taken away from the crime scene,' he said. 'How she survived is as close to a miracle as anything I know about.'

The greatest fear was the chance of the attacker striking again; the greatest worry was that they might not find him in time. 'We're looking for a needle in a haystack and you don't get a haystack much bigger than the Northern Territory,' said Fields, peering out at the world's press through his large, old-fashioned aviator-style glasses. 'One break and we will zero in on him. We're jumping on cars out of helicopters. It is going to be a battle of wits and survival. But let me say this. We will never give up the hunt.'

The story had everything: two young backpackers on the trip of a lifetime to one of the globe's top holiday destinations, and an unknown and armed predator out to kill and, presumably, rape, still at large somewhere in the vast, mysterious outback, the stuff of so many dreams and just as many nightmares.

BACK IN ENGLAND, JENNY AND Vincent James were having a normal Sunday morning in their village just outside Huddersfield when they happened to turn the TV on to a Teletext channel. Jenny was in the kitchen washing up, and shouted out to Vincent to take a look. A young British man had been shot in the Australian outback, and a woman had only survived by escaping into the bush. It had happened on the road running north of Alice – the road Joanne had phoned them the previous day to tell them they'd be taking.

The couple stared at the screen with their hearts in their mouths, reading, and re-reading. No, it couldn't be. But what if it were?

Vincent was the first to break the silence. 'I'll go to Huddersfield police station and see if they know anything,' he said. The officer at the front desk said he had no information, but that he'd phone the Foreign Office. With every minute passing, Vincent's optimism slowly dribbled away. When the officer returned from the back office, his face was grim. Vincent felt like he'd been slugged in the stomach. 'I'm sorry,' the man said. 'They've confirmed it is Joanne and Peter.'

Vincent called Jenny from the station. 'It's them,' he told her. 'Pete's still missing, but Joanne is okay.' He could hear his wife sobbing on the other end of the line and ached to go home to comfort her but knew he had another call to make first. He dialled the Falconios' number and Peter's father, Luciano, picked up. Vince was filled with dread but far better they hear the news from him than from the anonymous authorities over in Australia. As he told Luciano that his son had been shot and was presumed dead, he could hear Peter's mum Joan in the background. The sound of her scream tore at his heart. He would never forget the raw desperation in her voice, and the utter misery.

AS THE NEWS SPREAD AROUND the Northern Territory, there was a deep sense of shock, and shame, that something so terrible could happen to two young visitors. There was also panic. With the road north sealed off, knockabout, happy-go-lucky Alice Springs suddenly felt like a town under siege. At the Stuart Caravan Park where Peter and Joanne had spent their last night, owners Leonie and Rob Marshall didn't know what to say. The police were going through their receipts book and taking down the numbers of the registration plates on every vehicle to check that the couple's attacker hadn't also been staying there, and had followed them out.

'They wouldn't let people leave,' says Leonie. 'It was our busiest time of year, and we were so crowded. But more and more people kept arriving because they didn't want to be out on the road and, with no-one allowed to go, we couldn't cope. We had people coming out of our ears. If everyone breathed at once, the fences would all have fallen over.'

Tempers were beginning to fray. 'The police advised everyone not to travel but people were getting a bit aggro and frustrated,' says Rob. 'They wanted to keep on with their travel plans. Elderly people were arranging to travel in convoys … I thought they were mad! I was telling them, "But this guy's got a gun! What would you do if you met him?" They were all saying, "Oh, we'll be right." It was absolutely mad. I had to point out to them, what if they broke down on the road? No-one would stop to help them. They would have been there for days. And there were roadblocks everywhere. Even the shortest journey was taking hours.'

FOR THOSE PEOPLE ALREADY OUT on the road, there were plenty of tales of narrow escapes. Joanne Harle from the Northern Territory Tourist Commission was driving alone from Alice Springs to Tennant Creek at exactly the same time as the attacker had struck. Towing her horse behind her, she was on her way to Katherine, 280 kilometres south on the Stuart Highway from Darwin, to compete in time trials. She was on heavy cold and flu medication and felt sick and fuddled. She didn't turn the radio on to hear the news, and later couldn't get any reception when she tried. On the way up, she pulled over a few times to let the horse out of its box for a walk, and to have a quick nap behind the wheel. It was only when she was stopped at one of the roadblocks that she heard what had happened, and realised how lucky she'd been. A phone call to a friend confirmed it. 'Have you been out on that road on your own?' he shouted at her. 'You're a bloody idiot! There's a man with a gun out there!'

Harle was shaken, but hadn't thought twice about setting out on her own to make that long, lonely journey. 'I lived for eight years on a station, and I'm used to those kind of places,' she says. 'Most people out here are really friendly and hospitable. Things like that just don't happen here.'

IN HUDDERSFIELD, HOWEVER, ANOTHER family was also panicking. Teacher Ron Phillips' daughter Kate was out on the Stuart Highway with her boyfriend too, and her father hadn't heard from them for days. When the phone call finally came to say they were fine, he felt thoroughly exhausted from the strain. 'I was terrified for my daughter,' he says. 'She must have come within a hair's breadth of meeting that man. She'd been over there eighteen months, living in Sydney and then travelling around Canberra, Melbourne, Adelaide and up through Alice Springs. She was also on her way to Darwin at the time.

'She had to go through all the roadblocks with all the policemen with shotguns telling them not to stop for anything or anyone. They told her, "Just keep going, whatever you do! Don't pull over in any circumstances! Even if you see someone with a broken leg, don't stop!" She said it was like the Wild West. She says there were so many people manifestly psychotic up there, and everyone seemed to have guns.'

AS BACKPACKERS VISITING THE Northern Territory checked out of campsites and into hostels, and abandoned plans to hitchhike, buying bus, train and plane tickets instead, even the hardiest of locals, well accustomed to the vicissitudes of life in the Australian outback, were shaken by the news. They prided themselves on being friendly, trusting and hospitable, and everyone depended on neighbours for help at times, and on people passing through. Strangers represented not unknown dangers, but the chance of a good yarn with someone new, and lending a hand whenever you could was one of the unofficial rules of the outback.

But, suddenly, everything had changed. The Northern Territory was being portrayed as a strange, dangerous place, home to deranged souls on the run from the rest of civilisation, and as a vast, desolate stretch of nothingness where people came to hide out, and were rarely found. And, in some ways, that's true. The name the 'Never-Never', coined in 1902, still held fast. For together with that down-home hospitality comes a real tolerance for difference, and an acceptance of free spirits. On all the massive cattle stations in the area, drifters often turn up looking for casual farmwork and usually get it, no questions asked. They may be colourful characters with indistinct pasts but, in the outback, a talent for telling a good story goes a long, long way.

The outback holds a firm place in the Australian psyche. For most indigenous Australians, it's somewhere familiar, often quite unchanged with time, a place of sacred sites and ancient spirits. For most white Australians, it's immense, anonymous, untameable; a frontier of white imagination, a land that turns us all into vulnerable babes in the woods.

IN HUDDERSFIELD, PETER FALCONIO'S family was struggling to come to terms with the news that he'd been shot and was now missing. Luciano and Peter's second-eldest brother Paul had gone to the police station together because they couldn't quite believe what Vincent James had told them. It was the beginning of a long, uncertain nightmare. 'The family are going through hell,' said Paul. 'We are just waiting for the phone to ring and are just sitting tight and praying. We spoke to Pete on Friday and he said he was having the time of his life.'

Luciano and Paul were making urgent plans to fly to Australia, but Joan still couldn't seem to digest the news. 'Peter is a very outgoing man, who lives life to the full,' she told journalists. 'He's the kindest boy in the world.' No-one at that stage had told them the full story, and the Falconios were under the impression Peter had stopped to help a fellow motorist in trouble. 'He was just stopping to help,' Joan said. 'We thought that was just typical of him.'

THE NEXT MORNING, TUESDAY JULY 17, forensic scientist Carmen Eckhoff did more luminescence testing for blood on the Kombi van. More samples were sent up to the laboratory in Darwin; she'd collected some 380 items in all. Then she took some swabs to check for DNA on the steering wheel. She'd earlier noticed a police officer touching the wheel with an ungloved hand, so only took swabs from the part she was sure remained uncontaminated. Then she took samples from the gearstick and the seats.

Joanne's clothes were carefully tested too. There was blood on her shorts and T-shirt, which turned out to be hers, but a tiny bloodstain near the back left sleeve contained a different DNA. Eckhoff tested it against

Joanne's, against Peter's, against Millar's and Adams'. But it was none of theirs, and it was male.

And then came the icing. The steering wheel and gearstick swabs also contained samples of another man's DNA. Eckhoff smiled to herself. This was their first big breakthrough.

# PART THREE

# THE SEARCH FOR
# THE TRUTH

# CHAPTER TWENTY-SIX

# Strained Relations

IT HAD BEEN TWO DAYS since the attack in the desert, but the only people who had seen Joanne Lees were the police. More than 120 newspaper, radio, television and wire journalists had congregated in Alice Springs, and they were all waiting anxiously for the same thing: the appearance of a tearful young English woman, lost and alone in the Australian outback, pleading heartrendingly for any information that might lead to the rescue of her boyfriend.

But they waited. And they waited. And they waited.

In newsrooms across the globe, editors were screaming for a picture of Joanne, for a few words, for the definitive first-hand description of what had happened. Here was a real-life heroine, and a slip of a girl at that, who'd managed to evade a ruthless, cold-blooded killer. It was a powerful story. The only trouble was, no-one was getting it.

At the hurriedly re-equipped police media office in Alice Springs, Denise Hurley was fielding a call a minute. She'd had to install more phones and whiteboards in the tiny one-person office, and squeeze in another staff member from Darwin so there'd be three of them to manage the avalanche of interest. But even then, they couldn't cope with the demands for information from all over Australia, Britain, Singapore ... everywhere around the world. When Hurley slipped away to her hotel room one night for a couple of hours' sleep, she woke to find her mobile phone message bank full with another forty messages, all demanding she call back immediately. Nothing like this had happened in the Northern

Territory since Lindy Chamberlain's baby had gone missing. And even that wasn't on anything like this scale. 'It was difficult from every angle,' says Hurley. 'Another problem was that the mobile phone range wasn't that good there so often people became very frustrated that they couldn't get through. We were working twenty-four hours a day trying to keep up, and people were just falling apart.'

Media organisations were offering large sums of money for an interview with Joanne – one British tabloid was rumoured to be prepared to pay half a million Australian dollars – and everyone was trying to work out where she was staying. Journalists had travelled great distances, and were having to justify large expenses bills getting there and staying, only to sit around their hotel rooms, in the police station or in the town's many bars, with not a single glimpse of their quarry. It was a media feeding frenzy and, with no Joanne to feed on, they set their sights elsewhere.

THE POLICE HAD BEEN TOTALLY unprepared for the level of interest. The Northern Territory force was comparatively small with just 770 officers, 120 auxiliaries and fifty Aboriginal community officers spread over an area five times the size of the UK and twice that of Texas. Much of the area was remote and many of its communities isolated, with 25 per cent of the 200,000-strong population identifying as Aboriginal. In addition, in the four years from 1990, and again in 1997, there'd been a freeze on police recruitment because of budget cuts across the public sector. This had left the force rundown and depleted in experience at the critical sergeant and senior sergeant level.

Resources were already over-stretched by the extent of the searches with officers drawn from all over the Territory to travel to Alice Springs. In addition, normal community policing work had to continue; no-one who'd just been burgled would forgive the police for saying they couldn't investigate as they were too busy elsewhere with a couple of tourists. As well as the business of crime and managing the force, there were also the anti-violence programs and pioneering Aboriginal recruitment projects. 'We think we know our country, but you really don't know what it's all about until you go into a place like the Northern Territory,' says Brian Bates, who was the Northern Territory Commissioner of Police for seven-and-a-half years until Christmas 2001. 'You have to experience the size and remoteness and some of the horrendous problems before you can understand.' No-one had too much time left over to pander to the seemingly insatiable demands of a media who were growing positively obstructive.

As the search continued, furnishing little of interest, there was less and less to give the media. The release of a photo-fit image of a man with shoulder-length hair and a droopy moustache distracted them for a while, but ended up creating even more work when the police had to deal with a fresh torrent of calls from a public eager to help. The trouble was, while Joanne thought the man looked distinctive, some of the local press muttered that the man looked like half the male population up there. Any real breakthroughs, like the discovery of the DNA, had yet to be released. The police wanted to flush the attacker out, and they reasoned that those kind of revelations might scare him underground for good. Even some of the smaller titbits, however, appeared, by either accident or design, to be kept jealously under guard. No-one had, at that point, quite realised the significance of the Shell Truckstop video, amongst all the video tapes collected from a dozen sources around Alice, so news of that wasn't passed on. Worse, Hurley was frequently kept in the dark about developments that might have kept the media happy – if only she'd known them. 'One of the major difficulties for us was that we were not being kept fully informed ourselves in the media unit,' she says. 'Everyone was quite secretive. Our police spokesman was Commander Max Pope but sometimes I even questioned whether or not he was being told everything too.'

When black trackers were brought in, Denise Hurley was relieved, but much to the media's chagrin, they were sent home immediately after they'd finished their work. In addition, access to senior officers was initially limited and, with the paucity of sanctioned information, conjecture and rumour flourished. On Tuesday July 17 British newspaper the *Daily Mail* printed a spine-tingling description of Joanne Lees' ordeal, saying she'd been bound hand and foot, yet had managed to push enough tape away from her legs to stumble into the bush. Under the byline of its Australia-based correspondent Richard Shears, it said she then fell over and started wriggling across the rocks and sand 'like a commando on her elbows'. Despite the fact that Joanne had adamantly refused to speak to all press up to that point, and had never said her legs were tied, the paper even purported to have a direct quote from her, confirming this. 'It was the only way I could get away,' it reported her saying, 'wriggling along on my stomach because my hands and feet were still tied.'

JOANNE HAD HAD LITTLE EXPERIENCE of the media in her tiny Yorkshire village, and couldn't understand why they were so keen for her story. She'd lost the love of her life in horrific circumstances, probably made even more terrible by the guilt of her recent affair with Nick Reilly. She herself had been threatened at gunpoint, tied up and bundled into a stranger's car. She was in shock, on medication and drowning in grief and fear. She longed to be left alone to get on with helping the police find Pete. She didn't see any point in re-telling her story over and over again and viewed the media as an aggressive mob determined to make capital from her distress. They wanted her image and her words simply to sell more newspapers, attract more viewers, entertain more people. They were vultures feeding on her misery, and the more they pushed, the more she dug in. Joanne had used the opportunity of a fresh start in Australia to come out of her shell, to relax more, to be more vivacious. But she was only able to express that confidence around people her own age, her type, with similar interests. Out of that small circle, like many young women with sheltered upbringings and little experience of life beyond, she was completely lost. She didn't have the good communication skills that would allow her to easily cross barriers with people quite different to herself. She had little small talk, and she wasn't comfortable when forced to think on her feet, and talk off the cuff. In the situation in which she now found herself, she didn't have a clue how to behave. She responded by becoming withdrawn and defensive. 'She was a fish out of water,' says Bates. 'Take her outside the environment of her own young crowd and she was lost. In her own circles, she was fine. But with others …'

Hurley and Vanderlaan were trying to persuade Joanne to appear at a press conference. Joanne resisted. They asked if she'd do a couple of interviews. She refused. 'I think she was actually quite traumatised by the whole thing,' says Hurley. 'Not giving in to what other people wanted at that stage was her attempt to retain her own sanity and stature. She was never the kind of person who'd let herself break down in front of the world.' With her hardening attitude that the press was her enemy, she felt giving a press conference would be seen as a sign of real weakness, and she was determined not to appear any more vulnerable than she already felt. She was the victim here, and didn't deserve to be victimised any further. Ironically, her behaviour elicited the opposite effect to the one she imagined. 'It only served,' says Hurley, 'to create even more of a media frenzy.'

AS THE WORLD'S PRESS CLAMOURED for an interview, and the police put more pressure on her to talk, Joanne seemed to start taking grim satisfaction in outfoxing the media. While out eating in Alice Springs with Helen Jones at her old favourite Bojangles restaurant one night, a bunch of journalists came in and sat at a nearby table, not realising they were within a few metres of her. By the time they'd realised who she was, she was long gone. Then came one of the most bizarre episodes of the case. Joanne decided, albeit with a little encouragement from Jones, to give a single interview. And it was with the tiny Alice Springs newspaper, the *Centralian Advocate*, a local bi-weekly with a circulation of just 8000.

It happened partly by chance. The paper's chief of staff Mark Wilton knew Helen Jones from the time she'd worked for the newspaper, booking advertising space, and had a knack of being in the right place at the right time. A Tasmanian-born fitter and turner by trade who'd got into newspapers on the island state by dint of writing about his great love, cricket, he took the first call about the Port Arthur massacre. Similarly, when he found out from publican Les Pilton where Joanne was staying, he made the first call to Jones. He asked if Joanne might consider talking to him and was told maybe, but not yet. Wilton persisted, calling a few times a day and once even speaking to Joanne herself on the phone for a few minutes. She said she still wasn't ready to speak, out of respect for Peter's family. He could have written up the phone conversation, but decided not to use what he'd gleaned from her in the hope of building a relationship that could yield results later. It was a smart choice.

He rang Jones every couple of hours on the Monday, and again on the Tuesday. Jones said Joanne was still upset but that she was getting keener to speak. 'Helen said Joanne was monitoring the media to death, reading everything that had been written about her,' says Wilton. 'She wasn't happy with a lot of the stuff that had been written. Someone had written that Peter had been dragged out of the Kombi kicking and screaming, and all that sort of shit which wasn't true.' Doubtless Joanne had also read about her own fantastical commando derring-do.

At 3 p.m., Wilton finally received the call he'd been waiting for. 'Mark,' came Jones's voice down the line, 'can you come over now to have a chat?' Wilton put down the phone with a triumphant flourish. 'I've fucking got her!' he told the office. 'I'm going now!' It was the interview the world had been waiting for, but it was only by chance it didn't have to wait another three days. As Wilton was leaving the office, someone asked, 'Do you think it'll hold until Friday's edition?' They were immediately overruled.

There was only one condition placed on the interview: no photos. 'I didn't push it,' says Wilton. 'In some respects that was a shame. I probably could've made some money out of that.'

When he arrived at the house, Joanne was sitting in an armchair with her feet tucked up in front of her, and holding her hands tightly together. 'It wasn't quite a fully foetal position, but it wasn't far off,' says Wilton. 'Then she took a couple of deep breaths and let it all out. She was definitely still in shock.'

The interview wasn't easy. Wilton asked Joanne the same questions twice, three times, sometimes four times, in an effort to prise decent answers from her. After forty minutes or so, he switched off the tape recorder, and it was only then that she started to open up. 'I honestly do not believe this man would have let me go,' she said. 'He really needs to be captured. I do not think he would hesitate to do it again.' She found it hard to describe what she went through as the man hunted her in the outback. 'Everyone can use their own imagination about what it was like for me that night. But I was determined to escape and I feel very lucky to be alive.' She said she was convinced the man would have stopped her and Pete even if they had not pulled over. 'He would have shot our tyres or done something anyway.'

Wilton also provided a sympathetic ear to Joanne's feeling that the police were pushing her hard. One day, Helen Jones pointed out helpfully, Joanne had been picked up at 8.30 a.m. and she was still at the police station twelve hours later. He noted she wasn't going to be given access to a counsellor until the next day. By the time he left the house, he knew what he had in his notebook and on his tape was pure gold, but he still had a long day ahead of him before he could write it up. As chief of staff, he was also chief sub-editor and had to lay out pages, as well as make up the paper's biggest earner, the real estate section. While all around the world newspaper editors were biting their nails waiting for his copy and offering him five figure sums to leak material, Wilton diligently sorted out descriptions of three-bedroom houses.

He finished writing up the story just before 8 p.m. that evening. As part of the worldwide News Ltd group, his copy was then sent on elsewhere. Because the *Advocate*'s email system was rudimentary, the story was eventually faxed down to Sydney via the *Northern Territory News*, and then syndicated around the world. Those newspapers that didn't get the story legitimately, plundered the printed text for snippets they could use. One way or another, Wilton's interview found its way on to the pages of every newspaper in Australia, Britain and beyond.

Not surprisingly, Joanne was horrified. She had no idea how the global media machine worked, and had chosen the tiny local paper as a means of delivering a slap in the face to the big British papers who'd been offering her what she considered 'blood money', and the aggressive Australian journalists who'd been hounding her. She'd assumed that, by giving her story to the tiny *Advocate*, she would be denying everyone else. And besides, Jones had told her Wilton was a good mate, and was honourable. Joanne would never have agreed to the interview if she'd known what was going to happen. She considered she'd been tricked into speaking.

It spelled the end of her relationship with Jones, whom she now saw as having been party to what she interpreted as a 'deception'. Their bond had already been weakened when Jones told the media how Joanne had confided that she felt guilty at not insisting Peter ignore the man and drive on when he tried to stop them. That snippet had been picked up and flashed around the world. Joanne interpreted that as a betrayal, and later accused Jones of making mileage for the Barrow Creek Roadhouse out of what had happened, and of enjoying basking in the press attention. Others like Denise Hurley felt it was plain wrong that Jones had gone out on a limb to set up a press interview with someone who was clearly traumatised, without any help or support. In any case, Joanne severed their relationship completely from that day on. Today, Jones refuses to comment on the matter.

Rumours flew around that Mark Wilton had been part of an elaborate ruse and had been introduced to Joanne by Jones as a lawyer who was going to help her. That too was reported to police, and they demanded that he hand over the tapes, which served only to strain even further relations between the media and the police. 'I was accused of perverting the course of justice,' says Wilton. 'So I turned round to them and said you can do anything you fucking want, but you can only have it if I deem you should have it. It got very nasty.' Indeed, the transcripts of his interview show he's telling the truth. Although Joanne said she wanted legal advice, at no time during the interview did Wilton claim to be a lawyer.

Joanne's old Dymocks bookstore boss, Gary Sullivan, watching from Sydney, felt sure he knew what had happened. 'I think she thought that this guy was from a local Alice Springs paper, and she didn't expect that the story would go all through the country, and over to England,' he says. 'She was probably a bit naïve.' In Joanne's determined attempt to outwit the press, she just hadn't realised that the friend of her trusted comforter and minder worked for News Ltd, the most powerful media empire on earth.

# CHAPTER TWENTY-SEVEN

# Gum Leaves To Remember

THE BRIGHTLY-COLOURED POSTCARD LAY ON the mat inside the front door for a while before Joanne Lees' mum Jenny James could bring herself to pick it up. She turned it over to see her daughter's neat writing on the other side and, with her heart in her mouth, read the words slowly. Joanne and Peter were having a great time in Alice Springs, it said. Next, they were travelling north. In a few days, they planned to be in Darwin.

'All I could think of when I read the card was that I hoped Peter's mother had not had one too,' said Jenny tearfully. 'I don't know how she's coping, but we're praying for a miracle.' She'd watched the drama unfold on the other side of the world with despair. She was not well enough for a trip over to Australia, so she and Vincent agreed that he should go. Like her daughter, she too read everything she could about the case, and spoke to Joanne on the phone daily, but it still wasn't enough.

'At times she seems to be okay and handling it, at others she just breaks up,' she said. 'She just wants to help Peter and helping the police is the only way she can help him. I think she's still holding a glimmer of hope that he may still be alive.'

IN SYDNEY, GARY SULLIVAN WAS also trying to work out how he could help. When he'd first heard about an attack on two backpackers, it hadn't occurred to him it might be Peter and Joanne. 'You never expect those sort of things to happen to people you know,' he says. When he learned the next day that the couple had been driving a Kombi van, however, it didn't take long for his worst fears to be confirmed. The police phoned the shop to speak to him. 'Then everyone here knew about it and we were all upset,' he says. 'So we tried to see if there was something we could do to help. I think the thing that goes through your mind is that if that was one of your kids overseas and they were on their own and something happened to them, you would want to think someone might look after them.

'There was no point in me going up there. I thought it'd be much better if someone closer to her went. So I talked to her closest friend at the store, and asked her if she'd want to go.' Amanda Wealleans was keen to help Joanne and Sullivan was happy to pay her fare. She arrived in Alice Springs on the Wednesday July 18, the same day as another friend, Lisa.

Joanne was overjoyed to see them, and moved out of Helen Jones's place to stay at a safe house, as the police had urged originally. In the company of old friends, she felt confident enough to do so.

Sullivan kept in touch with Joanne via Wealleans. 'The whole thing had obviously had a severe effect on Joanne,' he says. 'She wasn't sleeping, and she was in a bit of a mess. She was on Valium or something too, so she was pretty much a zombie.' That also explained why, later, when she finally came face to face with the press, they all remarked on her lack of emotion and her blank composure.

JOANNE'S STEPFATHER VINCENT ARRIVED the same day. When she saw him, she ran straight into his arms. 'I'm so sorry,' he told her. 'We loved Peter too.' He was one of the first people around her to talk of Peter in the past tense.

THE POLICE WERE CROSS-CHECKING their criminal records for anyone fitting the man's description, as well as following up the 300-plus leads phoned in by the public. A charter plane carrying Tanami Mine staff reported spotting a white ute with a green canopy driving through the Tanami Desert. Heavily-armed police swooped, but were disappointed to find the driver was seventy-one. There was an itinerant near Katherine who fitted the description and who'd told a couple of fishermen he'd had to shave off his moustache and cut his hair as he was sick of being stopped by police. The men described him as behaving oddly but, when police tracked him down, they were again able to discount him. A man someone knew in Queensland a few years before with a reputation for violence was also found, but subsequently given the all clear.

Helicopters had joined the planes in conducting aerial searches, but with little success. Motorbike hunts of the area, 50 kilometres north and 50 kilometres south of the crime scene, had found only a kangaroo caught in a fence and a dead dog. There were no more footprints discovered on either the hard, stony surfaces or in the soft, loose sand. One of the sergeants covertly tossed a tiny five-cent coin into the scrub to test how effectively everyone was looking. It was found only an hour later.

By the late afternoon of Wednesday July 18, police decided to call off the search of the 10 square kilometres around the bloodstain and the 4800 square kilometres around that. If a body was there, it would have been found. They had to face facts: the body must have been taken a distance away. The hours between the incident and the time Joanne alerted the police would have enabled the attacker to travel many hundreds of kilometres, especially if he were familiar with the outback roads.

A note of desperation was beginning to creep into the words of police. 'This whole thing is really so bizarre, it almost defies belief,' Commander Bob Fields said. 'If we are dealing with someone who has some local knowledge of the Northern Territory, its back blocks and back roads, it's certainly not beyond the realms of possibility that he could have got out that way.' The words 'defies belief' would later come back to haunt him, however, in a situation where the media was still scrabbling for material to file. One UK newspaper wrote about 'Horror Trips Down Under', recounting the disasters that had befallen backpackers travelling in Australia, while other journalists were speculating, in the absence of any known leads, that maybe even the police were beginning to doubt Joanne's story. The words 'defies belief' came up in the discussion, again and again.

ON WEDNESDAY EVENING, POLICE asked Joanne to take part in a re-enactment back at the crime scene in the hope it might help her remember more details. She sat in a car beside a police officer playing Peter, as a white four-wheel-drive ute pulled up beside them, and another officer leaned over calling to them to stop. She then watched as the two officers moved behind the vehicle. They stopped short, however, of tying her up. Instead, a female officer took her place. Before darkness fell,

Joanne walked around the scrub where she'd hidden that night. 'We realised just how traumatic it would be for Joanne,' said Commander Max Pope. But they were desperate for any clues, however small.

To the assembled press, herded behind police roadblocks 1.8 kilometres either side of the scene, it seemed a perfect opportunity for photos, film and questions. Instead, they were kept for several hours so far away from Joanne and the officers that they could only just make them out. From that distance, no-one saw the moment, just after the fake attacker had pushed his gun into Joanne's face as she sat in the van, that she ducked down beneath the dashboard. She'd broken down in long, anguished sobs, and the play-acting had to be suspended for a few minutes to allow her to recover. The mock gunman patted her arm reassuringly.

One photographer alone managed to get a picture of Joanne as her police car sped through the barrier on its way back to Alice Springs. The rest froze in the cold and wind, watching police lighting their own bonfire to keep warm well into their side of the orange cones.

BUT IF RELATIONS BETWEEN THE police and media were chilly, between Joanne and the media they'd reached 10 degrees Celsius below. She put a message out to her friends in the UK not to speak to any media if approached, and asked the staff back at Dymocks in Sydney to refuse any interviews too. She'd lost so much, the only thing she felt she had left was her private grief. But, as it would transpire, that was the one thing she couldn't afford.

INSTEAD SHE LEFT IT TO Peter's brother Paul Falconio and their father Luciano to front the press as soon as they flew into the airport in Alice Springs. Grief was etched deeply on their faces, but they were calm, composed and dignified as they spoke haltingly of a beloved son and brother who was kind, clever and good. It couldn't have been a more stark contrast with the way Joanne had behaved towards the press.

'My feeling is that he is still alive,' Luciano said. 'Otherwise, I would not be here. I'm looking forward to seeing Joanne, but I'm looking forward to seeing my son even more.'

After the re-enactment, Joanne was driven back to Alice Springs to meet them. She'd told Senior Sergeant Helen Braam she didn't want to see them, but realised she'd have to. She knew how difficult the meeting would be, especially as Luciano was so eager to hold on to the belief that his son was still alive.

THE NEXT MORNING, THURSDAY JULY 19, father and son provided blood and DNA samples to help identify the blood found at the scene. Then they visited the actual site, while the press, again, was kept at a distance. The two men were plainly distressed as they walked up and down the road for some forty minutes, obviously trying to understand Peter's last moments and commit to memory the place with which he'd be forever associated. Then they wandered over to the scrub and leant down. Everyone craned heads to work out what they were doing. They were picking a few gum leaves as mementoes.

BEHIND THE SCENES, JOANNE WAS still working hard with the police. Art teacher David Stagg from the Charles Darwin University Secondary School in Alice Springs was rung to ask if he'd help with the investigation. He arrived the next day, Friday July 20, and was startled to find himself face-to-face with the woman the whole world seemed to be looking for: Joanne. The police wanted some drawings of the white four-wheel-drive ute, he was told, as well as the gun, and Stagg spent a total of six-and-a-half hours with her. Joanne described the vehicle she'd been pushed into once more, and went over every single detail she remembered. Stagg drew sketch after sketch, she pointing out where he hadn't quite captured an aspect, or rethinking her words to make them more accurately explain what she recalled. It wasn't easy. 'Ms Lees gave clear and precise explanations [and] she was composed the whole time,' says Stagg. '[But] at one stage we asked her if she wanted a break because we thought it was a bit too much for her. She rolled back in her chair and covered her face with her hands and came back forward and offered more information. She said she wanted to, that there might be something she'd missed that might be important.'

Joanne tried to remember everything she'd seen. She told Stagg she had a glimpse of a red fire extinguisher on the left-hand side behind the passenger seat, she described the passenger's seat as a bucket seat, and she said the headlights were square in shape. But when it came to describing the man's dog, Joanne hesitated. Stagg showed her a book of dog pictures and showed her a Blue Heeler. Joanne shook her head. 'It wasn't a Blue Heeler or typical bush dog or Territory dog,' she said. 'But I can't say what breed it was. Just a dog sitting in that seat, the driver's side.'

Stagg ended up with more than a dozen sketches of both the inside and outside of the vehicle. The pair followed the same process for a picture of the gun, with the main focus on the barrel and the engraved scrolling on the side. All the time, other officers were popping in to ask Joanne questions. But the one question Stagg kept asking her, over and over, was: 'Are you *sure* you saw that?' Because only the details Joanne said she remembered with absolute clarity were allowed to end up in the final pictures.

BY THIS STAGE, THE CLAMOUR for Joanne to appear at a press conference had reached a crescendo. Australian newspaper, radio, TV and wires journalists were jostling for position with the British media, including correspondents from the BBC, *The Times*, *News of the World*, *Daily Telegraph*, *Guardian*, *Independent*, and *The Observer*. 'It was an absolute feeding frenzy,' says *The Centralian Advocate*'s Mark Wilton. 'It was wall-to-wall journos everywhere.'

As everyone's frustration – and expenses – mounted, no-one could understand why Joanne wouldn't simply face the press, and get it over and done with. 'All we wanted was a picture and a few words,' says Phil Cornford, from the *Sydney Morning Herald*. 'It really wasn't that hard.' Barbie Dutter, the Sydney-based correspondent for the UK's *Daily Telegraph* felt much the same. 'Here we all were, sitting in Alice Springs, just waiting for her to come out of hiding. If she'd just speak to us, and allow a few photographs, it would have taken so much of the pressure off her.'

Rumours as to why Joanne was being so intractable intensified. A new one reared its head: maybe she'd actually been raped and that's why she was refusing to talk.

Police again tried to persuade Joanne to appear at a press conference, but again she refused. In the end, she agreed to prepare a written statement. Police assumed she'd read that to the assembled media but … no. Would she read it on a police video camera? No. She also rejected the suggestion of giving the media the chance to take film and pictures, giving them instead a photograph of her and Peter taken in the Kombi.

Media officer Denise Hurley tried to explain that that wouldn't be sufficient to placate the media. 'Well, that'll have to do,' Joanne replied stubbornly. She was close to tears, and Hurley left it. In the end, Paul Falconio, who, with his dark short hair and his soft brown eyes, looked eerily like Peter, agreed to read the statement for her. Joanne asked that Wilton not be allowed into the room.

The statement was only six brief paragraphs. 'I don't want to lessen the severity of what happened, but I believe there has been speculation I was sexually assaulted,' it read. 'But this did not occur. I consider myself very lucky to have escaped and be okay.' Paul then did his best to make excuses for Joanne. 'Joanne is still very distressed and she is withdrawn, which is to be expected,' he said.

But her message was clear, particularly to those sections of the Australian and British media who had written her letters, through the police, to buy the rights to her story. 'I am not prepared,' she wrote in another statement that would come back to bite her later, 'to sell my story to the media.'

CHAPTER TWENTY-EIGHT

# A Desert Shoot-Out

THAT SAME DAY, FRIDAY JULY 20, Geoffrey Nicholls, the armed man who'd been using a cow as target practice as he drove towards Peter Falconio and Joanne Lees' Kombi, was getting into yet another fight, this time 500 kilometres south of Alice Springs. He'd veered off the main road as he travelled south from Alice Springs to take the 200-kilometre dirt road to Oodnadatta, a tiny town in the heart of the Simpson Desert, north-east of Coober Pedy. The famous old track was used as a trade route by local Aboriginal people tens of thousands of years before Europeans arrived and built a railway through the town. Since the closure of that railway in 1981, however, Oodnadatta has become a quiet settlement – population just 120 people, mostly Aboriginal – with a general store, a museum and a hotel. Its most frequent visitors are long-distance trucks and four-wheel-drive off-roaders. Even the main road is a challenge to ordinary vehicles and it's a big deal when the council's road grader comes through a couple of times a year to keep it open.

Together with his Aboriginal girlfriend Judy Rose and her two children, Nicholls had been travelling rough in their white Ford stationwagon. They'd been stopped by police searches a few times, but on each occasion had been allowed to pass. They'd chosen to avoid the main road, calling into towns only when they needed petrol, and had been sleeping out in the open in the soft orange earth in parking bays. Nicholls, with his .22 Magnum rifle bolt action repeater by his side, and a

158

tomahawk and a large kitchen knife in the car, had been drinking heavily all the way. At one point, they stopped for petrol at Barrow Creek.

The family arrived in Oodnadatta at about 4 p.m., intending to wash the windscreen, and went to the hotel, the Transcontinental, in the middle of the town, to buy something to eat. At the front bar, they were asked to leave and sit outside because the children, at eight and two, weren't allowed on licensed premises. Nicholls asked for food, but was told they didn't start serving meals until 6 p.m. He was outraged, and accused manager Alan Wilson of being racist – even though, with the hotel Aboriginal-owned, Wilson was actually employed by black proprietors. Eventually Nicholls stomped out of the hotel, told everyone to get back into the car, drove nearer to the hotel, and parked. Then he got his gun.

Rose was alarmed. 'Don't be silly, Geoff,' she pleaded. 'Put the gun away.'

Nicholls looked at her strangely. 'Don't worry,' he replied. 'The welfare will look after you.'

He then walked to the front of the hotel. Wilson's wife Beverley Kemble spotted him and ran in through the back door. 'He's got a gun!' she shouted to Wilson. Together, they raced around the pub locking all the doors, and called the police. With Joanne and Peter's attacker on the loose, they weren't going to take any chances, and the two men on duty, Senior Constable Mark Sutton and Senior Community Constable John Coombes, grabbed a 12-gauge shotgun and a box of ammunition before rushing to the hotel.

FROM THE CAR, JUDY ROSE heard a gunshot and scrambled out and ran to the back of the hotel. She saw Nicholls standing on the corner, aiming the gun at someone. She screamed at him to stop. But standing right in his sights 30 metres away was Sutton who'd arrived and was shouting to Nicholls to put his gun down. Nicholls ignored him and, as Sutton walked towards him, he heard the crack of gunfire.

'I moved diagonally towards the hotel to get some cover,' says Sutton. 'I was still yelling but my shotgun didn't have the range of his rifle. I had capsicum spray too but I wasn't close enough.' The only bullet-proof vests back at the station had been too small to wear.

Nicholls seemed hellbent on shooting someone. 'I've got a rifle and you've got a shotgun,' Nicholls yelled to Sutton. 'I can shoot you, you can't shoot me.' He was right. He then fired another shot, and darted behind the fence. Sutton was torn; he needed cover, but he also wanted to be close enough to talk to him. By this point, Nicholls was 5 to 7 metres away. Sutton was intensely aware of all the people around too. At one stage, elderly local Nelly Stuart walked between the two men; at another, a tourist pulling a trailer drove through. There were drinkers standing on the verandah of the hotel, there were children in the nearby playground and there were fifteen or so people milling around the store 50 to 60 metres away. 'Police!' Sutton was shouting as loudly as he could. 'Put the gun down! Police! Put the gun down!'

Finally, Sutton came out from behind his cover, only for Nicholls to level the dark grey barrel of his rifle right at him. Sutton pulled his trigger first. Nothing happened. He hadn't disengaged the safety catch. He then flicked the safety off, aimed again and shot three times in rapid succession. Nicholls crumpled to the ground.

GEOFFREY NICHOLLS WAS PRONOUNCED dead by an ambulance officer on the scene at 4.45 p.m. on Friday 20 July 2001. A DNA sample request was filled in by the South Australian Police 'to be compared re possible sample from Barrow Creek shooting in NT'. Police investigating the Barrow Creek case also requested an image of Nicholls to check it against Joanne Lees' descriptions. 'It was a matter of waiting for that photo to come through,' says Superintendent Kate Vanderlaan, now back from Perth and in charge of the Peter Falconio case. That picture was emailed to Detective Sergeant Chalker from the NT police on July 23. 'We then realised it wasn't him,' says Vanderlaan. Nicholls was simply a bloke with a gun who was severely depressed, had been drinking heavily and hadn't been taking his medication. Police also discovered that he died on the actual day of the second anniversary of his son Troy's death.

A Commissioner of Police's inquiry concluded that Nicholls was suffering from a mental condition, and that the use of a firearm by police was justified. Nicholls' actions, they said, indicated that he had every intention of killing or seriously injuring someone. The coroner recommended that the police buy new bullet-proof vests.

But Geoffrey Nicholls' brother Shane was left in no doubt that Peter Falconio's murderer had now claimed his next victim. He feels today that Nicholls was only shot because, with the real killer still at large, police acted too quickly to resolve the situation. 'Police overreacted because of Falconio,' he says. 'They were hysterical. Geoff had drunk too much to do anything, and his hand had been injured by the first bullet – how would he have carried on firing?'

Nicholls' barrister Ralph Bleechmore was also critical of police. 'They shot at the centre of his body, so they were shooting to kill,' he says. 'From army experience, it's possible to disable someone instead.'

Others were adamant: Geoffrey Nicholls had been depressed and suicidal and his death was more a case of 'self-precipitated suicide', or 'suicide by police'. But however heartbreaking was his death, as was his life, Peter's killer was still at large. And no-one was safe.

# CHAPTER TWENTY-NINE

# The Lindyfication of Joanne Lees

ON THE SATURDAY EVENING A week after the attack, Joanne Lees was sitting with her chaperone, Senior Sergeant Helen Braam, in their Alice Springs hotel room, but kept getting up, pacing the room, and glancing at the clock.

'What's wrong?' asked Braam.

Joanne shook her head. 'It was about this time,' she replied quietly, 'that it happened.'

Seven days had passed since Peter Falconio's disappearance, and it seemed to her that little real progress had been made. But she didn't need to remind the police of that. They too were acutely aware of not having come up with any conclusive leads. They'd searched 800,000 square kilometres from the air – almost half the Northern Territory – vehicles had trawled 4800 square kilometres around Barrow Creek, and police and trackers on foot had covered 10 square kilometres around the scene. There'd been more than 500 calls from members of the public, but every one had drawn a blank. Dozens of potential suspects had been apprehended, questioned and set free. Pictures of the ute had been circulated and, despite police hoping such a distinctively customised vehicle might be easy to spot, nothing so far had been. They started to believe family or friends might be harbouring the gunman and appealed to them to come forward.

That same day, Senior Sergeant Jeanette Kerr had decided to begin an audit of the whole investigation. She also came to the conclusion that she needed to try to get more information out of Joanne.

In the meantime, the police had conducted a new search of the area and found another footprint, but it could still possibly only be but a tiny piece in the gaping puzzle. Then they played one of their trump cards. Top Aboriginal tracker Teddy Egan had finally been located in the outback and was brought to the scene.

From the harsh, sun-blistered deserts of Australia to the snow-blanketed forests of Europe, Teddy Egan Tjangala had plied his almost mystical trade as one of the last great traditional trackers of the Australian subcontinent. Aged around seventy-five – he's thought to be the only person in Australia who doesn't have his year of birth marked in his passport, merely a question mark – he's one of the most respected Aboriginal elders and one of the most in-demand black trackers in Australia. It had been a hard journey, however. At the age of three, Teddy, his mother and their relatives were cornered by police officers during the brutal Coniston massacre near Barrow Creek. His mother hid him in a cave and Teddy emerged as one of just two survivng Aboriginal people from his clan who ducked the white men's guns to live to tell the tale. Now his tracking skills are sought after throughout the world, including in Germany where he once helped police find three dangerous murderers who'd managed to escape from jail, tracking them through the snow, even though he'd never seen snow before. These days, he also plays a critical role in Walpiri ceremonies, with his talents as a traditional dancer much admired among his tribe. And he is a revered artist, painting not only on canvas, but in the old way, in the sands of the desert. Today Teddy lives as traditional a life as he's able. When he's not roaming the traditional lands of the Walpiri people in the Central Australian outback, he sleeps out in Alice Springs. He still speaks in the traditional Walpiri language and, with his halting English, prefers to converse in his native tongue.

At Barrow Creek, Teddy peered at the ground and complained about the vast number of police officers and searchers who'd left their own prints. 'If you got me more early, I find the man,' he said. He then walked straight to the mulga bush where Joanne had sheltered that night. 'She running, here, there,' he said, pointing to indiscernible signs. 'Here she fall down. She run away into night. And here she lay down,' he pronounced, pointing to the space under the bush. 'Many hours. She shelter here. She very afraid.' He bent lower into the space beneath the spidery branches of acacia. 'See, she keep very still. Five witchetty grub trees here in a row.'

Teddy was in little doubt as to the attacker's movements, he said he was a good hunter and that he knew the country well. He pointed out the places where he'd been, both in the scrub and where he'd walked along the side of the highway. 'Big man tracks. Size eight–nine boots.' And then he said something which startled the police. 'And here, he had a flat tyre. His car not good. He have to change.'

THE POLICE PURSUED THIS NEW lead vigorously. They also checked out the route of a gas pipe line in the area. Denise Hurley saw Teddy as the ideal person for the press to meet but, unfortunately for her, a new footprint in a burnt out campsite a distance from the crime scene was discovered, and police returned to whisk Teddy away again, leaving the media even more disgruntled.

'I predicted, right at the start, that as soon as the press had got over the first stage of the investigation, and all the excitement of that, they'd run out of things to write about, and they'd turn on us,' says Hurley. 'We actually sat down and strategised what to do for when that happened. One of our strategies was to give them Teddy Egan. But then something came up so we had to take him away, and cut all the media interviews. That didn't go down well.'

BY NOW, THE ASSEMBLED PRESS was running out of patience. They were restless and irritated that they weren't getting access to the big story – Joanne Lees – and they felt sure the police were hiding vital information from them. A low point was the re-enactment. In response to questions from journalists, police had denied they were planning such a thing; it was going to be a simple walk-through with just two police cars present. A press conference was scheduled in Alice Springs at about the same time, which many of the reporters therefore opted to go to instead. Then it was delayed when the keys to the pressroom were misplaced. Two journalists were stunned, standing out there waiting on the street, to see an orange and white Kombi driving past, en route to Barrow Creek.

They thought the police had deliberately misled them to keep them away and they later learned it had been a full re-enactment, complete with Joanne having a gun pushed in her face. 'We'd asked them if they were going to stage a re-enactment before they actually did, and they'd said no,' says the *Sydney Morning Herald*'s Phil Cornford. 'They'd lied about that, what else were they lying about?'

The press had also been tipped off about the Truckstop closed-circuit security video and kept badgering Hurley for details, convinced she was being deliberately obstructive. Mark Wilton asked a direct question about the existence of the footage, and was told no-one had knowledge of any such film. Afterwards, the journalists were furious to find out that the police viewed the footage the day after it was taken. But, at the time, the police he'd asked were telling the truth. They knew nothing about it. 'We kept getting told there was nothing, basically,' says Hurley. 'The media were really cranky about it but we couldn't get any information either. We were just passing on what we were being told.'

The journalists were leaked various bits of unofficial information from the police operation, sometimes from officers who were annoyed at not being a part of all the excitement, and sometimes from officers annoyed that they were, often far from home and operating in uncomfortable circumstances on an operation most had assumed would be wrapped up within a couple of days. There were also some officers who didn't like Joanne and had started to doubt her story. They passed their misgivings on to a media hungry for any scrap of information, whether real or speculative.

Some sections of the press picked up on it immediately. They'd been hanging around, day after day, chewing the fat and dissecting, scrutinising and re-assembling the story from every possible angle. Predictably, sooner or later, the spotlight would fall back on to Joanne, and this time as a suspect.

At a time when the world had become used to instant gratification over news events, when victims were usually grateful to enlist the media to help and when the media themselves were present, willing and able, it seemed bizarre behaviour at the very best and, at worst, downright suspicious. In addition, there were parts of her story that didn't seem to make sense to the press, especially when, of course, they hadn't been told the full story. With her feet bound, they asked, quite wrongly, how could she have crawled

30-odd metres into the bushes? Why weren't her injuries worse, and why hadn't she suffered more from the cold while she was waiting out there for her attacker to leave? And if he was searching for her with a dog, how could it possibly have failed to have sniffed her out? And what of this idea that she moved her handcuffed hands under her body from behind her to in front, surely that would be impossible? Then there was the fact that police had found no footprints from the man at the scene …

There was that one crucial aspect of the white ute that didn't make sense either. No-one had ever heard of a ute which had access from the front cab straight into the back. What's more, there'd been a report of Peter and Joanne having a row at the Melanka Backpackers' hostel. Maybe they weren't getting on and had fought on the road too. And as for Peter's body, why hadn't the searches found anything?

The strangest aspect to the story of all was Joanne's demeanour. She didn't look at all like a woman who'd been through a terrifying ordeal, and she certainly didn't behave like one either. No-one had seen her composure slip in public; she appeared stony-faced, impassive and bereft of emotion. It was a look a number of journalists in Alice Springs at the time remembered having seen once before. On the face of Lindy Chamberlain.

One of the main reasons that Chamberlain had been convicted twenty-one years before of murdering her baby at Uluru, outside Alice Springs, was that she just didn't match the popular image of a distraught mother who'd just lost her child in the most awful circumstances imaginable. She looked strange, and acted even more strangely, a view promulgated and shared from the media to the police investigators, from casual bystanders to the general Australian public. A Seventh Day Adventist, her pastor husband Michael had declared, in his first press interview, that Azaria being snatched by a dingo was 'the will of God'. Lindy hadn't cried on camera and had battled, as she thought she should, to contain her emotions in public.

It had the opposite effect to the one she intended. It might have allowed her to preserve her own dignity but, in the eyes of the public, it branded her a cold-hearted, dry-eyed murderess.

Now exactly the same thing was happening to Joanne Lees.

# CHAPTER THIRTY

# And the Dingo Didn't Do It ...

WAS JOANNE LEES HIDING SOMETHING? The speculation reached fever pitch, fed on itself, and grew more heated, and more concrete, by the day. It was only a matter of time before people started whispering about the chances of her being more complicitly involved. And as soon as you started from that premise, suddenly nothing appeared quite as it seemed.

Southern Commander Bob Fields continued to defend Joanne and moved quickly to dispel the gossip-mongering. 'The position of the police force is we have no problems, no cause to worry about the truthfulness and the accuracy of what Joanne Lees has told us,' he said at a press conference. 'We are proceeding full steam ahead on the basis that what Joanne Lees has told us is the truth and is an accurate and credible recollection of events that happened at Barrow Creek last Saturday night.' Yet earlier he'd spoken about events that night 'defying belief' – was he trying to cover his own tracks? And why had Commander Max Pope suddenly emerged as the main spokesperson on the case? Was this an attempt to sideline Fields?

Northern Territory Police Commissioner Brian Bates looked on with incredulity. 'The media saw something sinister in that, but there was nothing sinister at all,' he says. 'I had appointed Max Pope to talk to the media as I wanted to ensure they got what they wanted. I wanted to give them a focus. Bob Fields couldn't do that full-time. He was Commander in charge of the southern region, and his responsibilities went far beyond that particular investigation. He had other work he had to do. But the media thought I wasn't happy with Bob Fields, and that's why I put Max Pope there. That wasn't true. They just didn't understand our command structure.'

Yet on other aspects of Joanne's story, the message didn't seem to be getting through sufficiently clearly about what had happened. Fields and Pope appeared intimidated by the phalanx of world media that faced them every day and said the absolute minimum, sticking tightly to the script and volunteering no extra information. As a result, there were still sections of the media who thought – wrongly – that Joanne's legs were bound during her escape, and no-one from the police pointed out that Joanne had never even suggested the dog had left the ute. Even the re-enactment was taken as a sign that the police hadn't believed Joanne's story and wanted her to act it out to check she wouldn't slip up.

In addition, the police hadn't shown the cable ties with which Joanne's hands had been cuffed, or described how they enabled her to hold her hands apart with the tie in the middle. If they had, everyone would have understood how easy it had been for Joanne to move her bound hands from her back to her front, by stepping over the tie in the middle. In the absence of that information, Britain's *Daily Mail* reporter, Richard Shears appeared on TV saying he'd even spoken to a ballet dancer who confirmed that, despite all her intense training and agility, she wasn't flexible enough to step through. She'd have to dislocate a shoulder, step through, then pop it back. Another journalist, this time desk-bound in London, wrote: 'Here's a little party trick for you. The attacker taped Joanne's hands behind her but, she said, she managed to bring them to the front by putting her body through her arms. Can you equal this feat? And don't come crying to me if the ambulance men think it funny.'

The police knew the press wanted more information but, at the same time, they needed to keep certain evidence to themselves so they could distinguish genuine suspects from the attention-seekers. The situation was made worse by the way the British press in particular didn't seem to be able to convey adequately the size and remoteness of the area where Peter had disappeared, which made locating the body such a difficult task. Indeed, a man had once committed suicide in his car just 2 kilometres off the Stuart Highway near Tennant Creek and he wasn't found for seven years. Readers in Britain, especially, also couldn't understand how there could be so little traffic on a main highway, or how someone could apparently disappear off the face of the earth. There were still questions about the number of footprints and Pope didn't help things when he was asked whether there was any physical evidence of an offender and he replied in his slow, careful, unembroidered way, 'I'm not going to comment on that.' And as for the reports of a row between the couple at a hostel in town, they were allowed to fester for far too long before it was revealed to have been a case of mistaken identity.

Instead, the whispering campaign grew steadily in momentum. Burning in the memories of many British journalists was the story of former barmaid Tracie Andrews, twenty-eight, who received enormous media coverage back home in 1997 after she described how she and her twenty-five-year-old fiancé Lee Harvey were stopped by another motorist as they drove home along a little country lane in the British Midlands. After an altercation, Harvey was stabbed to death in a vicious road rage attack, and she was punched when she tried to intervene. The press went all out covering the story of the grieving, love-struck heroine who'd managed to escape with her life, especially when she tried to commit suicide later because she couldn't face life without her man. Two years later, she was convicted of the murder and jailed for life. Making that wrong call in the early days in such a similar situation played on those journalists' minds. By coincidence, in Australia just nine months before Peter's disappearance, a Sydney man, Patrick Joiner, made an emotional appeal on television for his missing wife. The body of Mary Seretis was found two weeks later in the boot of his car.

But with Joanne, it wasn't long before the quiet deliberations finally broke out into the public arena. The first sign was a question at a press conference asking whether police really did believe Joanne's story. The second was a query about whether Joanne had a history of mental illness. Pope unwittingly fanned the flames. He said she was 'free to go', but said he could not comment on the second matter. The rumour mill cranked up a notch.

BEHIND THE SCENES, THE ATTEMPTS to persuade Joanne to face the press were assuming an edge of desperation. There was only one way to stop all this innuendo, and that would be if she fronted up to the media and gave them the pictures, film and quotes they craved. But Joanne was still not cooperating. Sitting drinking tea in a café in Alice Springs, she was tipped off by another customer that just behind the nearest pillar, ten men with cameras were waiting for her to come out. Another day, she was walking back to her hotel and a camera crew drove onto the pavement to trap her so they could take some film. 'They then chased me down the street,' she says. 'It was all so intimidating.' She'd started to feel as though the press was trying to hold her hostage all over again, and she rebelled. She knew they were printing lies about her, so why should she bow to their demands? The two sides grew increasingly entrenched. There was a need for a circuit-breaker.

It came in the form of Bates. He'd had plenty of experience with the international media over his forty-five-year police career, most recently in 1999 with the mass evacuation of East Timorese refugees to Darwin. When the UN compound where they'd been sheltering in Dili came under siege from armed militia after the vote for independence from Indonesia, Bates oversaw the rescue operation for the 1300 terrified people. Ten years before, with the Australian Federal Police, he'd run the long investigation into one of Australia's most shocking crimes: the assassination of Assistant Commissioner Colin Winchester, after he helped uncover a complex tangle of a drug supply network and corrupt police.

On July 24, Bates flew from Darwin to Alice Springs to meet with Joanne personally. 'At that stage, no-one could convince her to do a press conference,' he says. 'So I thought I would go down and try.'

When he first approached Joanne in the corner of a little town centre café, she came straight up to him, avoided all eye contact, and declared, 'If you've got no news of Pete, there's no use talking to me.' Bates was taken aback but persisted. He had his own reasons. 'My background of many years in policing has taught me that it's important to keep the momentum of a case going,' he says. 'As much the media needs us, we need the media. I knew if I could get Joanne in front of the cameras and talking, it would keep things happening. The problem was that the days were flying by and there was no sign our suspect. The longer things go on, the more difficult they are.'

He sat down with Joanne and Superintendent Kate Vanderlaan, to try to explain how vital it was that she appear before the media. He was sympathetic to her reluctance, but felt it was vital. 'It was impossible to get close to her, to warm to her, to establish a rapport,' he says. 'But that wasn't important. It's no denigration of her, but I could see she was her own person, with her own personality, and she couldn't cope with what was happening. She'd got herself offside with the media, they'd taken an instant dislike to her, and she'd reacted in a particular way.'

Eventually, Joanne agreed, and everyone heaved a sigh of relief. But it wasn't to be straightforward. At first, she asked Denise Hurley to find out what questions the media would like to ask, because she'd decided she was only going to take certain questions, then she said she wanted only one journalist in the room, and the TV camera operators, no-one else. And, further, she wanted to ban all British media. 'We encouraged her to forget that, it would be a disaster,' says Hurley. 'But we got all the questions from the media, and then she started knocking some of the questions out. She said she'd answered some of those questions before, and that others were ridiculous.'

The press conference, on Wednesday July 25, was an unmitigated disaster. Only one ABC radio reporter was allowed into the conference room at the Alice Springs police station with the photographers and camera operators and, of the fourteen questions the assembled press had prepared for her, she'd whittled the list down to three. Those three questions gave the media little material to work with. 'If I could say one thing to the man who did this, I would ask him to let police know where Pete is,' she said, reading her written answer, with Paul Falconio on her right and Pope on her left. 'I am confident Pete will be found.' The re-enactment was 'unpleasant' but 'necessary'. 'I have asked police to tell me only positive news and remain hopeful of finding Pete.' As for her plans for the future, she said she hadn't decided how long she would remain in Alice Springs. 'At the moment I don't think further ahead than what I will do tomorrow,' she said.

She concluded by saying, 'Anyone who has spoken to me or had any contact with me, no-one doubts me. Only the media have asked questions about my story. I find it all so overwhelming and intimidating. I've got a problem with all press. They distort the truth and doubt my story. They misquote me, making up stories and accusations.' It was a hesitant, stumbling performance and she was breathing heavily, clearly nervous, but her answers made her look uptight and paranoid. She came away from the press conference feeling she'd done her duty; she'd given the press what they'd wanted. The press came away feeling more hostile and belligerent than ever.

One journalist talked of being phoned by an assistant editor on his newspaper, furious that they didn't have a decent story for the day, and outraged that Joanne had turned down all approaches for an interview. 'Right!' she's alleged to have barked down the phone. 'Let's get the bitch!'

Bates shook his head sadly. 'There was nothing I could do when she said she was only going to answer three questions,' he says. 'The media had expected her to open up to them, and she hadn't at all. At least I'd achieved the aim of getting her in front of the cameras, but it made things worse.'

Hurley couldn't understand Joanne's rationale. 'It was almost as if someone had planted the thought in her mind that the press were never to be trusted,' she says. Vanderlaan says Joanne never actually said she hated the press. 'I think she just didn't like talking about what had happened. She was overwhelmed, and didn't know how to react. I certainly felt for her.'

Bates, despite his disappointment, felt similarly. He was pleased she'd appeared – the police switchboard was flooded with more than 300 calls after her appeal, the biggest single response they'd had to date. And he was, to a point, sympathetic. 'She may not have got it quite right because of the trauma,' he says. 'But how would any of us react in the situation she'd been in?'

THE WAY LUCIANO AND PAUL FALCONIO were conducting themselves – politely, cooperatively and patiently, despite their grief – threw Joanne's behaviour even more sharply into contrast. Bates had decided he wanted to meet them as well as Joanne, to express his sympathy for their terrible predicament and reassure them that everything possible was being done. He saw them for lunch the same day as he'd met up with Joanne. Luciano was courteous and gracious while Paul was quieter but eager to do anything that might help. 'They were such lovely people,' says Bates. 'I felt so, so sorry for them. I said, "We're doing all we can", but I knew that really wouldn't be much comfort. It was important for them to know where we were at. That's part of the approach I'd always felt was so important.'

LUCIANO AND PAUL WERE HAPPY to speak to the press whenever they were asked to and it began to look as if Joanne was being deliberately obstructive. They'd covered all the obvious angles by now, followed every new lead and become endlessly inventive. One British journalist wrote breathlessly of Australia's 'Death Triangle' – a massive triangle drawn over most of Australia and the size of several European countries within which, in the past, a number of tourists had met their deaths.

Now it was time for a fresh angle. And that same journalist, Richard Shears, had no compunction about writing it. Under the provocative headline, 'Is the Outback Heroine telling the truth?' he wrote: 'Now in Australia they are beginning to talk about the "Lindyfication" of Joanne Lees, whose limited public accounts of the incident at Barrow Creek have given rise to rumour and speculation similar to that which grew up around Lindy in the early days of the Azaria mystery ... "Where are their prints?" the doubters ask. The Aboriginal trackers would find a dog's prints with their eyes shut. And why did the stranger tie up Ms Lees in such a way that she could escape? How could a woman stumbling away to hide in a clump of roadside bushes conceal herself so well from a man with a torch and a dog? ... It is disturbing questions such as these that dominate the dinner tables and bars of Alice Springs.'

Shears had reported doubts as coming from Australians and, in return, the Australian media reported the doubts as coming from the British. Both sides had effectively given voice to their speculative stories by quoting the other. It was a game of Chinese whispers, and the only real loser was Joanne.

Today, Shears remains defiant about his stand. 'I was suspicious about Joanne's story from day one,' he says. 'There were too many gaps in her story. It doesn't add up. Unless you shake a tree, nothing falls out. I felt I was justified in asking those questions. I got a lot of criticism for it; some of my colleagues said, "We've got to stick to the police line". To be honest, I don't know what happened, but I still don't believe her story. Why won't she talk to the press? What's she so afraid of?' Shears had once had similar doubts about Lindy Chamberlain and the death of her baby Azaria. It made for controversial, headline-grabbing copy. 'And I still don't believe the dingo did it,' he says.

Shears' story, with its raising of the spectre of Joanne somehow being involved in Peter's disappearance, created a sensation in the UK and other newspaper editors clamoured for similar reports from their correspondents. Some bluntly refused to file them. Sydney-based stringer for a host of British tabloids, Frank Thorne, was one. 'A few papers called me saying the editors wanted a story saying Joanne did it,' he says. 'I said I'm not going to write that. I don't believe she did it. There's no evidence at all to suggest she's involved. Then later, I got a call from a more senior person on one newspaper asking, "What's all this about?" I told him all the facts pointed to her not being involved at all. He was totally taken aback. I explained to him all the evidence and he said, okay, write that story. But it never ran. They just weren't interested. They were so carried away by the fact they'd all been conned by Tracie Andrews and here was another good-looking woman, so she must be a killer too. Everyone finds female killers fascinating, and it was much more interesting than the truth.'

THE DAY AFTER THE PRESS conference, the police launched a stunning new initiative by posting a record $250,000 reward. They said they were looking for 'someone who has knowledge of the gunman but who has so far been reluctant, or afraid, to come forward'. It was the biggest sum of money offered since the 1870s when an 8000-pound bounty was put on the capture – dead or alive – of outlaw bushranger Ned Kelly.

When Luciano Falconio went to pin up a poster for the cameras, he was overcome with emotion, and broke down and wept.

# CHAPTER THIRTY-ONE

# A Dead Body

THE BODY WAS LYING ON its front, sprawled in the dirt in a rest area some 30 metres off the Stuart Highway, 60 kilometres south of Alice Springs. Two Aboriginal men noticed it, and contacted the police the next morning. The area was sealed off and police chiefs raced to the scene. The body was male, Caucasian and in the right age range. At last, police hoped, they had found Peter Falconio. The decomposing corpse was wearing different clothes to those Peter had on when he'd gone missing, but that didn't matter. Anything could have happened in the interim.

Back at the police station in Alice Springs, Superintendent Kate Vanderlaan took the call and the atmosphere turned electric. 'We certainly thought it could be the body,' she says. 'I was just busting my guts to see the images of him sent through.'

When the photographs of the body came through later that day on Sunday 5 August 2001, however, there was a sigh of disappointment. But two murders within the space of just three weeks couldn't be a coincidence. This could well be the same killer, leaving his own personal calling card. Forensic officers performed a post-mortem, trying to ascertain the cause of death, the man's identity, and whether or not the cadaver held traces of another person's blood or DNA. The first signs weren't promising. This man had been stabbed several times in the neck, a completely different style of execution to Peter's probable killing. But, as the police put out the news of this next death, appealing for information as to his identity, the press also rushed to the conclusion it was unlikely to be pure chance. The story of Peter Falconio not so much caught fire once more, but exploded.

That rest area was where Peter and Joanne had pulled over with their new Canadian backpacker friends on board, to check the problem with their Kombi's steering.

BY TUESDAY, THE DEAD MAN had been identified as Stuart Rhodes, a thirty-nine-year-old chef who'd been working in Alice Springs. He was a popular man, gay, and with plenty of friends. He'd hired a white Proton Satria hatchback a few days before, and police speculated that he might have picked up a hitchhiker who'd turned killer. On Thursday August 9, the vehicle was spotted abandoned outside the Marla Bore Roadhouse, 450 kilometres south of Alice Springs, 170 kilometres into SA. The keys were in the ignition, and a motel room had been ransacked. Forensic samples from both the vehicle and the motel room were sent up to Darwin to be cross-referenced with samples from the crime scene north of Barrow Creek.

ANDREW HEFFERNAN, THE DRIFTER suffering from severe paranoid schizophrenia who'd set off on a journey from the South Australian riverlands to Alice Springs at around the same time as Peter and Joanne, had stopped at a local motel in Alice Springs to ask for a job. He'd just been evicted from a backpackers' lodge, because he didn't have any money. He'd filled in the forms, and then sat at the bar at the Gap View Motel for a drink. While there, he got chatting to Stuart Rhodes, who'd just arrived back in town after a time down south. It was Sunday July 29, and Heffernan, twenty-eight, confessed he had hardly any money. He'd sold his car for $400 cash, but was now broke until his disability pension came through. Rhodes felt sorry for him. He'd just checked into room 301, which had twin beds. He asked Heffernan if he wanted to crash on one of them.

Over the next few days, the two men formed a friendship. Rhodes allowed him to sleep regularly in his room – even though he was being charged an extra tariff for him to do so – and lent him $250. There were reports, however, that the friendship faltered after Heffernan overheard Rhodes, who was HIV-positive, telling friends the two men had begun a sexual relationship. Rhodes would have had no way of knowing that Heffernan had stopped taking his medication for his serious mental illness three weeks before.

On the evening of Wednesday August 1 Rhodes had been drinking heavily and was so drunk, he'd urinated in the motel bed. Heffernan says the chef then had the idea of going to visit Uluru, so he loaded him into the white hatchback he'd just hired, piled all the men's possessions in, as well as a fair few items like a mattress and bedding from the motel, and drove south. He then called into two supermarkets and bought prawns, ham, muesli bars and cigarettes ... and a very sharp hobby knife and a coil of thin, blue rope.

When the two men reached the rest area 60 kilometres south of Alice Springs, however, Heffernan pounced on Rhodes from behind, slit his throat, and stabbed him in the neck a number of times in an 'almost frenzied' attack. He then tied the rope around one of Rhodes' arms and one of his legs and dragged him across the cleared ground, under a barbed wire fence protecting a plant life regeneration area, and into the bush. With the body partially hidden, Heffernan then drove down to SA, withdrew $1000 from one of Rhodes' bank accounts and arrived at the Marla Bore Roadhouse, dirty and barefoot. The next day he disappeared, leaving the car behind, and catching a bus to Adelaide.

At the rest area, however, he'd left a cigarette stub bearing his DNA, and a number of bloodied footprints.

TWO WEEKS LATER, JOHN SHEATHER, the owner of a caravan park in NSW, was lying in bed. He was listening to the radio and wondering, he says, if anything interesting was going to happen that day. After a few minutes, he heard an item on the news about a man wanted in connection with the murder near Alice Springs of Stuart Rhodes. He sat up to hear the name of the man they were searching for. 'I thought, "Well, I'll be buggered!" he said. "'It's that bloke a few caravans away!"'

Heffernan had checked in under his own name because he'd applied for emergency assistance from the Housing Department and needed a valid address. But Sheather wasn't fazed. He calmly stepped into the shower. 'I knew he wasn't going anywhere,' he said. 'So I took a shower and then I rang the police.'

Two detectives crept into a spare caravan to keep watch then called for back-up. Heffernan was arrested a little over an hour later.

IN SEPTEMBER 2004, ANDREW HEFFERNAN was jailed for life after being found guilty by a jury of the murder of Stuart Rhodes. The judge, Justice Trevor Olsson, recommended a non-parole period of twenty years.

The Northern Territory police were disappointed not to have solved the biggest murder inquiry they'd ever had on their patch, but at least they'd taken another dangerous killer out of circulation. For Joanne Lees, however, there was still no solace in sight. The stormclouds of doubt over her story continued to gather, and grow blacker by the day.

# CHAPTER THIRTY-TWO

# A Breath of Fresh Energy

HE'D BEEN WATCHING THE STORY of Peter Falconio and Joanne Lees unfold from afar, but now it was the turn of the Northern Territory's police straight shooter, Assistant Commissioner John Daulby, to ride into town and take charge. Daulby, fifty-one, had been over in New Zealand for three weeks in July 2001, visiting his two daughters who were living with their mother across the Tasman. On his arrival back to Darwin, he was called into the office of the Commissioner. Brian Bates had been growing increasingly worried at what was happening down in Alice Springs. When he'd appeared at a press conference, and was asked about a man being questioned in NSW over Peter's disappearance, he'd been baldly accused by a journalist of lying when he replied that the police were 99.9 per cent sure he wasn't the one they were hunting. Bates shakes his head in disbelief. 'That was the sort of hysteria we found ourselves in the middle of. Joanne had got the media offside, and they were attacking everyone. I'd pick up my phone and there'd be a voice on the other end saying, "This is the BBC and you are live to air, Commissioner". Day after day in my diary, I had written down: Briefing re missing tourist. It was madness.' Bates asked Daulby to go straight to Alice Springs and take charge. 'He's a very down-to-earth officer, and very, very close to the community,' says Bates. 'He was the ideal man for the task.'

Daulby's arrival brought a draught of fresh energy to the investigation. He examined the progress so far and took immediate action: he announced the discovery of a mystery man's DNA on Joanne's T-shirt. The revelation on August 2, three-and-a-half weeks after the attack, instantly took the heat off Joanne. At last, here was tangible evidence that there may have been someone else at the scene, besides the two backpackers. Daulby still refused to say whether it was blood, saliva or sweat, but he was firm about its existence. 'We have found a DNA profile of a male person on the clothing of Joanne Lees,' he said. 'All that can be said in relation to this is that it could be the offender, and I can't speculate any more on that.' Privately, he felt the fact of the existence of DNA should have been released much earlier. 'Withholding it created real problems,' he says. 'Putting it out gave Joanne's story credibility.'

Daulby also released a new computer image of the man's face, this time showing him with his hair cut, without a cap and shaved of his moustache. It was a wise move. Fourteen years before, another man, twenty-six-year-old German migrant and former security guard Josef Schwab, killed a father and son who'd been camping in the bush. He'd used a semi-automatic rifle to shoot them both at close range in the back, the father once and his son twice. Their bodies were stripped naked before being buried. Police across the Northern Territory and WA released an identikit of the killer and set up a massive network of roadblocks to catch him. Unbeknownst to them, however, he'd shaved his droopy moustache into a thin line, and cropped his long hair short. Six days later, he murdered an engaged couple and their friend, shooting all three in the back. Schwab was eventually shot dead in a bloody gunfight.

Daulby warned that the man may also have altered the appearance of his vehicle, and disclosed that the gun he'd threatened Joanne with had been a revolver. A criminal profile was prepared, and the DNA was sent around to all the crime data banks in the Territory, NSW, Queensland and Victoria. When that failed, it was circulated further, to international databases in New Zealand, Britain, the US and other countries with similar programs. Daulby also threw his weight firmly behind Joanne. 'I have no doubt she is telling the truth,' he said. 'I've had no doubt from the very beginning.'

JOHN DAULBY WAS A COPPER'S copper, through and through. Tall, broad-shouldered and imposing, with a square jaw, neat grey moustache, an easy lope and a painfully firm handshake, he had the bearing of an army sergeant major, but softened with a quiet voice and a thoughtful manner. From country SA, he'd joined the local police as a cadet in 1967, took a break to work as an apprentice fitter, then signed up with the Northern Territory police in January 1975, just a month after Cyclone Tracy swept through the city of Darwin. Since that second start, he'd never looked back. He was in his fifth year as Assistant Commissioner, but still couldn't cross the road without picking up a stray tree branch that had fallen on the ground, or wishing knots of locals a brisk G'day.

When he took charge of the Barrow Creek investigation, he went back through all the files and came to the conclusion that there was too much territorialism between officers. 'Detectives weren't talking to the people running the search, and vice versa,' he says. As well, he perceived Joanne's unwillingness to speak to the press had created a welter of other difficulties. He wished he'd been there at the very beginning. 'If I'd have been there, I would have strongly urged her to talk. It would have stopped all the nonsense early on.'

In addition, he recognised that some of his police colleagues were turning armchair critics and promoting negativity towards Joanne. 'There were two very strong elements from the start: those who believed Joanne and those who didn't,' he says. 'The first were quite vocal, and dissected everything she said. But Joanne wasn't treated badly. She was the only credible witness we had, but there were just gaps in what she was saying. I think we had a duty to examine very closely those things, yet the disbelieving element were pushing a stronger stance against Joanne. So we decided to undertake a formal investigation, going through things with her again. She was upset by that, and eventually became exasperated, but it had to be done.'

The first exercise was hypnotherapy. Joanne was nervous about reliving her trauma, but agreed to take part. A psychologist from Sydney put the young woman in a trance on August 3 and 4, then asked her more questions. Police hoped she might come up with more details. Some took it as a test for Joanne's truthfulness about the incident. Three days later, on August 7, another interview was organised for Joanne, this time to sort out any lingering doubts over certain aspects of her description of the ambush. Senior Sergeant Jeanette Kerr was chosen to conduct the interview which lasted nearly three hours, and ranged over the whole spectrum of Joanne's evidence. The concerns were many and varied: none of the mechanics interviewed had ever seen a vehicle like the one she described; no-one knew of a four-wheel-drive ute with an opening between the front and the back; no gun that matched her description could either be found on the firearms records or was within the experience of ballistics experts; a doctor had said he'd expected her injuries to be worse than they were; and could Joanne really have heard a conversation going on at the back of the Kombi over the noise of its engine?

There were other doubts too: the electrical tape found was too short to go around her ankles; Aboriginal trackers said she wasn't in that single position under the mulga for anything like five hours; she hadn't suffered any sign of the frostbite that some said should have been expected on someone who'd been out so long at night; the police had found only her footprints; there was no forensic evidence to suggest that a body had been dragged anywhere; and the odometer on the Kombi read that it had travelled 6.5 kilometres further than police had measured the distance from Ti Tree. In addition, another detective mentioned that the scrolling she described on the gun was similar to a pattern on the door of the orange Kombi. In the same way, there were also worries about the dog and the canvas bag she'd had shoved over her head. Was it really just coincidence that the dog looked to be the same breed as the one at Barrow Creek, and what of the suggestion that the bag was similar to a mail bag that was in the roadhouse?

The exercise, says Kerr, was 'to clarify apparent inconsistencies in Ms Lees' account. It was conducted at that time based on the information and evidence that the Northern Territory police had at that point in time, and the information available to me.'

Lastly, police had arranged for Joanne's statement to be analysed by linguistic content experts, both in the Northern Territory and interstate, to assess whether it contained all the relevant information. All were of a view, Kerr was shocked to discover, that vital information was missing. They believed she was telling the truth about the attack, but they also thought she was hiding something. Kerr racked her brains for what Joanne might be concealing from the investigation team and instructed everyone involved to keep a closer eye on the young woman.

THE STRAIN MEANWHILE WAS TAKING its toll on the Falconio family. Peter's mother Joan appeared on TV from her Huddersfield home to make an impassioned plea for people to come forward. 'It's the only thing we can do,' she said. 'He hasn't been found and people are saying all sorts of things but he still hasn't been found. He might be alive. That's what we've got to cling on to. We've just been going through hell every single day. Today it's no better than it was the first day.' When she was asked about Peter's girlfriend, she didn't hesitate. 'I've known Joanne for six years,' she said. 'She wouldn't lie. She loved Peter.' She corrected herself quickly. 'She still loves him. She wants him to be found.'

Luciano went home a few days later. He said he was worried about his wife's health.

THE INVESTIGATION CONTINUED APACE. Wanted posters with the details of the $250,000 reward went up at all the truck stops, shopping centres, and throughout every police station across Australia. Commander Max Pope was still doing some 200 press interviews a week. The British police had sent over some snaps from two holidaying women who'd played pool with someone fitting the man's description in a bar off a different stretch of the Stuart Highway. Checks were being made of car body builders to see if anyone knew of utes being re-configured to allow access from the cab to the back. Detectives flew to Sydney to talk to people who knew Peter and Joanne, to double-check they hadn't made any enemies in Australia who'd perhaps stalked them all the way to the north before swooping.

There had been 2500 calls to Crime Stoppers, but still no definite leads. The sheer volume of information was proving both a blessing, and a curse. 'It was overwhelming,' says Superintendent Kate Vanderlaan. 'Trying to sift through it all was a huge task. But it was so frustrating because after a while I sort of felt you were dealing with so much information, but nothing concrete, and you wonder: when is it all going to end? I always felt it would eventually come to an obvious conclusion – but there wasn't even an obvious conclusion!

'We tried a lot of different approaches and lateral thinking and experimentation. We had a lot of brain-storming sessions. The investigation had so many different angles. We were looking at different types of cars around Australia, who deals with modifying cars, manufacturers of cable ties, which shops sold them, who owns pistols and which gun dealers or clubs might be able to help, where to place the media appeals, whether to put them in four-wheel-drive magazines … It was always difficult even finding a point at which to start.'

JOANNE WAS HAVING DIFFICULTIES of her own too. The press was still stalking her around town, and she was just as determined not to speak. On a number of occasions, she was caught holding hands with Paul Falconio as they strolled around town together, and rumours soon started circulating that she was now having an affair with Peter's brother. Others remarked that maybe she did have a motive for doing away with her boyfriend.

But Joanne had her mind on a completely different liaison. While she was being chaperoned around town, she called into an internet office to check her emails. Her police minder, under orders to keep a close watch for anything out of the ordinary, noticed that she was writing from a second email account. And she was emailing, and receiving emails from, a girlfriend called Steph.

She thought it was odd that Joanne should be operating another email address and she mentioned it back at the station. Just to be sure, an officer confronted her. Joanne was was eventually forced to admit that Steph was a pseudonym for Nick Reilly, the man she'd seen back in Sydney. She'd emailed him, suggesting they meet up one day in Berlin. The report went straight to Kerr: this must be the information the linguistics experts had detected Joanne being so frantically determined to hide. For Joanne, no doubt, it had been a desperate cry in the dark for companionship, from someone who felt she'd lost everyone, and everything, but she was devastated to realise that her secret was now in the open. She dreaded the press finding out. Bad enough that she'd betrayed Pete the first time; it would be horrendous if the wider world, and the Falconio family, discovered her deception.

That night, she wept as she often did. But this time, as well as the sobs of grief and of anger, there were also tears of shame.

JOHN DAULBY ALSO MADE ANOTHER major decision: he finally released the Shell Truckstop video, the snatch of film and series of

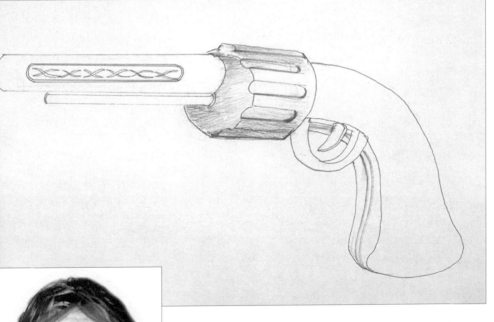

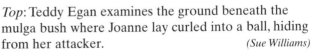

*Top*: Teddy Egan examines the ground beneath the mulga bush where Joanne lay curled into a ball, hiding from her attacker. *(Sue Williams)*

*Above:* An artist's impression of the gun with the distinctive scrolling pattern Joanne described to police. *(NT Police)*

*Left:* The police artist's drawing of the man being hunted by police, drawn from Joanne's description of her attacker. *(NT Police)*

*Top*: Joanne, Peter's brother Paul, and Northern Territory Assistant Police Commissioner John Daulby at the ill-fated press conference where Joanne refused to speak, leaving Paul to answer all questions. *(ABC News)*

*Above*: Northern Territory Police Superintendent Colleen Gwynne who worked 18-hour days in her determination to crack the case. *(Sue Williams)*

*Right*: Joanne was escorted by police into her next press conference. She would only answer a few questions.

...urdoch is re-arrested after being acquitted of raping a 12-year-old girl and assaulting ...r mother in South Australia. He was extradited to Darwin to face the charges in the ...lconio case.

*(Newspix/Lindsay Moller)*

*Above:* Murdoch was always studiously reading through his files whenever Joanne gave evidence at the trial. *Inset:* A lot of the rest of the time, he was staring at the witnesses, or peering at the monitors showing exhibits being tendered on his desk in the dock.

*(artist Liz Howell)*

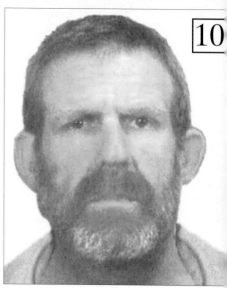

10

*Right:* Joanne took only a few seconds to identify Bradley Murdoch (number ten) as her alleged attacker from the 12-man ID board she was shown at a police station close to her home in Hove.

*(NT Police)*

*Top*: One of Murdoch's vehicles, which were constantly being altered. In this shot, taken shortly after his arrest, it is fitted with an aluminium cage on the back.

*(NT Police)*

*Above:* Jack the dog, Murdoch's pet Dalmatian cross, now living at the home of former friends. *(Sue Williams)*

*Left:* Jan Pittman, Murdoch's girlfriend who stood by him. *(Jimmy Thomson)*

*Above*: Northern Territory Director of Public Prosecutions Rex Wild QC who led the case against Murdoch, and two of his assistants, Crown Prosecutor Anne Barnett (middle) and DPP legal officer Jo Down (left). *(Jimmy Thomson)*

*Right*: Joanne arriving in Australia for the trial in October 2005. She was accompanied by old schoolfriend Martin Najan (right). *(Newspix/Brad Fleet)*

*ove*: Peter's mother and father, Luciano and Joan, holding hands, with Peter's others, Paul and Nick behind them, leaving the courthouse after the second day of rdoch's trial.

*(Jimmy Thomson)*

*ow*: The defence team. *Left to right*: Ian Read, Mark Twiggs, Grant Algie. They said ir client had been framed by police and former friends.

*(Sue Williams)*

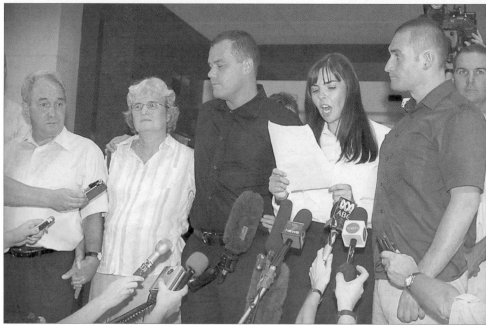

*Above*: The Falconio brothers, Paul and Nick (in the foreground), with Joanne. She had just finished giving evidence on the fourth day of the trial.

*(Jimmy Thoms*

*Below*: Joanne and the Falconio family finally face the world after Bradley John Murdoch, the man who robbed them of their beloved Peter Falconio, is sentenced to imprisonment. They were pleased with the verdict, they said, but it was not a celebration they still longed to be able to take Peter's body home for burial. *Left to right*: Luciano Falconio, Joan Falconio, Nick Falconio, Joanne Lees and Paul Falconio.

*(Newspix/Patrina Male*

pictures that showed a man, thought to be the Barrow Creek attacker, buying diesel, coffee and ice a few hours after Peter and Joanne had been ambushed. The disk had been sent over to police in Queensland to be transferred onto video and cleaned up. Police were hoping the process might allow them to work out the registration plates on the white ute pictured. But when the image came back, it was still not good enough.

The police had been in possession of the tape for more than three weeks, sometimes denying its existence or protesting it wasn't important, and its release after so long provoked a fresh wave of anger. If it had been released at the very beginning, critics argued, people would have been looking out for the attacker and his vehicle so much earlier, and there wouldn't have been such doubt about Joanne's account. Also, it instantly explained why there were so few footprints at the scene: the man was wearing thongs which would have made no impression on the hard, stony ground.

'The problem was that it got lost in the mechanisms of the investigation,' Daulby says. 'It's true we had that tape early. We treated it appropriately. We sent it to Darwin in the first week. Then they came back to us and said there was nothing they could do with it and it would have to go interstate. So it went interstate. To be frank with you, it should have been dealt with earlier. It should have been out there earlier. We received a barrage of criticism over that. I stuck to my line that there's a process that has to be gone through. There's nothing wrong with sticking to that process but if it goes wrong … we suffered. Another problem was that they had earlier discounted the person they thought was on the video, and so did not worry about it.

'It's difficult to explain, but once you've taken a line on something, that's it; you've got to justify your position. I had no problem with the time period of the investigation. It's just that it made things very difficult. You've got to face it: it was a stuff-up. That was one of the low lights of the investigation.'

But it also provided another of the darkest days. Daulby didn't say so at the time but two days before, Joanne had been shown a collection of ten photographs, one of which was a still taken from the security tapes at the Truckstop, by Senior Constable Anthony Henrys. He asked her if she could identify her attacker but her reaction disappointed everyone. When she saw the man in the Truckstop still, she said, 'No, that man is too old.' She didn't actually discount him, but she didn't immediately leap on him either.

Joanne's mum, Jenny James, explained that Joanne couldn't definitely say it was the man, but thought the likeness to him was very good. Over the coming weeks, the police kept asking, if the man on the video wasn't the attacker, why didn't the innocent customer filmed simply come forward to identify himself?

THE PUBLICITY OVER THE RELEASE of the Truckstop tape attracted even more calls from people with information. Toyota Australia had identified the vehicle as a 75 Series cabin chassis Landcruiser, a model nearly always supplied in white that had only been imported since 1985.

Joanne agreed to take part in another press conference, to appeal for anyone recognising the man in the tape, or his ute, to come forward. This turned out not to be so bad as the first, but still not much better. Joanne appeared, but refused to speak, leaving Paul Falconio to answer all the questions. She turned up in a tight pink sleeveless T-shirt that emphasised her large bust, with the words 'Cheeky Monkey' emblazoned across the front. Some of the press were aghast; media officer Denise Hurley admitted she had asked Joanne to wear a jacket over the top, but she'd refused. Even worse, she'd bought the T-shirt with police money.

When the pair sat down, they gave a much more definite response to the notion that the Truckstop man was actually the gunman. Paul said they both believed he was the one, and made an emotional plea to his brother. 'Just hang in there, if you can hear us, just wait,' he said. 'We will see you soon ... Anybody in Australia, or anywhere, if you see anything, or you know of any information, if you could come forward. This is from myself, Joanne and both our families.'

Joanne again looked nervous, and held Paul's hand tight, seizing it with her other hand when she turned around from her chair to leave the room. It was as if, having lost one Falconio boy, she was determined not to let this other one slip away.

# CHAPTER THIRTY-THREE

# That's You!

BRADLEY MURDOCH WAS SITTING IN his flat in Broome when his girlfriend Beverley Allan called round to tell him about a phone call they'd had that day at the office of the Broome Diesel and Hydraulics Service about the missing man, Peter Falconio. With a start, she saw him gazing at the front page of the *West Australian* newspaper of Tuesday August 7, with its picture of the man in the Shell Truckstop video. 'That's you on the front page,' she declared, 'and that's your vehicle.' Murdoch shook his head. Allan, however, was convinced. 'I just remember the way that he walked,' she said later. 'The way he held himself, his body posture.'

Murdoch had also had a call from his father that day, who'd seen the same photograph. 'He told his father it wasn't him,' says Allan. 'He sat me down and continued to point out all the differences between the vehicles. There were some differences on the tray, the canopy – which I can't remember precisely – and also he said he was towing a camper trailer, that it couldn't have been him.' Allan had never known he had a camper trailer, but later she actually saw one in the yard. Since he'd returned to Broome from Sedan, Allan says he'd overhauled his vehicle: the tyres were off, the back stripped and the canopy had been rebuilt with a new wire cage.

James Hepi was also surprised when he saw the photograph in the newspaper. He asked Murdoch, 'That's a picture of you, isn't it?' to which he claims Murdoch replied, 'Yes. But I had nothing to do with it.' When asked what 'it' was, Hepi explains bluntly, 'The murder.' Hepi says Murdoch would often wear glasses as part of a disguise, although his friend Brian Johnston says he needs them these days to read maps. Hepi is adamant, 'That's Brad Murdoch going through the door of the service station.' He was familiar with the place too, he used it regularly himself.

At first, Murdoch insisted the vehicle in the photo wasn't his. He pointed to the roof of the Landcruiser, which looked as if it had poles jutting from it. 'Brad said that can't be my car; it has the roof supports on it,' says Hepi. But Hepi subsequently saw another picture of the car, and realised those poles from the roof were actually part of the fuel bowsers, and weren't a part of the vehicle at all.

Broome mechanic Robin Knox had agreed to install a new, bigger exhaust system on Murdoch's Toyota Landcruiser. He knew Murdoch had been driving long distances across the red dirt roads of the area, so he was startled when he got a close-up view of the vehicle.

'It was in extremely good condition,' he says. 'It had been rebuilt or cleaned right up. It was quite unusual for a Broome car. You get a lot of red dirt and dust up here. The car was spotless. There was no dirt on the brakes or wheels or chassis, anything like that. We worked underneath the car and everything seemed very clean, like it had been rebuilt and tidied up.'

Later, Murdoch started a discussion about bodies with Hepi. It was fairly wide-ranging: 'How to get rid of them,' explains Hepi, 'to put them in a spoon drain on the side of the road, cover them with dirt, and soft diggings. [They're] on the side of the road, run-off so the roads don't flood.' Hepi was apparently unimpressed by the conversation. He replied, 'I didn't think I needed to kill anyone to carry on what I was doing.'

# CHAPTER THIRTY-FOUR

# All Quiet on the Northern Front

TOWARDS THE MIDDLE OF AUGUST 2001, the investigation was scaled down from 100 police to seventy, and then down to fourteen core people. Aware that it might be only too easy to lose impetus, the group decided they needed an inspiring name. They settled on Taskforce Regulus, after the brightest star in the Leo constellation. 'Lionheart,' they agreed enthusiastically. It felt apt. They knew they'd need all the spirit they could muster to keep wading through the oceans of information, with no firm lifelines or leads. With more than $1 million already spent, and 1700 cars and 200 potential suspects already excluded from inquiries, tip-offs from 6000 calls from the public were being carefully studied, filed and followed up. To maximise efficiency, the Taskforce was divided into three cells: intelligence; persons of interest; and vehicles of interest. They were still optimistic they'd find the perpetrator, but they realised it could take a long, long time.

Joanne Lees and Paul Falconio decided to leave Alice Springs and flew to Sydney on August 15, where Joanne went back to work at her old job, at the Dymocks bookshop, and stayed with her friend Amanda Wealleans at her flat in Manly. She said she was determined to remain in Australia while the investigation continued, while there was a chance of finding out something about Peter's fate. 'She said she thought that while she was here, she might as well be doing something,' says her boss Gary Sullivan.

'Initially, there was a lot of press hanging around, cameramen trying to shoot into the store, and people lurking in the shop. It was getting on Joanne's nerves. But all the staff were very protective of her.'

She used the pseudonym Anna for all phone calls, worked mostly in the storeroom away from the public and tried to avoid the weird guy who'd regularly come in to tell her he loved her. When a customer would approach her and casually ask her for an autograph, she would flee, astonished, upset, and angry.

'She was struggling to cope with everything,' says Sullivan. 'Peter's brother Paul started picking her up from work so she wouldn't get hassled. She was a really nice soft girl. She told me she didn't know how to cope without Peter. He did so much for her. The side others saw of her in Alice Springs, of wanting to be in control, none of us had seen. None of us knew that part of her. Here, she was just back to being an innocent young girl.'

EVERYONE WANTED A SAY IN the case. A British newspaper flew out John Stalker, one of the UK's most famous former police officers, and the man who unleashed enormous controversy by revealing an alleged Royal Ulster Constabulary 'shoot-to-kill' policy in Northern Ireland. Now the director of a large national security company and a crime specialist on TV, he visited the crime scene, and said it was no wonder there were so few footprints on such hard stony ground. He also revealed that he had never experienced such black nights before, and declared that the police were doing a fine job. 'For my own part, having spent two hours in [Assistant Commissioner John] Daulby's office, I can honestly say he is not the sort of cop I'd want on my trail if I were the gunman.' And his verdict on the villain of the piece? 'My belief is that the attacker is in his early middle-age,' he says. 'He is a loner and completely self-reliant – the kind of man who can take off into nowhere with his van and his dog and live off the land. He is a survivalist, the American Vietnam Veteran type. There are plenty of them in Australia too.'

A water-diviner from Queensland swore Peter's body was buried at Renner Springs, 150 kilometres north of Tennant Creek. The farmer who owned the land delivered a piece of dirt to the police for forensic testing. A psychic provided a fresh description of the Barrow Creek assailant.

Even loathed backpacker murderer Ivan Milat put in his tuppence worth. He said the description of the Barrow Creek gunman was the same as the description of the backpacker killer by the one man who got away, Paul Onions. The gunman, therefore, was most probably the same person as the one who stalked, raped and killed the overseas tourists. For Milat, of course, never did it.

IN THE MIDDLE OF SEPTEMBER 2001, Paul Falconio decided to return to the UK. There seemed to be little point in hanging around Sydney, with nothing he could do to help the police. There was another reason too. 'I think he thought Joanne was getting too dependent on him,' says Gary Sullivan. 'He felt it would be better if Joanne tried to cope on her own.'

IN OCTOBER, IT WAS DECIDED TO send a group of police officers from Taskforce Regulus to examine the crime scene. No-one at that point from the group had actually been there, so they took along Senior Constable Ian Spilsbury who'd been in charge of the area at the start to help them orientate themselves.

The group included Superintendent Kate Vanderlaan, Senior Sergeant Jeanette Kerr, Detective Tony Henrys and Detective Megan Rowe, and they arrived on October 15 to view the site. Spilsbury pointed out the mulga bush Joanne had hidden beneath and they walked over for a closer look. As Kerr casually bent down, she spotted something on the ground. It was three pieces of black tape, most probably the parts Joanne had described biting off the manacles. Spilsbury immediately photographed them and took them. But worse was to follow. As he moved a leaf aside, he found the lipbalm sitting there, just as Joanne had said. Everyone fell silent. It was hard to believe the intensive searches of the area had overlooked them.

THE INVESTIGATION HAD HIT A wall. Even though the public was still phoning in with sightings of the attacker and his vehicle, ABC TV's *Australian Story* had run a mini-documentary about the case, 'The Vanishing', and police were still churning through the mountains of information they'd amassed, there seemed to be little light at the end of the long tunnel. It was all painstaking work – checking people's vehicles, gathering bank statements, examining the receipts of suspects who'd been in the area at the time of the attack to rule them in or out – but there seemed, from the outside, not to be much to show for it. In Sydney, Joanne grew increasingly despondent. For her birthday on September 25, her workmates urged her to go out for a meal with them. She turned them down, instead sharing a takeaway with a friend at the flat in Manly. The days all merged into each other with the same routine: the ferry or bus to work, the bookshop, avoiding curious customers and then home again. Every day she hoped for a call from the police saying they'd found Pete or they'd caught their attacker. Every day she was disappointed.

On November 15, when the first anniversary of her and Peter's departure from England came, and went, without a phone call, she finally came to a decision. 'I don't want to leave Australia without Pete,' she said, but she knew she had to face facts. Peter must be dead, and it could take years, if ever, for the police to catch his killer. It felt a betrayal, somehow, to be leaving her boyfriend behind in Australia but, really, she felt she had little choice.

On 19 November 2001, she finally went home to England.

# CHAPTER THIRTY-FIVE

# Honour Among Villains

THE DAY IN NOVEMBER 2001 that the police called round to Bradley Murdoch's flat in Broome to question him about the Barrow Creek murder, he appeared unflustered. The officers were polite, but firm. Murdoch was known to drive a white ute similar to the vehicle that had been described by Joanne Lees, and to that captured by the security cameras at the Shell Truckstop. After seeing the footage and images, a few people had called the police in Darwin reporting that Murdoch resembled the wanted man. Darwin had checked him out, and their suspicions had been aroused. There was a register of corporate owners of the commonly customised 75 Series Toyota Landcruiser and a list of their secondhand purchasers – and he was on it.

But the day the Broome police visited Murdoch, they noted he had very short hair, and no moustache. His ute also at the time didn't have a canopy. And he appeared to have an alibi, putting him in Broome at the time of the offence.

'Thanks, Mr Murdoch,' they said as they left. 'That all seems to be in order.'

BUT ALL WAS NOT IN order with Murdoch. The work he'd been having done on his ute seemed to be taking longer and longer, and James Hepi was growing impatient. With his car not fixed up, he wasn't able to do his regular trips from Broome to Sedan and back again. And Hepi was becoming irritated.

For years, Murdoch had enjoyed messing around with his cars, but now the work seemed to be assuming a life of its own. In March 2001, he'd bought a 1993 white Toyota Landcruiser from a courier company which had purchased it originally from Telstra, at a government auction. In late July, he'd had welder Michael Somerville repair and extend the tray and order him some parts ready for building a new aluminium canopy over it. Somerville noticed Murdoch had shaved off his moustache.

He'd also called into Minshull's Mechanical Repairs, where he'd bought a new steel bull bar. Owner William Minshull saw there was nothing wrong with the original bull bar – in fact the one he was selling him was a lot older – but thought Murdoch perhaps wanted one that was more heavy duty. 'His was a bit more trendier,' he says. Powder-coater Wayne Holmes was then called on to treat the wheels, and then the bull bar. He was surprised at the condition of Murdoch's vehicle. '[It was] excellent,' he says. 'The leather had been resprayed, fully detailed, chassis freshly painted black, looked like a new car really.' A bloke Murdoch met in a pub, Robin Knox, then fitted a bigger exhaust system to the vehicle.

Towards the end of August, Murdoch finally had the new aluminium canopy built over the tray. He'd contacted Stephen Galvin to do the work for him. 'He provided 99 per cent of the materials; I just provided the rectangular hollow section that held the mesh for the doors,' says Galvin. 'It was a fully enclosed solid canopy, with hinged mesh doors on the side.' It was the kind of canopy that would allow no-one to get in, if he was carrying precious cargo – or no-one to get out.

His next port of call was Broome Tropical Upholstery, a company that had done some work for him before, making a canopy for a vehicle. Owner Louis O'Dore recognised Murdoch as a man who'd introduced himself as 'Doug' the first time. He also thought he recognised his ute, 'but it looked a lot newer, it looked done up,' he says. 'It looked like it had been detailed, it had new tyres, exhaust, a totally different frame from the first one.' That, of course, was the custom-built aluminium canopy, with a plate between the cab and the tray. 'The second frame had a hard front behind the driver,' says O'Dore, 'and a hard back where there was access for a spare wheel. And it had mesh sides, like security mesh, that was rolled and hinged at the top, and an aluminium roof.'

O'Dore reckoned he recognised his customer 'Doug' in another way too. He'd seen the pictures from the Shell Truckstop video on TV. 'I mentioned I'd seen a photo of the first vehicle,' says O'Dore. 'It was at the Truckstop ... I just mentioned to him that I'd seen the vehicle, and I believed it looked like the one we did for him. He said he was up there at that time and it could have been him, it could have been his vehicle because he made a stop at that Truckstop.'

Murdoch also said that someone else had asked him about the same thing. 'He said the police spoke to him about it and he told them it wasn't him, he didn't do anything,' says O'Dore. 'So I didn't think any more of it.'

JAMES HEPI, HOWEVER, WAS GROWING angrier. He'd hardly seen Murdoch since his return from Sedan in July, and he'd only done a few trips. It meant Hepi had been forced to do most of them himself.

Murdoch had his excuse: 'He said his car wasn't ready,' says Hepi, 'It took a few months to fix the car up.' But Hepi wasn't satisfied. Their partnership was beginning to fall apart. 'After that, things started to dissolve,' he says. Hepi started to look at his business partner more closely. One day they were both down in the shed at the Sedan property, and Murdoch was fiddling with something on the workshop bench. Hepi leaned over to see what he was doing. 'He was making handcuffs out of cable ties,' he says. 'I just asked him what he was doing. Then he put the shit in the bin and went out the back. He'd made them from three zip ties tied together, and extended by 100 mile-an-hour tape wrapped around the zip ties.' The handcuffs were very similar, Hepi said later, to the ones used on Joanne Lees.

IN LATE DECEMBER 2001, THE bad feeling reached a head. The pair met in a car park in Perth and had a heated discussion. 'I wanted to know where the money was,' says Hepi, who was also owed a cache of drugs by Murdoch. 'I asked him why he had not met me in Broome. He said he'd had trouble getting across a roadblock ... Because of the Falconio murder, police were waiting for him at the border.'

The pair were furious with each other, and traded insults and accusations about who might be cheating whom. 'You can get fucked!' Murdoch finally said to Hepi as he stomped off. That was effectively the end of their cosy drugs partnership. The ill feeling also spilled over to

Hepi's friends in the Riverland, the couple who'd given Murdoch his dog, Jack. Hepi accused the friend of stealing a heater from his house, and the row grew ugly. The friend then went off and sided with Murdoch, who decided to set up in the drugs business on his own from a shed he rented for the purpose in Angle Vale, 40 kilometres north of Adelaide. The friend admitted working as his gopher, locating amphetamines and cannabis, and dropping by to lend him a hand whenever he needed it. Soon after, in March 2002, the friend says Hepi turned up there, intent on taking some of the stockpile of drugs he insisted Murdoch owed him. The friend tried to stop him, and claims Hepi retaliated by assaulting him, threatening to cut off his fingers with secateurs or bolt-cutters and then saying he'd kill him. When Murdoch heard about the incident, he gave the friend a gun so he'd be able to protect himself in future.

He also put in a call to his old mate Darryl Cragan, now living in Katherine, and asked him if he too would be interested in coming over to SA to help with his new drug business. Cragan agreed, and Murdoch picked him up at Adelaide airport in the April, installing him in Angle Vale to pack cannabis, and then later in an old rundown stone farmhouse he also rented on 4 hectares just outside Port Broughton, a fishing town on the Yorke Peninsula. There, he gave him a Ford Falcon sedan and a Glock 9 millimetre semi-automatic pistol for protection. With his new team in place, Murdoch was now ready to start working his own business, doing his own deals, and making his own money.

But with that, Murdoch and Hepi were now effectively rivals in the drugs business, as well as deadly enemies. And the repercussions of that falling out would prove devastating to them both.

MURDOCH HAD BEEN FRIENDS FOR years with a young man called Benjamin Kotz, the son of some friends of his parents. They lived in Salisbury Downs in SA and whenever Murdoch passed through, he'd drop in for a cup of tea and a chat. Kotz, twenty years younger, grew up calling Murdoch 'Uncle Brad' and was devoted to the older man. With a similar obsession with cars, he looked forward to his visits. Indeed, sometime later, Murdoch helped Kotz out trying to fix up a rusted, unregistered Toyota Landcruiser he had. When it couldn't be salvaged, Murdoch bought it from Kotz for parts for $10,000. Murdoch then stripped the chassis from the vehicle and fitted the cab and drive train from the old Telstra Landcruiser on to it. Along the way, he also put Kotz's ute's build and compliance plates onto the new vehicle, and asked Kotz to go and register it for him in his own name. Kotz happily obliged.

But on one occasion when Murdoch called round, he didn't seem too happy. 'Me and my mum were there,' says Kotz. 'Dad was working away. He looked very pale.' It was easy for Kotz to overhear the conversation. 'He said to my mum that he's done something wrong and he's never done this before. He had dobbed in a Kiwi mate to the police. He was upset with his partner the Kiwi mate and he also told them there was drugs in his car.'

JAMES HEPI WAS ARRESTED BY the police as he drove into Broome on 17 May 2002, with 4 kilograms of cannabis that he'd brought up from Sedan. He was incensed. He'd been running a tight operation, and there was only one person who could have dobbed him in. But his immediate concern was the trouble he was in. This was serious. Four kilograms was a substantial quantity of cannabis and the police were clamping down on suppliers of the drug. Also, there were so many health reports coming out about how the cannabis now being grown was much stronger than before – and so much more dangerous as a result for young people, with links to depression and the country's spiralling youth suicide rate. In addition, Hepi was known to have crossed a border, thus importing the drug from another state into WA – once again, a much more serious offence. With a sinking heart, Hepi knew he was in for a sizeable stretch in jail. So when he was handed a phone at the police station in Broome to contact a solicitor, he told him to fix up a meeting with detectives. And when he was finally led into the police interview room to see them, he took a deep breath.

'I want do a deal,' he said. 'I've got some information you might be interested in. It's about that killing up at Barrow Creek ...'

# CHAPTER THIRTY-SIX

# A TV Confession

IT WAS THE MOMENT EVERYONE had been waiting for. Joanne Lees too. She looked nervous, tossed her head to flick her hair aside, and coughed a short little dry cough. 'Did you,' top British TV current affairs presenter Martin Bashir was asking her, 'kill Peter Falconio?'

Joanne looked at him, almost incredulously.

And then commercial TV did what it does so well – it went to an ad break. But not before freezing the image of Joanne's face so it looked as if she was hesitating forever, dumbfounded in guilt, caught in the full beam of the spotlights. It was a moment of extraordinary television and an incredible irony that Joanne, who'd be putting so much effort into avoiding the press, at the end of the day walked right into one of the oldest tricks in the book.

When the program resumed, however, she smiled and answered with a definitive 'No!'

Bashir then asked the same question in a different way, and again Joanne looked nervous, but this time composed. After all, being asked if she really was a killer could be the question, if the gunman was never caught, that might well dominate the rest of her life, exactly as it had Lindy Chamberlain's. 'There's no weapon, there's no gun, there's no body,' said Bashir. 'The attacker's footprints aren't found, but yours are. There's Peter's blood on the ground. So some people say the person who murdered Peter was Joanne. What do you say to that?'

Joanne's eyes narrowed and she swallowed. 'It's,' she said, with a grimace, 'totally untrue.'

For eight months Joanne had been pursued by the media but when she finally decided to speak publicly, she earned yet another tide of recriminations. She'd agreed to appear on the British ITV current affairs show *Tonight With Trevor McDonald*, produced by Granada Television, for the Bashir interview aired on 18 March 2002, and for a payment of $120,000 (50,000 pounds). After rebuffing the media in Alice Springs, saying she would never sell her story, she was described as having done exactly that. Not surprisingly, among those criticising her the most were those who'd had their offers turned down.

BASHIR WAS A STRANGE CHOICE, many onlookers thought, for her one and only interview. As one of the highest profile TV journalists in the world, he'd certainly had more than his fair share of attention-grabbing interviewees, including the historic Princess Diana audience when she'd revealed her 'three-person' marriage; the English au pair Louise Woodward accused of murder in the US; and the five young men suspected of killing Stephen Lawrence. Later, he was to garner even more attention with his Michael Jackson interview in which the pop star disclosed that he shared his bed with teenage boys. He wasn't without controversy himself, either, with Jackson later releasing a tape showing Bashir ingratiating himself with his interviewee, and a TV watchdog finding him guilty in 2003 of misleading someone to secure an interview.

Earlier, another TV team, this time from Britain's Channel 4, had tried unsuccessfully to persuade Joanne to talk to them for a documentary about the incident. Their program, *The Trials of Joanne Lees*, by filmmaker Ross Wilson, was centring more on the vilification of someone who might otherwise be treated as a heroine. It was believed to be taking a sympathetic attitude towards Joanne.

Bashir, on the other hand, was renowned for his hard-hitting style, and not allowing his interviewees, once they were on camera, room to be evasive. He was the same with Joanne. As well as asking her bluntly, twice, if she'd killed her boyfriend, he also put to her all the problems with the case. In the hour-long special entitled 'Murder, Mystery & Me', he quizzed her about the lack of her attacker's footprints at the scene; the fact that no blood was found on the vehicle; why the dog hadn't bounded after her when she escaped; how a speck of the gunman's blood had found its way on to her top; and why people should believe her when she stepped through her handcuffs, something not even a ballerina could do. She couldn't give satisfactory answers to many of the questions, and that was really not much of a surprise – she didn't know. It was a few days later that the police scotched one of the doubts by finally releasing a replica of the cable tie handcuffs, and a policewoman demonstrated how easy it was to step over the tie between each of the hands.

But it was only when Bashir asked Joanne how her hunter hadn't found her that night, that she sounded at all inspired. 'I believe someone,' she said, 'was looking out for me that night.'

She also warmed to the subject when she was asked about her attitude to the media, and why she hadn't simply agreed to media interviews, or answered more questions at that disastrous press conference. 'In hindsight, I could have done that,' she says. 'But I was just thrown into that. I haven't had any media experience before. I didn't realise how people were going to analyse every answer I gave or criticise me for questions I didn't answer, let alone the questions I did. I didn't realise I was on trial. And to me, they were ridiculous questions. I thought people should just focus on finding Pete.'

As to whether it would have helped the case if she had agreed to use the media, she replied that the case was already on all the front pages and at the top of every TV and radio bulletin anyway. 'I probably would have been willing to do more to raise public awareness but having had such bad treatment from the press, I did become withdrawn. I didn't feel strong enough at the time … I didn't really understand.'

She ran haltingly through the events of that dark night, yet came over as more deserving of compassion when, in a rare moment of candour, she said she blamed herself for the attack. 'I feel guilty that the man didn't want Pete … he just wanted me,' she said. 'He just wanted a female and he had to get Pete out of the way.'

She was also critical of the police, claiming that when publican Les Pilton first rang the Alice Springs station, the officer put the phone down on him, thinking it was a hoax call. 'He rang again,' she said. 'They asked me to describe the gun. They said, "No way!" Four hours later, I finally saw a police person.' That claim was denied by police, a denial later borne out by a review carried out into the police investigation, and the recollections of Pilton and truckie Vince Millar.

Strangely, considering the program-makers had paid to have Joanne on board and had flown her back to Australia, a re-enactment was performed by an actor. It was believed that, although requested to do so, she hadn't proved willing to do it herself.

Indeed, the first police learnt of Joanne's presence in Alice Springs was when she called them from her hotel room, asking them to be part of the program. 'We certainly weren't aware of it but I must say Joanne Lees is free to go about her business,' said Assistant Commissioner John Daulby, who later agreed to make a statement for the show, in the interests of keeping the case in the public eye. 'She doesn't have to tell us what she does.'

The return trip was reported in Britain by one newspaper, the *Daily Mail*, under the banner headline 'How could she go back?', using the opportunity once more to repeat factual errors about the police not finding any DNA evidence on Joanne's clothing, and claiming that the man had hunted her for several hours with his dog.

There were others with their noses out of joint too. During the filming in Barrow Creek, Pilton said he was disappointed Joanne didn't drop in at the roadhouse to say hello. Similarly, Millar tried to phone her in Alice Springs, but his calls were not returned. Helen Jones, however, came in for the biggest blast. In the interview shown in the UK – but in a part cut out when it was aired in Australia – Joanne accused her old Barrow Creek ally of 'getting off on someone else's tragedy', because she'd spoken to the media. Jones was hurt, angry and indignant, saying afterwards she'd only spoken to the media after consultation with police who thought it might help refresh someone's memory about Peter. In an interview with *New Idea* magazine, she hit back at Joanne, saying the 'black holes' in her story worried her. She said Joanne had claimed Peter was asleep in the back of the Kombi as they arrived at Ti Tree, which meant he wasn't seen. 'Joanne says no-one saw Peter because he was asleep in the back of the Kombi at the time,' Jones said. 'My question is: "Was he even there?"' She also pointed out the confusion over who was driving. 'I always thought Peter was driving the Kombi that night, but in the British interview Jo says she was the one at the wheel.' In addition, she said she was worried at reports of an argument between the couple in Alice Springs.

But Joanne had her reasons for returning to Alice Springs, quite apart from the TV program. One afternoon, she gave everyone the slip, rented a car and drove out to the Shell Truckstop where the video was taken. Owner Val Prior was the only one to spot her there. 'I caught sight of her, and watched her,' she says. 'She just drove around the diesel pumps in a hire car. We didn't interfere with her. We let her be. I guess she just wanted to see. Poor girl. I feel for her, and all the families involved. What must have she been thinking?'

DURING THE TV INTERVIEW, Joanne gave generally quite a controlled performance, as she recounted her ordeal in her slow, deliberate way of speaking, choosing her words carefully and obviously trying to keep her emotions in check. That thick bottom lip, however, although in normal circumstances considered so attractive, couldn't help but give her a look of petulance, a stubborn and obstinate appearance. As an exercise in winning over the public sympathy, it wasn't a great success. Even when she cried, it didn't come over terribly naturally. It wasn't her fault, of course, that she didn't cry gracefully for the cameras, but it didn't help. Fighting back the tears, the most moving moment of the interview was when she confessed that she still felt in touch with Peter. 'I talk to him every day,' she said. 'If I've got a decision to make, I ask him what he'd do. It's really difficult to talk about Pete before I start crying. He's the nicest person I've ever met.' Her face dissolved and she buried her face in her hands, still determined not to be seen crying on screen. 'Okay,' she said, wiping her eyes, 'okay.' When asked whether she could live without Peter, she was also reassuringly human. 'I don't want to. But I can. What's happened to me is I nearly lost my life and it's made me appreciate every single day. I do love life and I'm going to get on with it. I'd prefer it if Pete was by my side doing that but I think it would be a miracle for that to happen.'

Bizarrely, the interview wasn't aired in Australia by the Seven Network, which has all rights to Granada TV material, until 4 September 2003, some eighteen months later. 'We didn't think people would be interested,' said a spokesperson.

# CHAPTER THIRTY-SEVEN

# New Suspects...
# and Two More Killings

WITH A FLASH OF STEEL and a spurt of blood, the Barrow Creek investigation sprung back into life. An unemployed drifter called Michael Sorrell had lunged at two brothers with a large hunting knife as they left a Sydney electrical store on 3 June 2002. One, Michael Furlong, lay dead. The other, Glen, had only just managed to escape. Police in NSW had arrested the killer as he slept in his vehicle, early the next morning, with his victim's wallet. They'd then alerted the police in the Northern Territory. This man roamed widely around Australia. He seemed to have no motive at all for his sudden violence. He was obviously extremely dangerous. Could he possibly be the Barrow Creek gunman? It was a lead in a case that seemed to have gone cold, and police immediately requested a sample of his DNA and samples from his vehicle to compare to that which had been found on Joanne Lees' top.

Aged twenty-nine, Sorrell had been diagnosed with paranoid schizophrenia from at least 1994, and experienced delusional beliefs that made him unable to tell reality from fantasy. While serving time in prison in WA, he'd been transferred to Greylands Hospital for psychiatric help. He believed that he was under surveillance, had been drugged by a secret government unit using technology that enabled them to read his thoughts via vibrations in his larynx, and he was the victim of a complex plot involving the CIA, the FBI, the West Australian justice department and medical staff. He was prescribed anti-psychotic medication.

Later, during a period in the UK, he was admitted to the notorious Broadmoor Hospital for the criminally insane in Berkshire – the same institution as Yorkshire Ripper Peter Sutcliffe – until being deported back to Australia. More recently, he'd been in Townsville Hospital in Queensland after a suicide attempt, and was again treated with anti-psychotic drugs while in custody in NSW. Only when he took that medication, was his behaviour 'normal'. Without it, it could be, according to one of the psychiatrists who examined him, 'very alarming'. The killing of Furlong, forty-five, at Smithfield proved it. Could he possibly be the man being hunted for the disappearance of Peter Falconio?

Politicians in NSW, where there were tighter restrictions on the use of DNA, hurriedly passed legislation to allow Sorrell's DNA to be sent to Darwin for comparison, and the country waited with bated breath for an answer. It came just a day later. Michael Sorrell wasn't the gunman. Later, in February 2003, he was declared not guilty of murder by reason of mental illness, and was ordered to be detained in the psychiatric ward of Long Bay Jail.

SHORTLY BEFORE MICHAEL SORRELL, another possible suspect had come to light. English backpacker Caroline Stuttle, in Queensland on holiday, was pushed off a bridge during a violent robbery and plunged 10 metres to her death. The British press immediately linked her killing, in Bundaberg on 9 April 2002, to the Falconio case. It wasn't long, however, until her attacker was arrested: another drifter, this time drug-addicted and looking for cash to feed his habit. Ian Previte, thirty-two, was jailed for life in October 2004.

Assistant Commissioner John Daulby, despite the lack of leads, remained determinedly optimistic. 'We will catch this man,' he said. 'We won't be giving up at all. We are 100 per cent behind Joanne. We are going to resolve this case.'

Every week without fail, occasionally twice or three times depending on what was going on, he called the Falconio family to let them know of any developments. Sometimes, the phone conversations went smoothly. The week after the current affairs show *60 Minutes* ran a piece on the case on 26 May 2002, there were hundreds more calls from the public with promising information. But sometimes Daulby had so little to tell them, he dreaded the aimless chit-chat. But that had been his agreement with them, and he stuck doggedly by it. Joanne had been less keen to keep in touch, saying she only wanted to be contacted if there was anything positive to report. At times, Daulby was relieved at not having to call her too.

MEANWHILE, POLICE IN BROOME were talking to James Hepi about his assertion that they should be hunting his former partner in crime, Bradley Murdoch. They were wary as they'd lost count of the number of villains facing charges who'd tried to finger others to save their own skin, and it was Murdoch, after all, who dobbed in Hepi. In addition, there was that small matter of the $250,000 reward for information about the Barrow Creek killer up for grabs.

But as Hepi talked about his business partner, the police became more and more interested. He'd even had a friend visit his Sedan property collecting Murdoch's cigarette butts to post to him in Broome so the police could check his DNA against the blood on Joanne's T-shirt. The West Australian cops decided it was time to call Darwin.

BACK IN THE UK, JOANNE was living in Brighton but was finding life a struggle. The press continued to hound her, keeping watch on her old workplaces and hanging around outside her home for hours, waiting for the chance of a photograph, with one news crew even digging a satellite dish into the front lawn outside her apartment. Going back to her old travel agency job would have been impossible, and she had to move house every time they discovered her new address, which was often. Instead, she decided on a complete change. She moved to Hove, just out of the centre of Brighton, where a neighbour described her as 'very quiet. She seemed like a lost soul', and she changed careers, moving into social services. At first, she was an advisor for people with housing problems and later worked with people with intellectual disabilities. If she was going to take anything positive at all out of the experience in Australia, this would be it. 'I just want to give something back to people and help people who are struggling and need a direction,' she says. 'I can empathise with them and I think I would have appreciated someone like me to help me.' She also considered doing a course at university. For never far from her mind was Peter, and what he'd think of what she was doing. 'He'd want me to do this,' she says. 'He'd want me to go to university. I want to make him proud of me, like I was proud of him.'

She thought about going overseas again to escape the attention, but her mother Jenny James was getting sicker. Joanne travelled more and more regularly up to Huddersfield to see her, until Jenny grew so weak she knew there wouldn't be much time left. On 28 June 2002, her mother died, aged fifty-four. It was yet another blow for Joanne, and she wondered how much more tragedy she could take. But one of the cruellest twists was to come the day after her mother's funeral.

THE HEADLINE IN BRITAIN'S *Daily Mail* newspaper on 6 July 2002 made Joanne gasp. 'Did Outback Peter Fake His Own Death?' She read the story in a state of mild shock. The article said police in Australia were investigating a startling new possibility – that in order to collect an insurance payout, her boyfriend might have staged his own death and still be alive. The author, once again, was Joanne's tabloid nemesis, Richard Shears.

In fact, as part of their routine inquiries at the beginning of the case, the Northern Territory police had checked whether Peter had any life insurance. He hadn't. He'd merely had a small run-of-the-mill travel insurance policy. Police media officer Denise Hurley says Shears had been told this, but still he felt the story was valid. 'It was all speculation,' says Shears today. 'But I'd spoken to a particular fellow, I can't mention his name, who works for a company who works with people who fake their own deaths ... I don't believe Joanne's story. It doesn't add up. We phoned her for a comment but she's never given us one. She's just ducked and dodged.'

Even while Shears admits it was pure speculation, that still didn't stop the story from gathering momentum as it was picked up by other newspapers, TV and radio bulletins, and was reported all over the world. While it hit Joanne hard, it shocked and appalled the Falconio family even more. 'It's absolutely disgusting,' said Peter's teary mum, Joan. 'My son is not here to defend himself. No-one has ever had a bad word to say about him.' Peter's oldest brother Nick was also horrified by the claims. 'It's completely untrue, hurtful and insensitive,' he said. 'Peter would never have done that to our family. It's a fairytale, a load of rubbish.'

Even other journalists felt the story shouldn't have been printed. 'The police had investigated that already, and discovered Peter hadn't had any life insurance,' says Frank Thorne, the stringer for many of the British tabloid newspapers. 'We all knew that. And then that came out, and caused so much heartache and distress. I thought that was unforgiveable.' Onlookers also cringed to think of the Falconios' torment at such a story. 'The hurt that must be being felt by the Falconios would be really devastating,' says Les Pilton. 'There's no way their son would do that to cause such grief to his family.' At the end of the day, Thorne believes it was simply part of the game of 'getting Joanne'. 'The lack of information and the police's half-arsed answers made Joanne look guilty, and then the way she behaved aroused suspicions,' he says. 'Some people couldn't help adding two and two and coming up with five.

'Once the dogs of conspiracy are let loose, they're difficult to stop. If some people had their way, Joanne Lees would have been in a prison cell by now, like another woman once was.'

THAT OTHER WOMAN HAD INDEED been following Joanne's ordeal closely. Lindy Chamberlain, whose life was irrevocably altered by her ordeal out in the same desert, longed to help the younger woman. 'If she had given her consent, I would have liked to have helped,' she says. 'Can you imagine anything worse than being accused of murdering someone you love?' Chamberlain couldn't help but be affected as she watched Joanne suffering from her own 'Lindyfication'. 'People who love her and care for her are going to take her for what she is,' she told *New Idea* magazine on 29 June 2002. 'The ones that don't, that's their problem, and you can't do much about it. The sad thing is that even if they do find the murderer, the suspicion won't end. Some people have already made up their minds. They will still say she did it. "No smoke without fire" or "some funny business there". Yes, there was funny business but it was not you – but you have to wear it.'

Chamberlain also felt it was looking increasingly likely that Joanne would suffer the same fate as her, the longer the case went on. 'When you look at the huge areas of the outback ... it's no wonder a body hasn't turned up,' says Chamberlain. 'There are miles and miles of just nothing. I'd hate to be looking for a body out there.'

# CHAPTER THIRTY-EIGHT

# Policing the Police

TWELVE MONTHS ON FROM THE Barrow Creek attack, the largest police operation in the history of the Northern Territory had resulted in nearly 23,000 case note entries, with attachments, and DNA swabs from some 300 people. In addition, more than 2500 persons of interest and 2000 vehicles had been eliminated from their inquiries, and the computer system wasn't coping at all with the enormous workload. Yet in spite of the massive investigation, it seemed the police were no nearer to finding the killer.

Detectives had flown to Ireland to obtain DNA from the parents of one suspect and questioned another, only to find he was wanted for two cases of rape in Queensland. It was a win of sorts, but not in the main game: the Falconio case remained tormentingly open. There'd been massive publicity around the world, and Interpol and other countries' intelligence agencies had all been double-checked just to make absolutely sure Peter Falconio wasn't some kind of double-agent. The investigation had been forced, however reluctantly, to rely on other state police forces also doing their bit as they couldn't possibly afford to pay for their officers to fly off around the country to follow up every one of the 3000 interstate leads. And there'd been a virtual trial by media of the only witness, but there remained no body, no weapon, no motive, no clear suspect and no real sense that an end was in sight. It was the perfect time for an investigation into the investigation.

Just prior to his retirement at Christmas 2001, Commissioner Brian Bates had set the wheels in motion. The Colin Winchester case he'd headed had been the subject of a review and he felt a similar exercise could prove just as useful now. The new Commissioner taking his place, the former South Australian Assistant Commissioner Paul White, fifty-one, agreed. Two men were appointed to head the six-week project – White's old fellow South Australian Assistant Commissioner Jim Litster, now retired, and Northern Territory Superintendent George Owen.

Within the force, there was nervousness about the review; indeed, there was a lot riding on it. As well as the reputation of the Northern Territory force, with so much still to prove after the disastrous Lindy Chamberlain affair, there was also the pride of Australian policing at stake in the spotlight of a critical media both at home and away.

At the same time, however, police were intensely aware that, whichever way the review went, it was unlikely to be the end to the controversy over their handling of the case. If the review was disparaging, they'd have to take that criticism on board. If it was favourable, the police could stand accused of pulling off a whitewash. The man in charge of the investigation, Assistant Commissioner John Daulby, was in favour of a review, but wasn't keen on having Litster in charge. 'However professional the review was going to be, and however suited Litster was going to be to the task, having a friend of the Commissioner's, and someone user-friendly to the Commissioner, on board made it look like a farce,' he says. 'Outsiders might look at that and say he might just as well have conducted an internal review. If there was going to be criticism, I was more than ready to accept that but I wanted to have complete confidence in the process.' It didn't help that he received a call on his phone from a journalist for Litster, even before his participation had been publicly announced.

When it got underway, things got worse. It seemed to some within Taskforce Regulus that the terms of reference of the review were being blatantly flouted. Instead of sticking to the police's initial response, including its witness statements, its exhibits and searches, and reviewing the lines of inquiry and the resource requirements, it appeared the team was more interested, at times, in investigating the crime itself. 'We hadn't been able to solve it, but I think they thought they could,' said one insider. 'It was a very high profile case, and there was some jostling for position going on.'

Messages were constantly being sent over to the Regulus unit: We think you should be looking at this; Has it occurred to anyone to look at that; We've a new theory that should be checked out. The review was meant to be verifying the police had done their job, not giving them even more work on top of their own continuing lines of investigation. Daulby grew more and more annoyed as the lines of reporting between himself and the review team dissolved and the review team increasingly reported direct to the Commissioner. He was also taken aback that the review team failed to seek responses or feedback from members directly involved in the management of the investigation.

When the review's thirty-two-page report was finally completed, only the main findings were released. That created suspicion among the media that there had been a stuff-up, followed now by a cover-up. But, in fact, the final report was not overly critical of the investigation and the way it was conducted and found that, although the existing computer systems had encountered difficulties in processing the vast amount of information collected by Taskforce Regulus, a few police officers guarding the crime scene had not submitted statements and there was a lack of uniformity in record-keeping by police managing the roadblocks, generally the investigation had been as good as it possibly could have been. Yes, the crime scene had been trodden over by a number of police, but the review judged this 'justifiable and necessary in an attempt to locate Peter Falconio in the immediate vicinity'. Yes, the roadblocks had been 'set up in a timely fashion, taking into consideration the initial report of the crime', and the fact that it happened in such a remote area. And yes, the searches had been carried out 'in a logical and orderly fashion'.

In addition, the review delivered an interesting perspective on Joanne's recollection of events. 'Further, the team concluded it is perfectly reasonable to expect there will be inaccuracies in Joanne Lees's statement considering the undergoing trauma,' it wrote. 'For instance the review team undertook a re-enactment of the event utilising a female police officer. It was found that even under these staged conditions the female officer could not recall all events.'

ANOTHER CRITICISM OF THE investigation had come a short time before from Chris Tangey, a freelance cameraman and country music video-director, who'd been asked to video a much later examination of the Kombi by forensic officers. He was the only person known in the area who owned a camera that could film in the kind of low light that would pick up the glow radiated in the darkness by blood-sensitive Luminol, and was asked if he'd mind doing it for free to lend police a hand. 'I had no idea what they were talking about, so I looked it up on the internet,' he says. 'They said they wanted to run a test, to see if in the future it could be useful to film a forensic examination for court use later.' When he turned up, he was introduced to Joy Kuhl, the head of biology in the forensic science branch in Darwin, and the woman who'd become notorious during the Chamberlain case as the person who'd wrongly identified sound deadener in the family's Holden sedan as foetal blood which had proved critical evidence in Lindy's conviction. Six years later, at a Royal Commission, she'd admitted she'd been mistaken. She's always protested that the kind of testing she'd carried out at the time was somewhat in its infancy, and she is still mystified at how it had so misled her.

As Tangey was filming, he saw Kuhl spray Luminol on a door and heard the detective with her, Senior Constable Bill Towers, ask her if the resultant glow was blood. 'No, it can't be,' she replied. 'I went right over it this afternoon.' Carmen Eckhoff, as well as a team of crime scene examiners, had done a number of thorough investigations earlier in the case, finding no evidence of blood, but tiny amounts of DNA on the steering wheel and gearstick. Tangey, however, saw what he thought to be the blurred outline of a partial handprint on one wall of the Kombi, and felt that Kuhl was taking no notice of it at all. It was yet another echo of the Chamberlain case: the bloodied handprint on baby Azaria's jumpsuit that was later found to be red sand.

Tangey was alarmed. 'I thought, "why are they dismissing this?"' he says. 'Instead, they moved on quickly to the dash and carried on with an intense examination of the whole van. It wasn't until later that I mulled it over and thought, "What was that about?"' Tangey downloaded a digital copy onto Towers' computer, but kept the original himself. When he saw the story in the press criticising the police for not having seized the hard drive of the Shell Truckstop security camera computer, he phoned the reporter who'd written it, and sent him a copy of the tape. The newspaper ran an image of the alleged handprint. After that, it was given to the *Today* TV show, and a host of other media.

Superintendent Kate Vanderlaan phoned Tangey immediately, asking for the tape. 'No,' he replied. 'You didn't pay me anything for it, it's my property.' Later, Tangey spoke to another officer who arranged a conference call with the head of forensics, Dr Peter Thatcher, who told him the tape was of little value. That only ignited Tangey's suspicions even more. 'I thought, "So why are they going to so much effort to tell me this?"' he says. 'Steve Liebmann [of the *Today Show*] said it looks like a handprint too.' He then called barrister Stuart Littlemore, and arranged to store the tape in a safe in Sydney.

John Daulby was the next police officer to call him to ask for the tape, saying they didn't have an audio track, and therefore needed the original. Tangey didn't believe him, and the two had heated words on the phone. Tangey reported him to the Ombudsman. 'I feel it was a stuff-up by forensics, and a cover-up,' he says. 'During the Chamberlain case, they stuffed up and I thought this was another one. I couldn't believe that Joy Kuhl was still involved in forensics. But the police couldn't afford to be seen to stuff-up again.'

Yet it was purely by chance that Joy Kuhl hadn't been in charge of forensics throughout the entire Falconio investigation. As the call came through about the ambush early on the Sunday morning, she'd had guests for dinner and had been drinking. As a result, she sent her deputy, Eckhoff, to Alice Springs from Darwin instead. Another time, she happened to be in Alice on a different matter, and police asked her to do more Luminol testing on the Kombi. 'It had already been so closely examined, I said it was a silly idea,' she says. 'Luminol is very very good for an outside scene in detecting blood invisible to the eye, but in a car there are so many different compounds, metals, plastics, chemicals, that so much of it glows, it's frustrating. I kept trying to talk them out of using it, but I eventually said okay.' Kuhl went over the Kombi for a full six hours, testing every surface and finding nothing. Then she did the night-time test, with Tangey present. 'We wanted to see how it would be as we were thinking of buying a camera for future scenes,' she says. 'But it didn't work. He couldn't focus on me or on what I was doing. He'd never had anything to do with a crime scene before, but then he decided he'd found a handprint which is the most idiotic rubbish I heard. If there was anything there, it would have been found during all the proper testing by Carmen, then the crime scene examiners and then myself earlier. If there was real evidence there, why *wouldn't* I have taken notice of it? We were all so keen to get evidence. Then it became a real bone of contention. It was all so silly, a storm in a teacup. The press just needed stuff to write about.'

Daulby had similarly dismissed Tangey's concerns. 'I spoke to him on a couple of occasions and he went to the Ombudsman on the basis that we threatened him which is rubbish. People had to accept that everything that had to be done to the VW Kombi had been done. The significant examination was done by Carmen Eckhoff.'

The review organised a meeting with Tangey, looked at his video and examined his claims. They came to the conclusion that the vehicle had already been tested with the more accurate Orthotolodine and had been subjected to a fine fingerprint examination. 'The performance of forensic personnel was professional,' it concluded.

MORE CONTENTIOUS WERE THE review's recommendations on future media strategies. They recommended that media releases should be initiated by investigative teams as opposed to reacting to issues raised by the media themselves. They'd obviously learned little. Police in the early days of the case had done no favours at all to Joanne by ignoring so many media misunderstandings, and failing to correct them before they were given credence and repeated again and again. This looked like a recipe for similar problems in the future.

Daulby was critical too. 'The review said we should have had one or two press conferences a day, but that wouldn't have worked,' he says. 'You've got the major radio networks who have a fair degree of pull, then you've got people like John Laws. You had to talk to the local media to keep it alive because it's a Northern Territory crime, and then there's the interest nationally from those who all want to be party to the information. Then with the British press, you had to push home the remoteness of the scene. They'd started out saying we should have had police on every road within half an hour. It was a bloody difficult time for everybody. The community is worried and feels unsafe and the government worries about it. There's a lot of pressure, but I kept insisting I was briefed every hour and I had to make sure they didn't take things out of context. You have to treat every crime on its merits.' Media officer Denise Hurley feels much the same about the review's proposals. 'That was a disastrous idea!' she says. 'If you have a press conference at 9 a.m., the story's changed by 10 a.m. and there might be some story running around that the police stuffed-up that's not true and has to be countered. They'd learnt nothing from what had happened.'

But it was on one final recommendation of the review that Daulby saw red. They instructed Taskforce Regulus to pursue a line of inquiry they'd already exhaustively investigated, and finally discounted: the Kombi with its two women and one male passenger that had been followed by the man in a ute near Hughenden. A meeting between White, Daulby and media press officer Hurley became heated. Daulby voiced his criticisms of the review team, questioning why they'd been still sending materials to people who'd been eliminated from inquiries, and asking why they'd proposed that two detectives conduct an investigative audit on the job to date when they'd claimed earlier they had been through all the case entries. He was also angry that they seemed to have assumed a level of resources and personnel that simply hadn't existed. After all, the South Australian force from which Litster had come was a service with 4700 officers, compared to the Northern Territory's meagre 940.

'I believe it reflected the attitude of Litster and his "and what would have occurred in South Australia" attitude. It is apparent both Owen and Litster failed to appreciate the lack of seniority in the detective ranks that we currently have and have had for some time. We simply don't have a cadre of senior detectives that can be shuffled about.'

Litster declined to return calls.

JUST AS IN THE LINDY CHAMBERLAIN case, the misinformation had an effect. The documentary made by Britain's Channel 4, *The Trials of Joanne Lees*, was finally shown on 18 July 2002, and aired a number of vox pops from the general public, all suspicious of Joanne's story, all repeating half-baked, half-remembered half-truths. The program itself came in for criticism too for claiming that Adelaide was 'the murder capital of the world'. After protests from Prime Minister John Howard, South

Australian MPs and the public, the claim was cut from the tape, and an apology issued.

The documentary was revealing of the attitudes of some sections of the press, too. 'One of us was going to get her, because that's what happens,' said James Morgan, freelance photographer for the British *Sunday Times*. 'That's what we expect. We are the British media.'

# CHAPTER THIRTY-NINE

# I Want To Have Sex With Your Daughter

IT WAS A BEAUTIFUL DAY when German tourists Eva Obermeyer, forty-nine, and her fifteen-year-old daughter Sarah arrived at the vast Litchfield National Park, just off the Stuart Highway 130 kilometres south-west of Darwin, in their rented Toyota Corolla. They spent the afternoon driving around many of the park's beauty spots, gasping at the size of towering termite mounds and having lunch at one of the pools at the base of the rocky escarpments. As the light began to fade, they wandered down to the last of the four picturesque spring-fed waterfalls in the park, Tolmer Falls, to a lookout 500 metres from the car park. But they were not alone. A man had been following them and he slipped from his Toyota Landcruiser, pulled out a loaded Glock semi-automatic pistol, and stuffed some black cable ties and a pair of handcuffs into his pocket. He then crept over to the emergency phone in the car park and slashed the cable with a sheath knife, before sneaking back to the tourists' car and puncturing two of their tyres. He then sat down in the tourist information shelter, and watched the path, awaiting the pair's return.

When Eva and Sarah walked back up the hill, the man asked them for directions to the pool. And then he asked again. And again. They started feeling nervous, but smiled politely, and kept walking towards their car. But the man had other ideas. He stepped in front of them, produced the gun and told them he needed money. Eva quickly handed over all her cash – $150 – but then the man ordered them into the shelter. When Eva refused, he put the gun against her chest and told Sarah he was going to kill her mum. Both women suddenly realised he could be deadly serious. Sarah started crying, and Eva obeyed. But as soon as they entered the shelter, he motioned towards a rough track framed by Pandanus ferns leading away from it towards the creek. Again, he threatened he'd shoot if they refused. They stumbled down the sand and gravel path, and the man fired a shot in the air behind them, just to show he meant business. Halfway along, the man forced the pair to sit on a rocky outcrop while he went through Eva's travellers' cheques, credit cards and collection of odd notes in her rucksack. He then ordered them on.

When the three reached the clearing at the bottom, he stood by the water flowing into a shallow stream about 3 metres wide, and told Eva to stand next to one of the old grey ghost gums where he planned to tie her. He'd take Sarah, he said, back to the car. Eva shook her head. 'No,' she said, 'I won't let her go with you. You'll have to kill me.' She clung to Sarah as if she'd never let her go.

The man then tied both women to the tree, pulling the cable ties around Sarah's wrists so tightly that she screamed out in pain. At that, he slashed the ties with his knife, and snapped on the handcuffs instead. He made two attempts at tying Eva with the cable ties, but couldn't manage to tie her feet. He then offered them a drink of water from the creek. They both refused. 'You stay here,' he told them. 'I need an hour. Don't move or I'll shoot you. I'll come back to check.' He then left.

An hour later, it was nearly dark, but he was back with a torch. He removed the handcuffs from one of Sarah's hands and suggested they both go up to the car so she could get the key to free herself from the other. At the prospect of being separated, both women panicked. 'You'll have to shoot me first,' said Eva bravely.

The man looked at her, then sat down. 'I'd like to have sex with your daughter,' he said, calmly. 'What do you think about that?' Eva gasped. 'How old is she?'

Desperately, Eva, a psychotherapist, tried to talk him out of the plan.

'But I want to have sex with your daughter,' he replied. 'That's why I chose you. I saw your daughter, I saw you without a man, I watched you. That's why I picked you.'

Eva pleaded for her daughter, pretending she was twelve years old, and saying how being raped would destroy her life.

'Twelve?' he said, thoughtfully. 'That's too young.' He said he needed two hours and would come back and check on them. Then, finally, he disappeared.

After around three hours, Eva eventually managed to slip her hands from the cable ties, and broke off a branch from the tree to free her daughter. The two terrified women then spent the rest of the night hiding in the bushes, clinging to each other for warmth, fearful of the poisonous snakes and spiders they'd been warned about in the wilds, and jumping at every sound made by animals, and the orange horseshoe and ghost bats native to the area, thinking it could be signalling the man's return.

When the sun rose, they raced back to the car park, only to find their car undriveable and the phone useless. They then flagged down a passing motorist on the road who drove them to safety and contacted the police.

THE ATTACK ON THE TWO women sent alarms throughout the police force. It sounded so close in some ways to the Barrow Creek incident: the man was white, he was driving a Landcruiser, he had gone armed with a gun and cable ties and was planning to rape at least the young girl. An alert went out around the Territory. At last. This could be the man they'd been looking for.

A WEEK LATER, THREE PEOPLE were driving through the wilderness of Arnhem Land in their Toyota Troop Carrier, when they were waved down by a man on foot. He got into their car and asked them to take him to the nearest settlement. They started talking about the man wanted for an attack on two German tourists and he pulled out his gun and ordered them to drive on to where he'd left his car and hidden his Smith & Wesson .22 semi-automatic pistol and a .308 rifle. But the Northern Territory police had been prepared. They were not going to let their suspect slip through their fingers so easily twice. They'd set up roadblocks all over the area and when the tourists' car hit one, the gunman gave himself up.

THE GUNMAN TURNED OUT TO be Queenslander Matt Page, thirty-one, a keen member of the Australian Sporting Shooters Association and a former tour guide, manager of hotels in England and Scotland, and most recently a hospitality teacher in Queensland's Hervey Bay. His girlfriend had recently dumped him, he'd quit his job which he hadn't liked, he was heavily in debt and he'd just been turned down for a job with the Queensland police. He'd decided to go on a final journey across Northern Australia and commit suicide at Cape York. But then he'd changed his mind. He robbed the Obermeyers because he was broke, yet couldn't account for the rest of his actions.

The women were both badly affected by the attack. As well as fearing for her own life, Eva Obermeyer had to cope with the terrible prospect of her daughter being raped and murdered. 'I have lost the ability to enjoy life and will not be able to resume my work at full capacity,' she told Page's trial. 'I have become socially withdrawn, argumentative, stressed, tearful and insecure.'

In November 2002, Page was jailed for nine years. Another threat to life and safety had been removed from the highways and byways of Australia. But the other – the one the whole country wanted to see behind bars – was still on the loose.

# CHAPTER FORTY

# The Net Tightens

THE CALL FROM BROOME ABOUT the identity of the Barrow Creek gunman from an arrested drug runner brought some welcome traction to an investigation that, if it hadn't actually stalled, was certainly spinning its wheels. Okay, anyone arrested with 4 kilograms of cannabis in their car might be desperate enough to say anything to get themselves off the hook. They might even be desperate enough to tell the truth. And, of course, it would be just one more lead out of so many that had already been checked and rejected. But with each new suggestion came the fresh possibility of an answer to a case that had everybody stumped. And this one sounded interesting. Very interesting.

The lead landed on the desk of Superintendent Colleen Gwynne, the woman who'd taken over the day-to-day running of Taskforce Regulus after Superintendent Kate Vanderlaan was promoted to Commander of the Central Region, based in Katherine. Gwynne still reported to Assistant Commissioner John Daulby but, after the review of the investigation had been completed, was generally left to manage everything her way. It was a position she relished.

When the murder of Peter Falconio – for it was at last being described as a murder inquiry – had first happened, Gwynne spent the first forty-eight hours in the operations room, helping to coordinate the searches and the setting up of roadblocks. After that first flush of involvement, however, she'd gone back to work as an Acting Superintendent in Alice Springs, running everything else that was happening. She was adamant that Joanne Lees was telling the truth. 'As a police officer, you *can't* disbelieve,' she says. 'Otherwise, it's too easy to miss things. And you're busy dealing with the dynamics of the incident, checking that the victim is coping, working out what resources are needed, seeing how your officers are managing, looking for the offender. You don't have time to think about the bizarre-ness of the situation.'

By the time Gwynne had been brought in to run the Falconio case in March 2002, the review had recommended cutting the number of people involved from fourteen to nine. She took the opportunity to cull out everyone who wasn't 100 per cent behind Joanne. She felt she couldn't afford the doubters.

COLLEEN GWYNNE WAS THE YOUNGEST person in the Northern Territory Police ever to be appointed a Superintendent. Aged thirty-five by the time of the slaying at Barrow Creek, she was a tough, ambitious officer, used to surviving in what was still very much a man's world. She'd learned that lesson early. The second youngest child of eight, Gwynne's father was a big, hard-drinking man, who used his fists often. Her second eldest brother Phillip later wrote a kids' novel, loosely based on the family's life in the tiny South Australian coastal township of Port Victoria, 190 kilometres west of Adelaide across the Gulf St Vincent on the Yorke Peninsula. *Deadly, Unna?*, released in 1998, was an instant hit, winning awards all across Australia for its tale of domestic violence, racism, friendship and Australian Rules football in a small community. In 2002, it was adapted for a movie, *Australian Rules*, which caused massive controversy throughout Australia for its treatment of white–black relations – and chilling violence.

When Gwynne was older, she went back, with two of her siblings, to rescue her mum. She packed up all her belonging and moved her out of the house and to a secret location. When their father came home, everything had gone. He drove around the streets, looking for his wife, until eventually being forced to give up. 'I have enormous respect for my mother,' says Gwynne. 'She virtually brought up eight kids single-handedly. She worked sixteen hours a day. She's so strong, yet she's tiny and so timid.' When the film eventually premiered, Gwynne took her mother along and they both watched, spellbound, as the tale of a family of eight kids growing up with a violent, alcoholic, racist father, played by Simon Westaway, unfolded on the screen. Some scenes were almost too painful to take. Her mother sat quietly, and obviously felt very emotional. 'She loved it,' says Gwynne. 'It was her story up there. It was somehow freeing.' Later, however, she ticked off her brother for not warning her about what it contained. 'I couldn't believe what I was seeing,' she says. 'He said it was fiction, but it was us up there.'

Phillip says he too still finds it painful. 'Maybe because I grew up with all this as a kid and got over it, I find it very painful to go there again,' he says. 'My brothers and sisters saw the movie and some scenes for them, particularly where the children escape from the house out of the window and spend the night in the hen house, were too unbearable for them.' The film went on to be shown at festivals all around the world, including Hollywood star Robert Redford's prestigious Sundance Film Festival. Phillip heard later that his father had also been to see it. Appropriately, having been the one who finally rescued her mother from that real life living Hell, one of Gwynne's first promotions in the police force was to run the Domestic Violence Unit.

COLLEEN GWYNNE HAD JUST RETURNED from a one-year stint in Papua New Guinea when she was called into the office of Commissioner Paul White in March 2002 and told to take on the Falconio case. Her first thought was, 'What have I done wrong?' The case had been running for a year, and there was still no suspect arrested. She felt this could be the end of her career. The investigation was slowing down and many on the team were disillusioned and unmotivated after working so long without a result.

She decided, however, to make the best of a bad job, and soon won the respect of the Regulus team with her determination and dedication. A tall, slim, wiry, straight-talking woman with short brown hair flecked with blonde, she took over the task of talking to Joanne whenever there was positive news. She immediately warmed to the young woman, and felt for her. 'I got to know her and liked her,' says Gwynne. 'She's never faltered, even though she's had such a tough time.'

On the desk of Gwynne's office in Alice Springs is a picture of the red desert and a desert flower blooming in the midst of the harsh sandy terrain. On her whiteboard is a photo of the village of Hepworth in

Huddersfield, where the Falconios live. 'It looks nice, doesn't it?' she says. 'It keeps me going. It reminds me all the time why I'm doing this and what I'm doing it for.' She has become obsessed with finding Peter's killer. She nods and pauses for a moment. 'There's not a night that I don't wonder where his body is.'

JAMES HEPI'S INFORMATION ABOUT Bradley Murdoch had fired Gwynne's interest, and galvanised her into action. Murdoch was still a person of interest in the investigation, despite the earlier report from Broome that he didn't resemble the photo-fit image and that his ute was different. There were still some things about him that hadn't added up. He was on the police list for further questioning and now, with the extra information Hepi had supplied, the police were keener to talk to him than ever. But when they returned to Murdoch's flat in Broome to pick him up for questioning, there was no sign of either him or his vehicle. They started asking for him around town. He was nowhere to be found. No-one seemed to know where he was. In late May 2002, the Northern Territory police put out a nationwide police alert. The whole country was on the look-out for Bradley Murdoch.

JAMES TAHI HEPI, THIRTY-FOUR, appeared in the district court of WA sitting at Broome on 29 July 2002 to answer the charge that in the May he'd had in his possession a prohibited drug, cannabis, with intent to sell or supply. He pleaded guilty. Judge Antoinette Kennedy told him that being in possession of 4 kilograms of the drug was extremely serious, particularly as it was imported from another state. 'Under normal circumstances, I would sentence you to an immediate term of imprisonment, but I take into account what [your lawyer] Mr [Gordon] Bauman has said, that you have pleaded guilty, that it's a fast-track plea, that you cooperated with the police in the way in which Mr Bauman has outlined, and that you have really a fairly good record. I also have an absolutely glowing reference for you and one hopes that you will now return to leading a law-abiding life. This warrants an eighteen-month term of imprisonment and so you are sentenced to eighteen months' imprisonment but that sentence is suspended for a period of twelve months.'

Hepi had done his deal and had got out of jail, almost free. And now the police were in possession of a great deal more information about Bradley Murdoch.

THE ONLY PROBLEM WAS finding him. Once again, he appeared to have slipped through the net. When the national police alert failed to produce any sign of him, police visited his parents and his brother, Gary. They all said they had no idea where he would be. Then, desperate to be sure that they weren't wasting time chasing false leads, police asked if Gary would be prepared to give a DNA sample to compare with the DNA on Joanne's T-shirt. It's unclear whether Gary agreed purely in order to rule himself out of inquiries, or because he was so convinced his brother was innocent it would help him too. But on 14 August 2002, he had a swab taken. If the DNA on the shirt was Bradley Murdoch's, Gary's would show up as a close match.

But even that wasn't much good if they couldn't find Murdoch himself. And he seemed to have vanished into thin air.

# PART FOUR

# THE PURSUIT
# OF JUSTICE

# CHAPTER FORTY-ONE

# A Tale of Abduction and Rape

NO-ONE WHO HEARD THE LITTLE girl's terrifying story would ever forget it. One moment, the twelve-year-old was baking a batch of cakes with her mum, and offering one to the family friend who was staying in the annex of their house. The next, she was being handcuffed, blindfolded with a seatbelt cover, gagged with tape over her mouth and round her head, chained to his bed, stripped and then raped. 'If you move,' she claimed the man had threatened her, 'I'll give you brain damage.' And her assailant, she alleged to police, was someone she'd known for eighteen months. His name was Bradley Murdoch.

But that wasn't the end of her ordeal, she claimed. After that, she said Murdoch had grabbed her thirty-three-year-old mum too and, with his gun clearly visible in his body holster, bundled them both into the aluminium cage canopy at the back of his white Landcruiser, chaining them up by the hands and feet and securing them with cable ties to ensure they couldn't escape, and drove off through the backblocks of SA. During their next twenty or so hours of imprisonment, the pair alleged Murdoch had hit the mother and sexually assaulted her, before giving them both $1000 in cash, dumping them at a service station just outside Port Augusta, 300 kilometres north of Adelaide, and threatening to shoot them with a high-powered rifle if they went to the police. When the mother had asked Murdoch why he was doing such a thing, she claimed he'd replied he wanted hostages because, 'I need some insurance to get away from this place.' He'd threatened to shoot her if he didn't do as he'd ordered and went on to say he was on the run from the police. 'He said the police were after him for the murder of Peter Falconio,' the woman claimed, 'and had framed him for it.'

Murdoch would later deny all their allegations, with his lawyers saying the girl and her mother had made the whole thing up as part of an elaborate ruse to deliver him to the police – and claim the $250,000 reward on the head of the killer of Peter Falconio.

THE TERRIBLE STORY TOLD BY the mother and child was the big break police all around Australia had been waiting for. At last, Bradley Murdoch had surfaced. As soon as the girl's mother had reported the alleged crime, police circulated descriptions of Murdoch's white Landcruiser and canopy. It was eventually spotted later that day at 4.50 p.m., Wednesday 28 August 2002, on Highway One outside Port Augusta. Senior Constable Robert Michael followed the vehicle until it turned into the car park outside the massive Woolworth's supermarket, came to a halt, and Murdoch climbed out and walked into the shop. Michael called for back-up and within minutes heavily armed police were on their way.

While Murdoch wandered around the shop buying himself a chicken, sausages, soup, rice, custard, milk, safety pins, and batteries, all shoppers and bystanders were herded into nearby shops while police in bullet-proof jackets took up their positions outside, police snipers crawling underneath cars and crouching on neighbouring rooftops. They feared their target might choose a shoot-out with police rather than being taken into custody. When he finally emerged carrying two bags of groceries, three officers raced over to confront him. As he appeared to reach for a loaded semi-automatic pistol in a shoulder holster, Senior Constable Sean Everett raised his 12-gauge pump action shotgun and yelled at him to stop. 'Get down on the fucking ground,' he shouted. Murdoch let his shopping bags fall and dropped to his knees. Everett ordered him to lay face down on the ground but, when he didn't move, put his foot in the small of his back to force him down. Then the rest of the contingent pounced, handcuffing him and tying his ankles together. His time on the run was finally over.

SEARCHES OF MURDOCH'S VEHICLE and possessions revealed a prize haul of drugs, guns and cash, a court was later told. The arresting officer, Senior Constable Andrew Dredge, found a loaded gun in his shoulder holster, with a spare magazine containing seventeen rounds. In Murdoch's wallet were two bags of white powder which were tested and found to be amphetamines. In the Landcruiser, police found a backpack with a Beretta semi-automatic .38 pistol, together with a box of bullets, and a rifle. In addition, Senior Constable Peter McKenzie found a knife by the steering wheel, cable cutters, a number of chains, rolls of tape, an electric stock prod, shovels, $5000 in cash, some pearls and camping gear. There were also five containers of cannabis inside the canopy's lockable steel mesh. Senior Constable Charmaine Cowling found a piece of a pair of black tights and a quilt stained with the young girl's urine. There was also a bag containing a number of highly detailed maps showing even the most obscure dirt tracks across Australia.

THE TWELVE-YEAR-OLD GIRL was the daughter of the friend James Hepi had introduced to Murdoch, who was now helping him in his own drug-running operation. Her mother was the man's de facto. None of them can be identified for legal reasons.

The three had been living in a rundown house on an isolated backblock of the Riverlands of country SA, 100 kilometres outside Adelaide, for the past eight years. With neither mains water nor mains electricity, or a phone they could afford to ring out on, they only just got by from year to year. Times had got harder since the mother's de facto, a much older man for whom she'd once worked, had been diagnosed with terminal lung cancer and found it much harder to hold down a job. He was therefore grateful when his friend James Hepi offered him a few jobs around his property, helping him clean up his block, and organising generators and water tanks. Later, he started packaging cannabis for Hepi's drug-runs, and acted as a scout, sniffing out new sources for the lucrative trade. Occasionally, the girl's mum would clean up after them but she refused to have any drugs prepared in their home, although she did smoke cannabis herself.

About six months later, Hepi introduced them to another friend of his, Bradley Murdoch. They'd see Murdoch regularly at Hepi's place, and then sometimes Murdoch would come and stay at the annex they had on their ramshackle property, 8 metres away from their house.

After Hepi and Murdoch fell out, and then Hepi and the friend fell out in March 2002, the woman said Murdoch started employing the friend himself to help out with his own drugs business he'd just set up, giving him a car and a gun for protection. Murdoch then started staying more often at the annex, and the girl said she often went over to help him with little jobs. She said he always had a lot of cash on him and, for her birthday in July that year, he'd given her a present of $500, delivered with a hug. Her birthday was five days after the first anniversary of the Barrow Creek murder.

BACK IN ENGLAND, JOANNE LEES was unaware of the latest developments. Instead, she was wrestling with a fresh outrage: it had been revealed that she'd put in a claim for up to $28,000 in compensation from the Northern Territory government as a victim of crime. In August 2002 two claims had been lodged on her behalf under the Territory's victims of crime assistance legislation. While she stood to receive $3000 for the grief of losing her de facto, there was also the possibility of an award of up to $25,000 in personal injury as a victim of crime.

When Luciano Falconio was phoned by the media for his reaction, he said he'd had no idea.

FOR THE GIRL AND HER mother, everything had been sweet with Murdoch until the last time he'd come to stay in the annex on Saturday August 17. The reason was simple, claimed a lawyer for the woman and her daughter: Murdoch had just discovered his brother Gary had given a DNA sample to police and was getting worried that they might be on their way to arrest him. His paranoia was exacerbated by the heady cocktail of drugs he'd consumed.

That evening, the two women said they were mystified to see Murdoch putting black plastic up at the doors and windows of the annex. But they hadn't had much time to think about it. The girl's stepfather was in hospital, having fluid drained off his lungs, so they visited him the next day, the Sunday, staying overnight in the nurses' quarters. On Monday, the pair returned. The girl said she'd been chatting to Murdoch and showed him an article in an old copy of a *New Idea* magazine, headlined 'Mystery At Barrow Creek'. At another point during that day, a car had pulled up in the driveway of their house and then pulled out again. The mother said Murdoch thought the police were coming after him, and stormed into the house to confront her about it. 'He said the police were getting too close to him and he's got to move, keep being on the run,' the woman told a court. But, she said, the motorist had simply been using the driveway for a U-turn.

The next evening, August 20, the girl claimed she'd gone to the annex to help him unpack his shopping, and seen him cutting up medical tape. She also happened to ask him where he'd got one of his T-shirts from. It was an innocent question, but Murdoch responded, she said, with a statement about Peter Falconio.

Over the next two days, the mother claimed she noticed Murdoch smoking cannabis 'countless' times, and either snorting speed or drinking it in tea or other drinks. The next day, Wednesday August 21, there was no school, so the girl baked some cakes and asked Murdoch if he'd like to come over to the house for some. He did, and then asked her to visit him in the annex later to help him with something. When she arrived, she said he asked her to sort out his map bag. He was smoking cannabis and drinking Jim Bean and Coke, and was 'a bit weird, grumpy and picky'. When she finished, she went to go, but she alleged at Murdoch's trial later that he became angry and said she had to stay. He got a pair of handcuffs from the bag, put a blindfold on her, pushed her to the bed, handcuffed her hands behind her back and put tape over her mouth, wrapping it all around her head. The girl, at that time a virgin, alleges he then pulled off her clothes, put his finger into her vagina, and then had sexual intercourse with her. After that, she claimed he shackled her ankles which he connected to the handcuffs on a chain. He left for a few minutes then returned to try to dress her, and carry her out to the Landcruiser, where he chained her up.

Murdoch then woke the mother up, she said. The woman asked where her daughter was, but he told her to shut up and put some warm clothes on. She saw he was wearing his shoulder holster. When she went outside, she alleges she was horrified to see her daughter chained in the back of the ute. 'What are you doing?' she asked him. 'Why are you doing this?'

'He said he needed hostages for his insurance to get out of there,' the woman alleges. 'He said that the cops might be there any minute and he's got to get out of there. I went into shock. I was so scared. I thought he might shoot us.' She alleges that her daughter, 'was as white as a ghost and she was terrified. I've never seen her terrified like that in my whole life.' As they drove Murdoch's mood worsened. He was 'like a raging bull' the woman later told a court. 'To me, he was verging on psychotic, like really angry and terrifying. I didn't know whether he was going to shoot us or what.' She said Murdoch was convinced James Hepi had told the police he was bringing drugs into Broome and that the police were after him. Now, he said, he planned to go to WA to shoot Hepi and a couple of bikies, and then shoot himself in the head, 'because he couldn't take being on the run any more'.

When she and her daughter were finally freed, they called the hospital, and then a taxi, from the service station. Manager Derek Riding remembers seeing them, huddled together, sitting on the kerb, waiting for the taxi to pick them up.

MURDOCH, BY NOW FORTY-THREE, was charged with two counts of rape, two counts of false imprisonment, two counts of indecent assault and one count of common assault. He would deny all the charges, saying they were all part of a conspiracy to frame him for the rich reward. But at last, he was back behind bars – and in circumstances no-one could possibly have imagined.

# CHAPTER FORTY-TWO

# A Glimmer of Light

IN ALICE SPRINGS, SUPERINTENDENT Colleen Gwynne was sitting in her office waiting for the phone to ring. She'd been trying to work all morning, but hadn't been able to concentrate. Every file and document she picked up from her in-tray, she went through and put down again impatiently, having no idea at all of what she'd just read. She picked up the phone receiver and heard the familiar burr. Reassured it was working, she put it down again carefully on its cradle. She glanced at her watch. Only five minutes had passed since the last time she'd looked. It had felt like an age.

Five weeks and six days had passed since Bradley Murdoch had been arrested in Port Augusta on 28 August 2002 on charges of rape and abduction. And since the South Australian police had taken blood samples from their prisoner, it had been … five weeks and five days. Gwynne knew. She'd been counting every single one of them.

Murdoch's lawyers had argued that police had no right to send a DNA analysis of their client's blood to the Northern Territory to be matched against the speck found on Joanne Lees' T-shirt. The magistrate had disagreed, and South Australian Attorney-General Michael Atkinson said he would sign a ministerial arrangement with his Northern Territory counterpart Syd Sterling to allow the interstate transfer.

Murdoch's lawyers appealed the ruling in the South Australian Supreme Court. On October 2 they lost again, with Justice Ted Mullighan saying that the public interest served in profiling Murdoch's DNA outweighed his right to protection from unwanted interference. But solicitor Mark Twiggs immediately announced that he'd also appeal that decision. It was only on October 8 that Twiggs decided not to take the matter further, and the DNA was couriered to Darwin. The forensics team had told Gwynne they'd call her as soon as they had a result. She'd be the first person to know. It was just that the wait was proving interminable.

They'd been close to bringing in Murdoch three times before: firstly, when he was questioned by Broome detectives and let go; secondly, when he'd risen close to the top of their top ten list of suspects as a result of following up on the initial set of inquiries and questioning people who knew him; and thirdly, when James Hepi was arrested, and named him as the Barrow Creek killer – and then he'd just disappeared.

But at last Murdoch was sitting in a cell in Adelaide's Yatala Prison awaiting his fate and the answer to the question that had been haunting Gwynne for the past fifteen months – not to mention the rest of Australia and Britain – could be just within her grasp.

When the phone suddenly rang, it sounded so loud, Gwynne jumped. She stared at it a moment before reaching over to pick it up. She noticed her hand was trembling.

A FEW MINUTES LATER, she was dialling Assistant Commissioner John Daulby's direct line. He picked it up straight away. She guessed he too had been unable to concentrate on much else that day. 'John,' she said, 'It's Colleen. I've got something to tell you. I want you to sit down ...'

Gwynne forced herself to stay calm but, inside, she was dancing. 'I wanted to do a big Toyota jump in the middle of the crime squad,' she says. 'I was jumping around, saying, "We've solved it!" It was so exciting. It was the big breakthrough we'd been waiting for so long. It had been a glimmer of hope but the DNA was a match, and we felt we'd got our man. We'd all been under so much pressure, and had so much criticism, it was a wonderful moment.'

Yet while they had a DNA match, that only showed that, at some point, Murdoch's DNA may have rubbed off on Joanne. Proving he had killed Peter Falconio was another thing entirely. But Gwynne allowed herself the luxury of savouring the pleasure of this latest breakthrough.

'When you are dealing so closely with victims, you are living what they are going through to some extent. It felt so good. John was so happy too. To some extent he was going through Joanne's experience. The media had been so quick to make assessments of what the police were doing, and he took everything to heart. It was a really personal thing for him. He speaks from the heart and works incredibly hard and really *cares*. He's such a great team-player, and was always sympathetic to people affected by the investigation.' Despite this breakthrough, Gwynne felt the ongoing saga had bruised Daulby: 'I think the whole thing left him a little bit disillusioned.'

Daulby called the Falconio family and spoke with Nick, the eldest son. Luciano and Joan were away visiting relatives in Italy. 'They were relieved, but you couldn't say they were happy to hear the news,' he says. 'It was a sad occasion for them really. Their biggest hope was that we'd found the right man, and he might lead us to the body. That was always their priority. They still wanted to find their brother, to find their son.'

He tried to call Joanne but got only a message bank. He also sent her an email. He hadn't known, but she was over in Sicily, working. When she received a number of messages from friends, she went on to the internet to look at reports of who it was that had been arrested. 'I thought that I should just have a look on the internet to see what people were writing about,' she says. On the BBC website, next to a photo of herself and Peter, she saw her first photograph of Murdoch. It would be something his defence team would later hold against her.

The police had intended to announce the development the next morning, but soon they were deluged with calls. Nick Falconio had spoken to a journalist, and suddenly everyone wanted confirmation. The press conference was hurriedly re-scheduled for later that evening, Wednesday 9 October 2002.

In England, Joanne's stepfather Vincent James was relieved. 'I just hope the man arrested will tell us what happened to Peter,' he said. Nick was cautiously optimistic, but sombre. 'We had been expecting to hear, but I am still a bit shaky to be quite honest,' he said. 'Realistically, we don't think Peter's alive but deep down that is what my mother thinks. But we are hoping we will know the answer soon. My mum has been in a terrible state ever since it happened and she will never be the same again. It's been an agonising wait. You think about it every day. It comes into your head whatever you're doing. Hopefully this is the start of some sort of close or conclusion so we can get on with our lives.'

For legal reasons, Daulby couldn't say the DNA was an exact match, merely that Murdoch couldn't be excluded by the result. Everyone knew, however, precisely what he meant.


THE PRESS TOOK IT AS vindication of Joanne and her story; the doubters were faintly apologetic, while the believers took pleasure in watching them choke on humble pie. Joanne's chief adversary, the *Daily Mail*'s Richard Shears, wrote in his story that appeared the next day, 'I am happy for Miss Lees, for I am the first to admit that there were elements of her story that caused me to doubt her. Today she will be able to face her critics and hold her head high.' The *Sydney Morning Herald*'s Phil Cornford put it succinctly. 'Ms Lees's only mistake was surviving and then refusing to tell the media about her ordeal,' he wrote. 'A number of reporters, mostly British but some Australian, decided her silence signalled guilt. The pariah instincts of the talkback jocks found an echo in their audiences.'

At the same time, legal writs from Murdoch's lawyers kept arriving at newspaper offices on their stories linking Murdoch with the crime. Some people favoured theories that Murdoch wasn't the one; he was merely a bloke who happened to be in the wrong place at the wrong time, just as the Northern Territory police had become desperate to find someone, anyone, to frame to take the heat off them. The real killer just hadn't been caught. Others still preferred to believe that there was something suspicious about Joanne. Questions remained in Shears' newspaper copy, for instance, about the movement from the front to the back of the car, and Joanne's recollection of the man's dog. With Murdoch to be charged for the attack at Barrow Creek, wasn't Jack, a Dalmatian, quite different to Joanne's description? But, if Murdoch *were* her attacker, at least it cleared up another doubt. A Dalmation, or even a Dalmation cross, wouldn't be the best kind of dog to let out of your car on a dark night in the outback to help you look for someone. 'They're daffy dogs which aren't the smartest,' says vet Meredith Phillips, whose family has always kept Dalmatians. 'They're very energetic and excitable, particular when they're puppies, and they're not the best at obeying commands. They're very friendly and loyal, but they like to run and they tend to be submissive. They're not aggressive at all.'

THE MAN OF THE MOMENT, however, was still saying nothing. Superintendent Colleen Gwynne and Taskforce Regulus head Sergeant David Chalker flew down from the Northern Territory to Adelaide to interview Murdoch, but left empty-handed. Just as he'd refused to answer any questions from South Australian police about the alleged offences against the girl and her mother, he remained resolutely silent on the Barrow Creek killing.

There are some who believe alleged offenders in Australia should no longer be able to retreat to the right to silence. Just as it's long since been abolished in England, so should it be abolished in Australia, they feel. Victorian barrister Ken Marks QC is one. 'The "right" prevents a court or jury from applying common sense to a refusal by a suspect to answer important questions by disallowing any inference whatsoever to be drawn from the silence,' he says. 'This is one of the tiny minority of places in the world that maintains the "right" – [and] it is a luxury which an increasingly crime-ridden society cannot afford.'

But with Murdoch declining to speak, the detectives instead travelled over to the annex where he'd been staying in the Riverlands to look at what the South Australian police had found. While they were there, they took a DNA swab from Jack, the dog, hoping they might be able to compare it with the dog hair found on Joanne's body that night at the roadhouse.

Senior Constable Tim Sandry also examined the items found in Murdoch's vehicle: the guns, the cable ties and the drugs. Later, after the rape trial, Regulus member Sergeant Megan Rowe took out a warrant to have all the exhibits found that day sent up to Darwin. When they arrived, Rowe noticed a black hair tie on the board, identical to the one Joanne had lost that night. It was shown to Joanne. 'That's my hairband!' she cried immediately. 'Where did you get it?'

GWYNNE DIDN'T STOP SMILING for the next few days. The whole Taskforce Regulus team had been working so hard on the case that it felt an immense relief that they at last had a suspect and, they felt, a good case against him.

Over the long period of the investigation, so many police had fallen by the wayside. Some of those who'd been working on the case far from home, had eventually packed up and asked to go back as they'd been away from their families for so long. Some officers just couldn't be spared from their regular areas, both geographical and spheres of expertise, for any longer. With such a small force, there were only ever a certain number of people who were experienced, willing and able to help at any one time. There were a few officers who'd become disheartened that there had been no quick result. Others had argued over the best way to achieve an outcome and had quit the investigation when their colleagues disagreed. Promotions had been put off. Relationships had broken down. Gwynne had been no exception. Her steady relationship had also finished, midway through the case. 'Falconio cost me my relationship,' she says. 'You just have no time together. You're never there for them, and they eventually aren't there for you. It can't survive.'

But Gwynne, now thirty-seven, had absorbed herself so completely in the case, there wasn't much time left over for a private life anyway. On Sunday mornings, Daulby would call her to ask, 'Have you thought about this?' Or 'how about that?' And 'What do you think of the idea ...' Gwynne relished talking through every possibility with him. 'Sometimes the thoughts would be really off the wall but there were always some really good suggestions there that they were so quirky.'

In November, with Murdoch in prison in SA and with the extra information that had been gleaned about him, Colleen Gwynne flew to England with one of the taskforce members who'd been there from the beginning, Sergeant Megan Rowe, to re-interview Joanne Lees. The pair wanted to check that she could identify Murdoch, and to clear up the last few nagging queries. It was tough on Joanne. With a suspect behind bars she'd felt that everyone would finally believe her story and leave her alone. But now she was having to face even more questions. At one stage, she broke down in tears all over again. 'Why won't people believe me?' she cried, with such pain in her voice that it tore at the two officers' hearts. 'Even now you've caught him, you don't believe me! Ask my friends. They know I don't lie.'

While recounting events yet again, however, Joanne mentioned one detail she'd never revealed before. When she and Peter were watching the sunset in Ti Tree before the darkness, they'd shared a joint. Gwynne looked at her in amazement. Why hadn't she mentioned this before? Joanne shrugged. She hadn't thought it important. How on earth could it be relevant? Gwynne made a note of it. Now she had been told one more fact about what had happened, she'd have to report it back to the investigation. She didn't see it as particularly significant, either, but she'd have to include it.

The main matter, though, was the dog Joanne had seen that night. She'd described it as a Blue Heeler. Murdoch's pet was a Dalmatian cross – although probably crossed with a Blue Heeler. Gwynne and Rowe arranged a room at the local Hove police station, and handed her a book of photos of dogs and asked her to pick out one that was most similar to the dog she'd seen. She chose photos of cattle dogs which she said were similar in 'its size, its face, shape, ears'. When asked about its colouring, she replied, 'Patches of dark colour.'

The pair also showed her a photo-board of pictures of twelve different men, and asked her to pick out the man who attacked her. She went straight to number ten: the photograph of Bradley Murdoch.

JOANNE WAS STILL DOING IT tough. She loved her new job helping care for people with intellectual disabilities, but the pressure of the police, media and public attention was getting to her, and she was not coping with the grief over the loss of Peter. When she took on the problems of others, sometimes she found she could forget her own, but she was jolted sharply back into reality all too often. She'd be in a shop one day, when someone would ask her for her autograph. She would wander through Brighton's lanes and a camera flash would suddenly flare in her eyes. She'd be sitting drinking coffee in a café and notice she was being stared at. Even worse, she would be out with one of the people she was caring for and be approached by someone wanting to ask her all about the case. She'd get upset and flustered, and her charges would also start getting distressed. At times she feared she'd be sacked. At others, she wondered if she'd ever lead a normal life again.

'She wants closure,' says Gwynne. 'She's been an incredibly strong woman. She's done everything I've asked of her. We told her how SA is trying to fast track the case, how it shouldn't be too much longer.'

Similarly, the Falconio family were also still reeling from the tragedy. Joan really wasn't well at all, and Luciano was trying hard to keep it together. Everyone was focussed on finding Peter's body, but often they had different ideas about how best it could be achieved. One member of the family asked, if Murdoch was convicted, could police do a deal that would give him a lighter sentence if he told them where the body was? Another wanted him to receive the heaviest sentence possible. No concessions.

'I'm still hopeful of finding the body,' Gwynne told them. 'I won't give up.' And she wasn't just spinning them a line. She knew she'd do anything to try to find it, even if it wasn't strictly within the rules.

ONE DAY, GWYNNE DECIDED TO have another go at interviewing Murdoch. She went into the interview room at the jail, walked right up to him, and lifted up her shirt. 'Look,' she said, 'no wires. I just wanted to ask you, tell me where the body is. This isn't permissible as evidence. Just tell me.'

For a moment, Murdoch stared at her in silence. Their eyes locked. She held her breath. And then his eyes slid away. He said nothing.

She realised that, if he were the killer, he still might never tell. It was a moment straight out of *Silence of the Lambs*.

'His image has never left my mind,' says Gwynne. 'There's something about him … He's one of those people you just wonder what's going on inside his mind. I've never let anyone get to me like that. I was glad to get out of there, basically. I've interviewed murderers, rapists, paedophiles … but this was worse, somehow. I couldn't get his face out of my mind.'

# CHAPTER FORTY-THREE

# The Price of a Life

AT THE BARROW CREEK HOTEL, two years on from the murder of Peter Falconio and the attempted abduction of Joanne Lees, there's a party in full swing. Publican Les Pilton is serving behind the bar, and his girlfriend Helen Jones is sitting on a stool on the other side. She's had too much to drink, and her words are slurred.

'You'll have to forgive her,' says Pilton amiably. 'These anniversaries can always be hard. Somehow, this second is worse than the first. It's made more of an impact because there's still so much happening, and it's still not finished.' He and Jones spent the afternoon looking at their watches and saying, 'They'd be just leaving town now.' 'They'd be at the Camel Cup now.' That evening, they both watched the sunset and remembered the one at Ti Tree that two backpackers, so much in love and with their lives in front of them, had watched together. At 7.20 p.m., Pilton remarked, 'They'd be south of Barrow Creek now.' That night, they hadn't wanted to go to bed. At 1.30 a.m., they said, 'Everything unfolded just about now.' And at 4 a.m., they finally lay down. 'I'll always remember it until Peter's body is found,' says Pilton, sadly. 'That's the only way that closure will come along.'

For life has changed irrevocably for the couple since that dark night two years before. Now, visitors often mention the case, and they still get calls about it from overseas. Yet the place has lost a little of its heart, somehow. Pilton had always adored Barrow Creek. 'I've got the biggest backyard and front yard in the world!' he'd declare. 'When you see the setting sun behind the windmill across the road, and the cloud reflects the light, the whole canopy is absolutely beautiful. Yes! That's why I love it here. Sometimes, the stars are so bright you can even see their light at the bottom of the fireplace coming down through the chimney. There's nothing like the stars around here.' Now, however, there's a sadness that tinges his words. He's even thinking of moving on. On Boxing Day 2001, he took part in the annual Sydney to Hobart Yacht Race and enjoyed it so much he's planning to buy a 40–50-foot yacht and go to the Whitsundays and beyond.

'I want to experience more of the rest of Australia,' he says. 'Eventually, I want to sail around the world.' If Jones wanted to come, she could, but it was all the same with him if she didn't. 'It's up to her,' he says. 'Who knows? If it's to be, it will be. It's a case of "Do it my way, or hit the highway". It sounds callous, but I'll never allow myself to be hurt like I was with my wife again.' Pilton and Jones split up soon afterwards.

Pilton, however, is left with nothing but fond memories of Joanne. 'I always liked Jo,' he says. 'I've got good instincts for people. I always felt she was telling the truth. I only hope one day she can find peace.'

THE NIGHT OF THE PARTY, Aboriginal tracker Teddy Egan is out too, trudging around the area where Joanne hid beneath the mulga bushes. 'She has good spirit here,' he says, thumping his chest. 'She strong.'

Nearby, he lights a fire, and stares into it long and hard, as if somewhere in the flames he can find an answer.

FOUR KILOMETRES UP THE ROAD, former PR consultant turned writer and private detective Robin Bowles is with a few friends. She has her hands tied behind her, and is crashing through the bush.

Egan smiles in delight. 'She is in wrong place,' he chuckles. 'Strange lady.'

Obviously in her private re-enactment of the chilling crime, she's clearly taken the police at their word when they told journalists where the crime scene was; they didn't want the spot turned into a circus. Three months later, Bowles announced she was travelling around the desert with a shovel and a psychic to find Peter Falconio's body. That hunt was abandoned soon after.

But even if Bowles was traipsing around a different patch of bush, Teddy Egan knew exactly where it was: 'She run from here … then here she fall down, get up run one bush, two bush, three bush and lie down under this one.' And just when you're wondering if this man who seems as old as the hills and cast from the same clay is simply spinning a good yarn, there it is, under the bush, a metal spike with police tape tied round it. It's a unnerving moment – this is exactly where death came looking for Joanne Lees but couldn't find her.

BACK TOWARDS ALICE SPRINGS, at the Shell Truckstop, manager Val Prior still can't stop watching the video that was taken that night of the mystery man buying diesel. 'I don't know how many times I've watched that video,' she says, gloomily. 'I downloaded it on to my PC and watch it over and over, trying to see *something*.'

The man who operated the till and also appeared on the video that night, Andrew Head, no longer works there. Prior had to change his shifts around because he was constantly being approached by journalists. He would get anxious about the safety risks of having electronic cameras around the fuel bowsers and worried about somebody getting knocked down by a car. Prior would call into the station, twice a week during the nightshift to check he was all right, and spend an hour with him. She offered him counselling too, but he refused.

'He just had trouble handling it,' says Prior. 'He was just an ordinary bloke. Police kept asking him questions that he couldn't answer. He felt like he was letting someone down because he couldn't recall anything out of the ordinary.' He now works in a shop in SA.

Two regular customers don't call by any more, either. Vince Millar gave up driving trucks soon after that fateful night, spooked completely by what had happened and Rodney Adams left the company and went to stay in Adelaide.

OVER IN THE WEST OF the country, in a pretty seaside town south of Perth, Bradley Murdoch's parents are also in mourning. They don't stray far from the dark, cramped brick-built bungalow on the subdivision where they live, and they rarely open the door to strangers. Colin, Murdoch's father, used to be a big man, but now he's shrunk with age, and hunched with worry. He's walking with a stick after he fractured his toe when he stubbed it against a wall. His passionate belief in his son, however, remains undimmed.

'He knows he's innocent, he didn't do anything,' he says, the pale blue eyes under the mop of white hair hot and fierce. 'The trouble is, he's just too good-hearted. He tries to help people, and they take advantage. He had to really battle his way through school. He got into a lot of fights, but he was a good fighter. He was really good at sports, too.' A cloud passes over his face, and his wife Nancy hobbles over to him. In one of those terrible blows of fate, at about the same time as Colin's accident, she had a fall soon after a hip operation, and is still recovering. She's walking with a frame.

'This whole business has cost him $75,000 so far,' says Colin. 'He could get out of prison if he wanted to, but he doesn't want to yet because then he can get more money in compensation. It's terrible what people are saying about him. He would never do anything like that. He's a good boy. It's just that people pick on him. He didn't do it. He told us. He's too kind-hearted. This is a set-up, and they'll prove it soon.'

The couple live in the town of Falcon – a name so close to that of a young man from the other side of the world that it will forevermore haunt them.

FURTHER NORTH, WHERE THE intense blue of the Indian Ocean meets the vivid red cliffs of Broome, Bradley Murdoch's friends also wait to see what his fate will be. Some are convinced he'll beat the charges in SA, and then go on to defeat his accusers in Darwin. Others are not quite so sure. His current girlfriend, Jan Pittman, who works in the town's bakery, is a big blonde with her hair caught up in a perky ponytail. She looks weathered, anxious and exhausted. She hands over a blurred photograph of Murdoch holding a fishing rod, standing in the shallow surf on Cable Beach with his dog, Jack, gambolling by his side. She echoes the same affectionate tones of an earlier girlfriend. 'He's a gentle giant; brusque on the exterior, but underneath, he's really good. If a woman is in trouble in a bar, he would help. A lot of people don't get past the brusqueness, but I did. We're very close.'

She says he used to spend his time off fishing, and in other such harmless pursuits. She was introduced to him by mutual friends at his old favourite drinking hole, the Beer and Satay Hut. 'Far from being a loner, he was very sociable,' she says. 'He worked hard. He used to cook for me, and we'd go out for dinners together. And he loved his animals, his dog and his cat. We were living together and sleeping together. If something's a bit odd about a man, you find out then. But with him, there's never been anything.'

Down at that bar, the air is filled with the scent of frangipani, and talk of 'Big Brad'. 'He was a good bloke,' says Jeff, one of the regulars. 'He never did it. He never had it in him. I knew him for two years, we drank together every night. He'd come for a drink, go home to feed his dog and cat, then come back for the night. He'd tell you if he didn't agree with you, but he never caused any trouble.'

Greg, a silver-haired Aboriginal man, says he was a steady drinking buddy too. 'He was always fine,' he says. 'Sure, he was a drug dealer, but he never pushed to kids. He got angry if a dealer pushed to kids. The ones who did sell to kids were shit scared of him. He was a big bloke. He wouldn't ask too many questions; he'd just go and do his business. But you could have a joke with him. He wasn't racist. He only shot at those Aboriginals down at Fitzroy Crossing because they wouldn't get out of his way.'

Over in the sports bar in the Roebuck, John is another mate who doesn't have a bad word to say about Murdoch. He too thinks he's been framed. 'Peter Falconio – I don't believe he's dead,' he says. 'Nah, I bet he's in Malta or the Mediterranean or something. There's no dead body, otherwise the Aboriginal trackers would have found him. They're really good. They can find anything. They look for food every day. Only some of them go to supermarkets.' His friend Albie, however, has a different take on the case. 'That girl did it,' he says. 'I know someone who knows she did. And, tell me this, how comes she married again last year?' When it's pointed out to him that she certainly didn't, he's insistent. 'What would you know?' he says. 'It was in the newspapers, I read it, everyone knows about that. She's the same as Lindy Chamberlain who killed that baby. She reckoned a dingo cut the matinee jacket with a pair of scissors. Come off it. They're both the same them two.'

Albie is obviously one of those people who listens to too much late-night talk-back radio and believes way too much of what he hears. But he's indefatigable. 'The police in the Northern Territory, they're terrible. They take all the misfits, and never check them out. They took on one police officer once and didn't realise he was on their wanted posters all around their stations. They only noticed after he'd left.' But John agrees. 'Yeah, they don't know anything,' he says. 'They just wanted someone to pin that Falconio murder on.'

JAMES HEPI HAD MANAGED TO wipe his slate almost clean. After his fateful arrest by West Australian police, the police in South Australia had searched his property in the Riverlands and found seven cannabis plants, charging him with producing a prohibited substance. In February 2003, he appeared in the South Australian court, before a magistrate at Berri. He pleaded guilty and was fined $439 and his plants and equipment were seized by the Crown. He then went back into hiding, waiting nervously for Murdoch's committal hearing. After all, none of the kind of people he usually associated with much likes a dobber.

AT THE ALICE SPRINGS police station, working late again, Superintendent Colleen Gwynne sits sifting through the day's reports from Taskforce Regulus. 'I think we did well, despite the criticisms,' she says. 'We've been through so many people and so many vehicles ... We've been working hard crossing all the 't's and dotting the 'i's ready for the trial. We don't want anything to go wrong. And, you know, I still feel confident that one day we'll find Peter. It might take us a while yet, but it'll happen. It'll happen.'

In Darwin, Assistant Commissioner John Daulby is still phoning the Falconio family every week but plans to stop that when the trial gets underway. After nearly thirty years in the police service, he's also considering leaving. 'It's made me bitter about certain things,' he says, sadly. 'I think I'm very professional, but I do take things personally. If I'm responsible for a mistake, I say so and take responsibility. And things do go wrong. But with this Falconio case, if it all happened again today, I would do and say all the same things. My difficulty was coming in so late. If I'd have been there at the beginning, I would have tried much harder to persuade Joanne to talk to the media. She would then have been treated differently. We chaperoned her around Alice Springs for quite a considerable time because we weren't sure of the stalker element. But after a while, she should have been left alone.

'I really want to see this case through to the end. I would really like to find Peter. There will always be people who want to say you weren't successful, to say you were wrong all along, and that the investigation was a stuff-up. But it hasn't been. It's worked. For the trial, who knows? We have a good case, but there's always an element of never knowing what a jury is going to do at a trial.'

IN ENGLAND, JOANNE LEES battles to rebuild a normal life. There were rumours of a new boyfriend, but they turned out to be about simply a good platonic friend of her's and Peter's from far happier days. In the Brighton electoral register, there's a Joanne Lees living with a David Murdoch in Park Street which could, given the right circumstances, spark yet more rumours about Joanne being part of a plot to do away with her boyfriend to set up home with the beloved brother of his alleged assassin. When I call round, however, they have no idea what I'm talking about.

Relations between Joanne and her stepdad Vincent James are said not to be as close as they once were. A friend says he's spoken once too often to the press for her liking. James, however, insists they're still good mates. He smokes roll-up after roll-up as he looks through photos of happier family days, when his wife and Joanne's mother was still alive, and no harm had come to his stepdaughter, safe at home. 'I'm angry that the police aren't in touch with me more,' he says. 'I don't talk to Joanne so much. She has email.' He says she's thinking of writing a book, one day.

At the Falconios' house a short drive away, Peter's mum Joan is home alone. She looks weary, and her face is lined with care. 'The pain never goes away,' she says, softly. 'It's pain all over your body. It never stops. It's there all the time. We have friends who do their best, and family, but no-one can stop the pain. I tried counselling at first, but it didn't do any good. I went to a support group, but everyone else just wants to talk about their problems and their sorrow. You don't want to hear it. You just want to be on your own, with yours.' She says she keeps forgetting what she's doing. She can't find anything. She can't even read a book, as she can't concentrate. 'I'm not right in the head. I'm not right in the body. I'm ill. I can't imagine ever getting over this. It will never end.'

Joan says her sons are coping, they have each other, but she doesn't believe she ever will. 'It's different for a mother,' she says. 'And because they haven't found the body, you can't ever give up properly. You never know. I can't even think about Peter without thinking of the horrible things that might have happened to him. I can't think of him. It's too horrible.'

The killer has even robbed her of those, her memories of her son.

# CHAPTER FORTY-FOUR

# Bradley Murdoch's First Trial

THE MURDER OF PETER FALCONIO, the attempted abduction of Joanne Lees and now the rape and false imprisonment of a twelve-year-old girl and an assault on her mother – but far from being simple, the charges against Bradley Murdoch were a morass of contradictions and interstate legal complexities, and issues critical to the fundamental principles of providing a fair hearing to anyone accused of a crime … or several. The biggest hurdle was that Murdoch was now facing charges in two different legal jurisdictions: the Northern Territory and SA. Naturally enough, they both wanted the chance to try him first. The Northern Territory felt they'd been hunting Murdoch for a long time, and were keen to see their suspect tried in such a high profile case. But SA argued that their alleged victim was now thirteen and if the matter was delayed for much longer, with a trial in Darwin on the Falconio matter and then possible appeals, it could feel like an eternity for a young girl longing to get on with her life. Some legal experts believed if Murdoch were convicted of the South Australian charges, his trial in the Northern Territory would have to be put off until he'd served his sentence. Only then could he be extradited to Darwin. On the other hand, if the Northern Territory trial went first and he were convicted of murder, he could end up in jail for life, which would make it highly unlikely he'd ever be allowed out of prison to face charges in Adelaide.

To break the deadlock, South Australian Director of Public Prosecutions Paul Rofe decided to talk to the mother and daughter, to ask them how they felt. They were anxious for their case to be finalised and so a date was set first for the trial on allegations of rape, false imprisonment and indecent assault in the South Australian District Court in Adelaide.

WHEN ADELAIDE SOLICITOR MARK TWIGGS received a call from the mother of a man he'd successfully defended against rape allegations, asking if he'd represent a friend of hers, Bradley Murdoch, he wasn't keen. He was still embroiled in the gruesome long-running Snowtown 'bodies in barrels' case, and was representing one of the accused, Robert Wagner, later to be labelled one of Australia's worst serial killers. Manchester-born, but having migrated with his family to Australia at the age of eight, Twiggs had been working in law for twenty-five years in total, and practising as a lawyer for ten. The Murdoch case didn't particularly interest him until the woman phoned back the next day to tell him Murdoch was also going to be questioned about the Barrow Creek murder. Twiggs, forty-six, was then a great deal more interested. He had Murdoch brought to Adelaide, agreed to be his lawyer and approached local barrister Grant Algie to represent him in court. 'It's a case that excites me,' says Twiggs. 'It's intriguing. It's the kind of case any good defence lawyer would like.'

WHEN ALGIE ENTERED THE DISTRICT court in Adelaide on Monday 13 October 2003, a ripple went around the courtroom. If central casting had come up with a barrister, they couldn't have done any better. Algie walked on to his stage as if he owned it, back as straight as a rod, head held high and chin raised haughtily. With blond hair rippling over his collar, an impeccably neat goatee and silver rimmed glasses on the tip of his nose, enabling him to look down, if he cared to, on everyone he passed, he swept in with a stately flurry of black gown, his furled black umbrella leading the charge. Immediately, there were frictions with the assembled press. Algie had laid his gown out carefully on one of the press benches, together with his brolly and extra bag of papers, taking up two or three seats in the limited space over which the media contingent were already fighting. When one reporter asked him if he'd be so kind to move his possessions forward to the legal benches, he ignored him completely. An usher was asked to approach him instead. With a pained sigh, he finally transferred his belongings to a vacant chair. He didn't deign even to glance at the press after that. As he took his expensive fountain pen out of his neat black briefcase and dipped it fastidiously into a bottle of ink on the bench before him, Twiggs sat beside him, short, stout and with the outline of his vest showing through his shirt. They looked for all the world like a modern day Pancho Villa and Don Quixote, ready to take a tilt at another windmill. But looks can be deceiving.

AS JUDGE MICHAEL DAVID ENTERED the room, the next set of legal problems arose. Murdoch's defence team argued that if the prosecution were allowed to mention that their man was also facing charges in the Falconio matter, the jury would naturally be prejudiced against him, and he would never receive a fair trial. Grant Algie said he could find no precedent where one person faced serious charges in two jurisdictions at once. After long legal argument, the judge ruled that the Falconio matter could be mentioned – after all, it was the prosecution's case that the reason Murdoch had attacked the women was because of his paranoia that the police wanted to talk to him about Falconio – but that mentions be kept to an absolute minimum.

The second issue related to the press. Algie argued that if the Adelaide case were fully reported, that would prejudice the jury at the Darwin trial later. The difficulty there, however, was that a judge in SA only had the power to suppress the mention of certain matters in SA alone. Algie, at one point, argued that Murdoch's name not be permitted to be used. Then he objected to his image being reproduced in newspapers. In any case, one of his alleged victims, the twelve-year-old girl, couldn't be identified which also prohibited naming her mother, her stepfather and the place where they lived.

The case started and stopped, started and stopped, until it finally stuttered into life at a point where many had despaired that Murdoch would ever be allowed to face his accusers. Overshadowing everything was the front page news that a torso, possibly Peter Falconio's, had been discovered in a remote dam near Marla, between Coober Pedy and the border with the Northern Territory. Five divers, a plane carrying a number of detectives and a host of volunteers scurried to the scene to look for clues. Eventually, a pathologist in Adelaide examined the remains and declared they were of a large animal; they were definitely not human.

THE PROSECUTION CASE DELIVERED by crown lawyer Liesl Chapman was simple: she alleged Bradley Murdoch had learned police had obtained DNA from his brother Gary, had panicked over the prospect of his arrest in connection with the murder of Peter Falconio and, fired by drugs, had taken the two women hostage as 'insurance' for when the police arrived.

In reply, the defence, however, was just as straightforward: there was a reward of $250,000 on offer for information that would lead to the arrest of Peter Falconio's killer, and the mother and her de facto, together with her daughter and possibly Murdoch's old friend Darryl 'Dags' Cragan, had contrived a plan to frame Murdoch in the hope of making a great deal of money. Algie neither admitted nor denied allegations of drug-dealing against his client.

The styles of the two barristers were a study in contrasts: Chapman, small, pretty and blonde, was softly spoken, sweet and likeable – seemingly the perfect choice of prosecutor in a rape case. Algie was much more strident, verbose and passionate, frequently growing red in the face when he stormed in with an outraged point – 'It's an absolute furphy!' – and was ticked off by the judge for not getting to the nub of an argument more quickly. But he was obviously a very smart operator.

Appearances, too, in middle-class, prim and improper Adelaide, that old city of churches and corpses, can be particularly important. The mother, known to be a former escort, was on medication for anxiety which slowed and slightly slurred her speech; her daughter, dressed up for court looked much older than her thirteen years; and her wizened, sick and much older stepfather, later revealed to be a former brothel owner who'd employed his de facto, had already admitted to having been involved in the drug trade. They weren't exactly the fine, upstanding members of the community a prosecution case would like on its side. Of course, they might have stacked up to Murdoch, but he was exercising his right to silence and didn't say a word. They became, instead, a marked contrast to the cultured, confident and highly intelligent Algie.

WHILE THE MOTHER AND DAUGHTER had both provided graphic accounts of their alleged ordeal, the stepfather – to whom Murdoch gave out $100 payments every now and again – claimed Murdoch always had plenty of cable ties around and lots of rolls of tape. In addition, GP Dr Susan Taylor examined the girl and found a split of hymenal tissue consistent with penetration by a finger or penis eight-and-a-half days before, and an injury to her right wrist consistent with being bound by cable ties. The girl, however, refused a full internal vaginal examination. Dr Taylor said that nervousness wasn't unusual among young female victims.

Amphetamines had been found in Murdoch's bloodstream and Adelaide University pharmacologist Professor Jason White said taking high doses of speed over a long time could lead to psychotic symptoms, hallucinations, delusions, aggression and paranoia. At their extreme, the symptoms could be the same as those of a paranoid schizophrenic.

Algie, however, alleged that the girl's stepfather had asked Murdoch to come to stay in the annex to look after the two women while he was in hospital, and suggested he put up black plastic at the windows in case Hepi came over. With that action, Murdoch looked paranoid – and had thus been set up as part of their conspiracy.

Algie then pointed out inconsistencies in the pair's accusation. He said that mother and daughter each described the position they'd been handcuffed in the Landcruiser differently, and had varied from each other in the way they'd said the cable ties were tied. He also drew attention to the six-day gap between the two women being released at the Port Augusta service station on Thursday August 22, and phoning the police on Wednesday August 28. The mother had said on their release the pair had caught a cab to the hospital, where her de facto had phoned Cragan. He'd taken them to the Bolivar Caravan Park on the outskirts of Adelaide while they worked out what to do. The reason they hadn't called the police earlier was that they were frightened of Murdoch and thought he might act on his alleged threat to shoot them if they went to the authorities. 'We were terrified of Brad,' the woman said. 'Everything was just getting on top of us, like, we didn't know how to handle it and [my daughter] needed attention, the doctor and everything.' Algie argued they'd in fact stayed at the Bolivar working on their ruse to frame Murdoch. He claimed that her partner had advised her to delay going to the police, thereby giving Murdoch time to 'get' Hepi – whom her de facto hated following his death threats – before the police arrested him.

In addition, there had been no DNA or sperm present on the quilt on which they alleged the girl had been raped, and they'd thrown out the girl's clothes, which could have proved, or disproved, the rape allegation. Algie said her partner had not kept them because he knew they could not offer any evidence. The girl's mother protested, 'We weren't thinking straight, we were in shock.' But Algie insisted that her partner had told her to get rid of them to help his plan to make money out of the allegations. As well as the reward on offer, Algie said, the man also planned to sell their story to the media. His partner admitted making a statement to police saying that he was looking at Murdoch as 'a money-making type proposition'.

She'd previously told the police, '[My de facto] is looking at the Bradley Murdoch thing for the money, like he always does. He thinks he can make some money from what happened and keeps talking about going to the media, saying I knew Brad. But talking to the media does not interest me. I want [my daughter] and I to be able to talk and feel safe in our home.'

She'd also said that she'd consider leaving him, if she were financially secure. 'If I had not signed the mortgage on our house I bought with [my de facto], I would have left him years ago,' she said in her police statement. 'It was sort of the case that I was happy with what I had with my house, daughter and animals, whereas [my de facto] always wanted more and couldn't be content with what he had... [He] was out for whatever he could get and he has been like that in all the time that I've known him ...'

As for Cragan, when the woman's de facto phoned him, Algie says he drove to Port Broughton and took exactly half the cash stashed in the shed – $12,000 – and half the cannabis, weighing 1.8 kilograms (4 pounds). He then used $3000 to trade in his Ford Falcon for a Fairmont Ghia to drive back to Katherine in. It could have been part of a pre-arranged plan to rob Murdoch but, equally, by leaving half the money and drugs there, it could have been a scheme to make sure the police found evidence against his old hometown friend. Then again, it could have been honour between drug mates that Cragan took what he believed was his fair share, no more, no less. Perhaps, with the police alerted by the woman, Cragan believed that it was all going to be over for Murdoch very soon, and the cash and dope would at least pay for him to get well away.

Chapman, summing up the prosecution case, protested at Algie's allegations. The women hadn't reported Murdoch earlier because they were scared, she said. The woman's partner was dying of cancer, and Cragan was certainly no master planner – he'd simply got out of there, as any drug dealer would, taking what remained of the business. '[The de facto] isn't the driving force, the mastermind behind any complicated conspiracy, set-up, whatever you like to call it against the accused,' said Chapman. 'Back in August 2002, he was so sick he had to go to hospital.' She said the women lived in a very isolated property that Murdoch knew well. It was all very frightening.

On a trip to view that property, it became evident how rundown it was. The annex was a mess of upended furniture, with broken blinds and scattered rubbish. Outside, a group of dogs barked in a cage whenever anyone walked past. One of the pack was a thickset Dalmatian cross, answering to the name of Jack. It would turn out to be Bradley Murdoch's dog.

Later, an old girlfriend of Murdoch's came on to the property to try to take Jack. The outraged mother and her de facto had her charged by police, and ended up getting the dog back.

THE MAIN FACTORS IN THE case against Murdoch were the cable ties, the drugs, the two women and the girl's urine on the quilt from the back of his ute. Ranged against that was the conspiracy theory, discrepancies between the two women's recollections, the disposal of her clothes, and the eight-day delay in calling the police.

On Monday 10 November 2003, the jury took two hours and ten minutes to deliver a not guilty verdict on all counts.

THE JUDGE TOLD MURDOCH HE was free to go, but the scent of freedom was tantalisingly fleeting. As soon as he'd received his acquittal, he was led down to the basement cells of the court building before being re-arrested for the charges awaiting him in the Northern Territory. He was then taken by police outside, as officers forcibly restrained him, and eased into a waiting car. For those sitting every day in court, gazing at the silent defendant and wondering idly what his voice might sound like, there was at last some satisfaction. A journalist shouted after him, 'Did you kill Mr Falconio?' and he finally broke his silence to utter just two words: 'Fuck off!' It may have been a show for the photographer and reporters, as the defence team darkly muttered, but it at last gave everyone a glimpse of the new-look Murdoch, with clipped short grey hair, cleanly shaven and without the droopy moustache many friends talked of him having. He was then driven to police headquarters where he was served with a provisional warrant for the murder of Peter Falconio.

The next day he appeared in the Adelaide Magistrates Court for an extradition hearing, and two days later he was flown to Darwin. A gaggle of journalists were waiting all day at the airport for him to arrive. Growing bored, they amused themselves by competing to find the silliest questions they could ask. But he then appeared so suddenly, that some ended up asking the questions that were freshest in their minds – the dumb ones. 'What have you got to say for yourself now, Mr Murdoch?' asked one. 'Where's the body?' asked another. And, 'Did you kill Peter Falconio?' Murdoch grimaced at all the questions, glowered at his accusers, and returned to his state of sullen silence.

The press having been given, and missed, their moment, he was promptly whisked to Darwin police headquarters in a police van. There, on 14 November 2003, he was formally charged with murder, deprivation of liberty and unlawful assault.

THE NEWS TRAVELLED INSTANTLY TO the other side of the world. In Huddersfield, Vincent James said Joanne was relieved and pleased to hear the end might be in sight. But Joanne suspected, quite rightly, that she was just starting on a different phase of the same ordeal.

# CHAPTER FORTY-FIVE

# The Committal of Sin

THERE HAD BEEN TIMES OVER the past two years and ten months when Joanne Lees felt she was drowning in her own tears. But as the date for the court hearing to commit Bradley Murdoch to a full jury trial steadily approached, Joanne had never known such anguish. She was fearful, sure enough, of the proceedings themselves, when she'd be forced to face the man she believed had attempted to abduct her and had shot her boyfriend Peter Falconio in cold blood. She was also increasingly anxious about the spotlight from the world's press falling on her once again, with all those accusing faces trying to ask her questions and shoving cameras in her face. But, most of all, she was afraid of the Falconio family. It wasn't so much them, she was scared of. It was their reaction to what she was about to tell them.

Bad enough that they'd lost their son to a brutal outback killer, and even worse that his body had not been found. But perhaps the fact that his girlfriend had lived to tell the tale was some small comfort. How would they feel now when they learned that, while in Sydney with their son, she'd also been sleeping with someone else? Yet she knew there was absolutely no alternative: she had to tell them.

When the police discovered her guilty secret over her email account in Alice Springs, they'd had to question her about it. They didn't know; it could have proved important to the case. In the event, they also spoke to Nick Reilly, and quickly discounted the affair as irrelevant to their investigation. But the betrayal lay, quietly burning away among the police documents – which all would have to be revealed, in due course, to Murdoch's defence team. The prosecution had discovered the defence planned to bring it up at the committal to cast doubt on the 'perfect' relationship she had with her boyfriend and cast doubt on her credibility, and warned Joanne.

She knew there was nothing for it, but to confess all to the Falconio family. The irony of it was that it wasn't a full-blown love affair, she didn't even term it an affair, really. It was just two young people, both far from home, who'd casually fallen into bed together a few times. Peter had never known, and would never have known. It just hadn't been all that significant. It's what young people on holiday far from home do. The Falconio family listened quietly to her confession. They tried to understand, but it was hard. They could imagine how much courage it must have taken Joanne to tell them about it, though. And they appreciated being told before reading it in all the newspapers.

By the time Joanne arrived in Darwin on Sunday 16 May 2004 ready for the five-week committal to start the next morning, she was completely wrung out.

THE NORTHERN TERRITORY IS ONE of the few legal jurisdictions that still holds a full formal hearing before committing someone to trial. The hearing is before a magistrate who must be convinced there is a strong enough case to answer for the matter to proceed to a jury. Usually, the prosecution briefly outlines its case, calls a few witnesses and the committal is a mere formality. For the defence team in Murdoch's case, however, it would be an important testing ground for so much of the evidence for the charges against him. With some 150,000 documents tendered in evidence, and nearly 600 witnesses named, they could decide how many of those people they would like to see, and work out which ones were the most important to the police case – or the least convincing.

Mark Twiggs and Grant Algie were again Murdoch's legal team. After their success in Adelaide at having the charges of rape, assault and false imprisonment thrown out, they were on a high. Privately, they said they were far more confident of beating the Darwin allegations. Their case hinged on the fact that Joanne had identified her attacker's dog as a Blue Heeler rather than a Dalmatian; that she said she'd been pushed from the front of a vehicle to the back, with no such vehicles thought to exist; that she'd described her assailant's gun as having a distinct pattern, and none of those had been traced; and that the DNA discovered at the scene could have been contaminated. Furthermore, without a body, it would be difficult to prove murder.

The pair had enjoyed some degree of notoriety as a result of their coup in Adelaide. 'It does raise your profile, but probably only among lawyers,' says Twiggs. 'It might not even do your business any good. If you have a high profile, people think you might be too expensive to hire.'

Murdoch's case was being paid for by Legal Aid, with a top-up. It was imperative he be seen to be getting a fair trial and normally legal representation in such a complex case would be paid more.

Algie was enjoying himself. It felt like somewhat of a David and Goliath battle – two lawyers from Adelaide up against the might of the South Australian police force, and now against that of the Northern Territory in the most talked-about case in Australia. He was a boy from small town country Australia, born in Edithburgh, a small farming community at the bottom of the Yorke Peninsula, just 80 kilometres from the childhood home of Superintendent Colleen Gwynne. His forebears had scrambled ashore from the shipwrecked migrant ship the *Marion* in 1851, which had set sail from Plymouth four months before, to become peasant farmers. He grew up being told by his father, 'Don't worry about lawyers, boy, they aren't for people like you and me.' But after winning a scholarship to Immanuel College in Adelaide, the Lutheran church school also attended by Australian tennis champion Leyton Hewitt, and then doing the unthinkable for a boy from his town – going to Adelaide University – he'd become a lawyer in the steel town of Whyalla, and been called to the bar in 1991. Now forty-four, he knew, apart from anything else, that the Murdoch case could be the making of his career. 'Every successful case is a landmark,' he says. 'You are certainly conscious of the fact that it's going to change your life.'

Up against them was the Northern Territory Director of Public Prosecutions, Rex Wild QC, sixty, who had opted to take on the case himself. He was an old-fashioned kind of lawyer, softly spoken, gentlemanly, humble and with a real passion for justice. Born in Sydney to a professional soldier father, he'd been appointed a QC in Victoria in

1991 and come over to the Northern Territory to practise in 1992. Two of his three children are also lawyers.

'I would like to think I'd be regarded as a fair man,' he says. 'It's not a question of being an easy mark, it's a case of being fair. It's very difficult for a defence lawyer to criticise to a jury someone who's patently fair. Being courteous and smiling is a big advantage.' One disadvantage for him in the Murdoch case is that he already had a large workload to juggle. At the time of the committal, he had on his plate no fewer than nine murder cases at different stages. But, for him, the case wasn't the biggest he'd been involved with. He spent four years with the Costigan Commission, a Royal Commission of inquiry set up as a result of disclosures on murder and mayhem within the Ship Painters and Dockers Union, which successfully exposed a 'bottom of the harbour' tax fraud, and he'd been an investigator into BHP and Elders IXL, and into Laurie Connell's Rothwells. With the Falconio case, however, he realised the stakes were high. 'There'll be a lot of criticism if we lose this,' he says. 'The first question will be: "How much money have you spent on losing this case?" That'll be difficult. We're aware the world is watching us. There'll be no other suspect, ever again, in this case. There he is; you've got one chance.'

THE COMMITTAL WAS HELD IN a courtroom in the Supreme Court building newly fitted out, at the cost of $1 million, with all the latest technology, including a screen on the wall to display evidence, and screens before all the witnesses, lawyers and journalists. It was billed as the country's first paperless court, but there were still mountains of paperwork in evidence. With 550 witness statements, fifty witnesses being called and seventy journalists in attendance, it was set to be one of the biggest cases ever. And it was always going to be controversial. On the first day, an order was made to withdraw the board game 'Trivial Pursuit' from the Northern Territory after a new edition was found to have included a question about the case with the given answer yet to be proven.

But the first day started well, with Wild outlining the prosecution case. There was a murmur at the quality of the DNA evidence found on Joanne's T-shirt – DNA 640 billion times more likely to be that of Murdoch than from any unrelated person selected at random from the

Northern Territory. It had also been the first time the DNA on the gearstick and steering wheel had been revealed too.

Murdoch, now forty-five, sat between two prison guards with his silver hair closely cropped, wearing a pale blue shirt and fawn trousers. He'd taken the opportunity of prison to have his dentistry problems sorted out and no longer had the unsightly gap with missing front teeth. He listened to the proceedings frequently shaking his head. Sitting across from him were Nick and Paul Falconio, who had previously applied for permission to sit through the whole proceedings. When it was granted, the brothers, now thirty-six and thirty-four and both dressed in black, arrived late into the courtroom which made their entrance all the more dramatic, creating a ripple around the room. Magistrate Alasdair McGregor, one of the Territory's most senior magistrates who'd been brought out of retirement to preside over the case, muttered later that he thought the Mafia had arrived. They took seats in the jury box 10 metres directly in front of Murdoch and, separated only by a sheet of glass, the pair stared fixedly into his face. Murdoch never met their gaze.

Paul Falconio later gave evidence that neither he nor his family had heard from Peter since July 2001. 'We have tea together at least once a week and just generally keep in contact,' he said, in an unfaltering voice to the court. They'd never seen him again after his departure for Australia.

Joanne, now thirty, was next to take the stand. Her appearance shocked onlookers. Whereas on her last visit to Australia she'd looked as young and as fresh-faced as she had before the attack, this time her pale skin was mottled with angry red acne that even heavy foundation couldn't hide. 'Stress,' confided a friend, later. 'She'd been dreading that day for so long now ...' But she'd obviously learnt well the lessons of the past as far as her clothing was concerned: she was dressed as conservatively and unremarkably as possible, in a white blouse and black knee-length skirt, with her black hair tied back in a neat ponytail.

She'd previously been driven into the court building at speed, with an unprecedented posse of police, security guards and TRG officers shielding her from the press. She elected not to be hidden from Murdoch with a screen, and looked at him only briefly when she began giving evidence. He glanced at her when she took the stand, but then averted his eyes. Joanne then looked resolutely straight ahead, but coughed nervously, sipped at a cup of water, and looked close to tears on a number of occasions. She gave a chilling account of the night her life changed forever but when she mentioned the marijuana joint she and Peter had shared watching the sunset before the darkness, there was another murmur around the courtroom. No-one had known. Outside the courtroom, it set off another flurry of speculation from the conspiracy theorists that perhaps Peter and Joanne were somehow involved with drug dealers or had perhaps known their attacker via a drug deal gone wrong, or had previously met Murdoch or Hepi through drug connections. And much to Joanne's horror, after everything she'd been through, it was that one small detail of the lone joint that earned the biggest headlines in all the newspapers.

Murdoch only looked back at Joanne towards the end of her evidence.

AS IN ADELAIDE, THE CASE quickly ran into difficulties with the various suppression orders over issues such as the photoboard, the Shell Truckstop video and photo-fit imagery and the DNA evidence that were placed on the press reporting the proceedings so as not in influence a future potential jury. Murdoch's role as a drug-runner was also never mentioned for fear that too might prejudice the jury – except for one slip by a witness. The Nine Network appealed against one of the orders, which went to three judges of the Supreme Court, leading to concerns that the court might end up closed to the media, or might even derail the whole process. As the case was delayed, and delayed again, Paul and Nick Falconio looked on in increasing bewilderment. 'But why can't they just get on and try him?' asked Paul one day, outside the court, in despair. Everyone just smiled sympathetically, and moved away. Joanne wasn't able to resume giving her evidence for another week, after the appeal was eventually dismissed.

Murdoch wasn't happy either. Fed up with being ferried to court each day and having to wait in the cells downstairs when the case was halted, rather than in the comfort of his Berrimah Jail cell, he leapt to his feet to deliver a catalogue of complaints about his treatment. 'I'm back and forth all the time,' he said gruffly at the glass partition around the dock. 'It's half past seven, quarter to eight by the time you get back to your cell … I'm in travel [sic] all the time. No-one knows where I am.' He also protested that his lawyers were forced to speak to him at a cell below the courts when he was in the precinct, rather than in jail, and that the court paperwork wasn't coming through quickly enough. It was a fitting end to another farcical day of legal manoeuvrings.

In the meantime, the press was still desperate for a photograph of Joanne, trying to snap her as she sped in and out of the court car park below the building, and, when court was out, cruising the small town looking for her. 'If only she'd just walk from a car into the court like a normal person, that would give us all a picture and we could stop this ridiculous circus,' said one photographer. 'But she's not a celebrity or a politician whose position waives the right to privacy; she's simply the victim of an alleged crime,' responded a court official.

Joanne wasn't in a conciliatory mood, anyhow. 'You know, I went through all that, and all the media could talk about was the dope!' she'd exclaimed to a friend. 'They've never done me any favours. Why should I do them one?'

Eventually, fears that someone might end up getting hurt led to Joanne making an offer to the press, saying she would pose for a photo for a donation to charity, the victims support program, from the media groups. It foundered, however, after some organisations that had strict policies against chequebook journalism said that was tantamount to paying for a picture, and a blow to the freedom of the press. One person suggested making a donation instead to put up a reward in the local newspaper for anyone who could tell them where Joanne was staying. Another person phoned police officers, offering them cash for information.

When Joanne did eventually take the stand again, there was another sensation in store: the revelation, under cross-examination, of her affair with Nick Reilly. She handled it badly, at first denying she knew a man called 'Steph', and then denying it was an affair. She probably felt she was being honest – there was no man called Steph, and it was less of an affair, more a casual fling. But her pedantry only succeeded in making her look evasive and shifty. As the press seized on this new titbit with gusto, and British journalists offered rewards for anyone who could lead them to Reilly, onlookers remarked that the prosecution hadn't done her any favours by not bringing the issue up in the first place and trying to control her responses. 'They protect her with everything they've got outside but in here, they've thrown her to the dogs,' remarked one journalist bitterly.

SUPERINTENDENT COLLEEN GWYNNE looked on anxiously. She felt protective of Joanne, but could never tell her so. 'She doesn't understand why the press won't go away,' she said. 'I wanted to hug her, but I couldn't – we're both involved in this case, and we're both witnesses. If I saw her, I had to talk about the weather. It felt bizarre and was obviously confusing for her, but I had to do it.'

Gwynne lost her cool just one day, on the court steps. Walking past the press contingent, she lashed out verbally at them for having nothing better to do than to hang around trying to take photos of Joanne every day. She was worried that what she saw as the excessive media attention might derail the case. 'I ticked them off,' she says. 'I realised then that I needed a holiday.' Instead, she went to yoga class that night. One of the press contingent was taken aback by her spray. 'We're standing there, and this bird comes up and blasts us,' he says. 'Who was she?' They had no idea.

WHEN JOANNE FINISHED GIVING evidence on Thursday 27 May 2004, she was told she was free to go. There was a flurry of photographers chasing her, for the last time, out to her car. This time, they continued on. She was taken to the Darwin RAAF base and from there whisked in an unmarked police car across the tarmac, so she wouldn't have to check in, to a waiting plane. Some journalists bought tickets on the same flight, but Joanne was given a special flight attendant's seat behind a curtain. She then sat on board for twenty minutes while everyone else, including the attendants, disembarked, and was taken to a connecting flight. The media was dumbfounded at the measures taken to ensure they wouldn't, once again, be able to take a decent photograph of her.

THE NEXT DAY IN COURT, there was an eerie silence as a video of the crime scene was run. Peter's eldest brother Nick had returned to England because he couldn't get any more time off work, but Paul watched silently as the camera showed the abandoned Kombi and then zoomed in on the pool of his brother's blood.

That evening, he approached Twiggs as the lawyer sat by the pool at the hotel they were both, by unfortunate coincidence, staying. Twiggs lifted his head from his papers as the young man drew level. But Paul didn't smile. 'I don't know,' he said softly, 'how you can sleep at night.'

OVER THE FOLLOWING WEEKS, with the committal split into two blocks divided by six weeks because the magistrate had a prior engagement to attend a conference elsewhere in the middle, the police witnesses talked in minutiae about the search for Peter and the hunt for his attacker. Forensic scientist Carmen Eckhoff discussed the DNA evidence. While the DNA on Joanne's T-shirt had such overwhelming odds of being Murdoch's, the DNA samples on the steering wheel and gearstick were less conclusive. Eckhoff said she was still doing statistical calculations on elements of the first sample which was 378 to one times more likely to be from Murdoch than any other unrelated person in the Northern Territory, while those in the second were also consistent with him.

Many of the rest of the witnesses trailed tirelessly through the endless detail about Murdoch's changes of ute, and all the modifications he'd carried out on them. They were tough men looking out of place in T-shirts and jeans, or uneasy in shirt collars, with oil-stained hands who could remember the smallest details about the colour of the spokes on the wheels but genuinely could not remember what Murdoch looked like. Friends and enemies of Murdoch came and went, with varying degrees of reluctance. One, old mate Darryl 'Dags' Cragan refused to answer any more questions until he was threatened with being in contempt of court. Another, the former bikies club barmaid who'd travelled behind him just before the Barrow Creek killing, was desperate to keep her identity a secret as she'd changed her life since. Ex-girlfriend Beverley Allan tried to hide from Murdoch behind a mane of hair, while saying the last time she'd seen him was when she was running down the driveway of the house, 'because, yeah, we'd had a bit of an argument and I had to get out of there'. It was as colourful a gallery of characters as you'd find in any outback town, and often just as rough.

The day James Hepi gave evidence, however, was the one everyone had been waiting for. When the big man ambled into court, he didn't look happy to be there, but he knew he had his side of the bargain to keep. As Murdoch glowered at him, he held his gaze steadily once, then concentrated on the proceedings, talking about their drug-runs, his suspicions about Murdoch being on the Truckstop video, the day he saw him making handcuffs out of cable ties and the way he'd changed his appearance, and car, straight after the events of 14 July 2001. Under cross-examination, Hepi, thirty-seven, admitted he'd done a deal with police, but denied it was an agreement to set Murdoch up, with the lure, not only of the suspended prison sentence, but of the $250,000 reward for information leading to the conviction of a suspect.

'If your evidence assists in securing a conviction of Mr Murdoch, you'd be proposing to make inquiries about the quarter of a million dollars?' he was asked by Algie.

'I reckon I would,' Hepi replied.

'You would say, I suppose, that you wouldn't be involved in setting up Mr Murdoch,' said Algie. Hepi flatly denied it but admitted that agreeing to give evidence had its recompense.

'I would say,' replied Hepi, 'getting my skin off the line.'

As he left court, he nodded to Paul Falconio, as if to say he'd done his bit. Paul smiled back at him.

THE PRISON OFFICERS GUARDING THE defendants who appeared in court were interested in Murdoch. They'd never seen so many press there before, and wondered what kind of man would excite such interest. One female officer asked for the chance to escort him to and from the dock, and sit there with him. 'I never want to do that again,' she said, at the end of her shift. 'He really interfered with my headspace. He played games. I couldn't handle it.'

THE WILD CARDS IN THE pack of witnesses turned out to be a young couple who used to work in a petrol station in Bourke, way into the NSW outback. Robert Brown and his girlfriend Melissa Kendall, both twenty-six, said they'd served Peter Falconio a week after he'd allegedly been killed. They said they recognised him from a photo in a newspaper, and that he'd bought a drink and a chocolate bar. 'I could tell he had a bit of an accent,' said Brown. 'The only English accent I know is on the telly.' Kendall said the man was 'identical' to Peter. Their only gripe was that they were giving evidence from Bourke over a video link with the courthouse in Darwin, rather than having been asked to make a personal appearance. 'You could've flown me up,' grumbled Brown, cheerily. 'I could be sitting next to you and I would have had a holiday.'

Predictably, the couple's claims made headlines around the world but few who'd been present in court that day took them seriously. Part of the hearing process was to expose and discredit witnesses who might prove distractions in the trial proper. Brown was asked also about sightings of Elvis.

IT WAS LEFT TO THE last witness of the hearing, Senior Sergeant Megan Rowe, who'd been with Taskforce Regulus from day one, to clear up any remaining misunderstandings. She promptly demolished two of the main pillars of the defence's arguments. Rowe said the team had found revolver-type guns with the kind of scrolling pattern Joanne had described, and there had also been similar vehicles to her attacker's discovered, with front to rear access.

MANY NIGHTS, ALGIE AND TWIGGS had gone out drinking with journalists. Algie was now a great deal more relaxed, laughing at descriptions of him having the best mullet hairstyle in the country. Wild, in contrast, rarely spoke to journalists outside the courtroom. Much of the press discussion centred on how smart Algie could be, and wondering if Wild was simply too gentlemanly – not 'mongrel' enough – for the fight ahead.

On 18 August 2004, Bradley John Murdoch was committed to stand trial on all charges by magistrate Alasdair McGregor. The date would later be set for May the next year.

On the last night of the hearing, a group of journalists got together to play their own ghoulish version of 'Trivial Pursuit', with all the questions and answers centred on the committal. Sample: Whose blood was found on the Kombi? For the answer, choose from the following: Peter Falconio, Azaria Chamberlain, Skippy the Kangaroo. Answer three was the correct one: the Kombi had earlier hit a kangaroo on the road. Whose DNA was it on Joanne Lees' shirt? Answers: Peter Falconio's. Bradley Murdoch's. Forensic scientist Carmen Eckhoff's.

And what are the odds on a conviction at the trial? Answers: 640 billion to one, 378 to one, or evens. The most popular answer was lost somewhere amidst the laughter.

# CHAPTER FORTY-SIX

# DNA and The Letters of The Law

THE TRIAL OF BRADLEY JOHN MURDOCH was at last due to start in May 2005, but the agonisingly long eight-month wait was making everyone jittery. Murdoch had now been behind bars for more than two years and, sitting in the confines of his Berrimah Jail cell, couldn't understand why the run-up to the trial was taking so long. Seventeen thousand kilometres away in Brighton, England, Joanne Lees was impatiently thinking exactly the same thing. But both sides in the case were painstakingly combing through all the evidence, witness statements and mountains of paperwork to find any gaps in their knowledge that needed to be filled, any holes in their evidence that required plugging and, in the case of the defence, anything that might suggest their client's innocence. The court prosecutors and the police were determined to make sure every 't' was crossed and every 'i' dotted before the case would eventually rumble back on to centre stage; and Murdoch's defence team was similarly anxious to make their challenges as forceful, and their denials as watertight, as possible.

For the case as it stood against Murdoch was certainly not conclusive. There was no actual witness to the murder of Peter Falconio – as even Joanne hadn't seen exactly what had happened behind the Kombi that fateful night – no body, no murder weapon and no apparent motive. Instead, the allegation of murder was purely circumstantial. It rested on

Joanne's identification of Murdoch; the fact that he'd changed his appearance and that of his vehicle so dramatically after the attack on Peter; the possibility that it was him pictured on the Shell Truckstop video which placed him in the area at the time; the discovery of a hairtie matching Joanne's in his Landcruiser; James Hepi's testimony that he'd talked about hiding bodies and had made manacles similar to those used against Joanne; and, lastly and perhaps most importantly, the DNA on Joanne's T-shirt, on the Kombi steering wheel and on its gearstick.

The police were utterly convinced they had their man, but knew that at best there was only a 60-40 chance of a conviction on the evidence they'd presented at the committal. They desperately needed something else. And, one evening, working late in the lab, it finally dawned on forensic scientist Carmen Eckhoff that she'd perhaps overlooked something quite critical.

A year before, she'd read about the pioneering work of a scientist at the UK Forensic Science Service DNA unit at Wetherby in West Yorkshire, England, who was an expert in a new method of analysing DNA, called Low Copy Number (LCN) testing. A technique sensitive enough to produce a DNA profile from just a few cells of a tiny sample left at a crime scene or on a victim, it had first been discovered in 1999, and Dr Jonathan Whitaker had since become the foremost scientist to perfect the method.

Because this kind of testing required only a miniscule amount of DNA, it had revolutionised police forensics investigations in Britain. Dr Whitaker had personally been involved in bringing a number of offenders to justice years after their crimes. In 2004, for instance, tiny dandruff flakes left in a discarded stocking mask finally led to the conviction of one man, Andrew Pearson, for staging an armed robbery – in 1993. Another, Anthony Ruark, was jailed for life following the analysis of a tiny amount of semen left on the clothing of his murdered girlfriend eighteen years before. Even more famously Dr Whitaker had also been called in to re-examine a case that had happened more than forty years ago. He found tiny specks of a man's DNA on his female victim's clothing and was able to confirm that James Hanratty, the man later hanged for the crime but whose family and friends had long protested his innocence, was indeed the villain of the piece.

In layman's terms, his tests amplified minute traces of DNA and the findings which, while no longer having the billions-to-one statistical odds of good clear samples, could still tell investigators that the chances of it being anyone else's DNA were millions to one against.

As a result, Eckhoff had travelled to England five months before to take Dr Whitaker DNA samples from the Kombi's steering wheel and gearstick. He'd found traces of Murdoch on both. But just before the voir dire, the preliminary hearing of legal issues before the trial itself started, Eckhoff looked at her files again. His tests had proved impressive and it suddenly dawned on her that maybe she should also have given him the cable ties with which Joanne had been handcuffed to test them for traces of Murdoch's DNA to see if he could be linked even more closely to the attack on the tourists.

It was only a few days before the voir dire and, in all honesty, that kind of testing should have been done well in advance. But, she decided, it was still worth a shot. It was late evening in Darwin, but still early morning in England. With a trembling hand, she picked up the phone and dialled the number of the UK forensics service.

MURDOCH'S DEFENCE LAWYERS were also focussing on the DNA found by the Northern Territory Police in the Kombi and on the T-shirt. Their client was still protesting his innocence and insisted the presence of his DNA merely meant that the police had tried to set him up.

The massive world attention on the case had put incredible pressure on them to find the tourists' assailant. Murdoch told his solicitor Mark Twiggs that he'd simply been in the wrong place at the wrong time. The big reward being offered for information leading to the arrest of their attacker had already given plenty of his enemies $250,000 worth of reasons to try to frame him and now, he said, people – either the police or adversaries like James Hepi – were planting his DNA on the scene. He could easily have brushed up against Joanne at the Camel Races, or by the Red Rooster chicken shop in Alice Springs where the couple had eaten beforehand. He had receipts to show he'd been at the Repco motor parts shop on the other side of the road, for God's sake. His DNA in the Kombi? With his mechanical skills, he was always helping out motorists in trouble, particularly when they were driving such vast distances in such obviously unsuitable decrepit old vehicles.

Grant Algie and Twiggs mulled over the DNA evidence together, day after day. They'd already pointed out that the Darwin forensics lab hadn't been accredited until much later, something the prosecution countered had merely been a technicality due to a lack of fire exits rather that any flaws in the testing procedures. But they felt they needed more. And finally they came up with a name: Ian Barker QC.

Barker is one of the sharpest legal minds, and most forceful court personalities, in Australia. His masterful prosecution of Lindy Chamberlain at the 1982 trial led to a jury convicting her of killing baby Azaria – a conviction later overturned on new evidence – and the extraordinary sentence of life imprisonment with hard labour. He is, however, widely recognised as a fiendishly acute intellect, a marvellous orator and a first-hand expert on the unreliability of DNA evidence. Despite his star turn as the Crown Prosecutor, Chamberlain was later acquitted when it was found that the 'foetal blood' Sydney forensics expert Joy Kuhl had testified was splashed around the family's Holden Torana and in Lindy's husband Michael's camera bag, was actually standard vehicle sound deadener.

With Kuhl playing a small role in the investigation into Peter's disappearance by examining the Kombi after everyone else had run tests, that faint tinge of doubt about the dependability of the DNA evidence was already there. If Barker were onside, that doubt could well be intensified to Murdoch's benefit. Algie and Twiggs agreed, and signed up the QC to help with their attack on the DNA evidence, to try to discredit it at the voir dire so that it could be ruled out for the trial. When the prosecution heard about Barker's appointment, they were stunned.

THE NAME OF THE JUDGE for the Falconio case – Brian Martin – was finally announced, and sparked a fresh frisson of excitement among the journalists. In even further echoes of the notorious Chamberlain case, Brian Martin had been the Northern Territory's Solicitor-General at the time, the man who'd played a pivotal role in bringing the original murder charges against Chamberlain. When pressure mounted for an inquiry into the conviction in 1985, he travelled to Germany to visit the maker of the forensics test that had identified the presence of 'blood' in the van. When he returned, he declared there was no grounds for a judicial inquiry. The makers of the test later wrote to him saying he had 'misunderstood' some of their points.

Immediately, the press were jumping to all sorts of conclusions. With Joanne already compared to Chamberlain, and claims floating around that perhaps she'd had a hand in her boyfriend's killing, how on earth could the case proceed fairly under the charge of a man who'd once been so convinced of another woman's guilt in similarly mysterious circumstances in the Australian outback? The agitation was, however, short-lived. The DPP's press officer immediately jumped in to explain: this was a *different* Brian Martin.

This indeed was Brian Ross Martin QC, appointed as Chief Justice of the Supreme Court of the Northern Territory in January 2004. Before that, the former Commonwealth DPP had been a judge at the South Australian Supreme Court where he'd presided over the infamous Snowtown 'bodies-in-a-barrel' murder trials. It had been a long and infinitely complex series of hearings but he'd acquitted himself with great aplomb. He had a reputation as a man as firm as he was fair, who brooked nonsense from neither prosecution nor defence. The stage had finally been set for the legal jostling that would immediately precede the trial proper.

BRADLEY MURDOCH'S FATHER COLIN had been unwell for some time, and the strain of having his son behind bars wasn't helping. As the first stage of the voir dire began on 7 March 2005, he took a turn for the worse. Four weeks later, he was dead. Murdoch was devastated. He applied for permission to attend his father's funeral. It was refused. His lawyers were outraged: after all, their client was only on remand, he hadn't been convicted of an offence. But their protests fell on deaf ears. On April 19, Colin Murdoch was buried without his son in the congregation to mourn him.

JOANNE LEES WAS STUNNED when she received a call from a friend about an article in Britain's *Daily Mail* newspaper by her old foe Richard Shears. She'd assumed all would be quiet in the lead-up to the trial, due to begin on 3 May 2005 in Darwin's Supreme Court. She couldn't have been more wrong. She tore open the newspaper to see her own and Peter's faces smiling back out at her. The headline chilled her. 'Why I *still* have huge doubts about the Outback Killer', it ran in huge, bold type.

The article went on to say that lawyers in the case would say that Murdoch, a man with a bad reputation, had been the perfect fall guy for police. And the reason they'd be able to do so with such confidence was because of all the discrepancies in Joanne's story. Joanne, already dreading returning to Australia for the trial, felt sick to her stomach.

ACROSS THE SEAS IN THE world's newest nation, East Timor, John Daulby, the senior police officer who had headed the investigation for so long into Peter's disappearance, was watching developments closely. He'd taken extended leave to fill a post as an advisor to the East Timor police service, based in the capital, Dili. As his year overseas came towards its end, he was asked if he'd consider extending his term. Eventually, in April 2005, just after the 30th anniversary of the beginning of his police career, he decided to resign from the Northern Territory force, in order to keep on making a contribution to the developing world.

The job was tough, but it was rewarding. 'Working with a nascent police force, which only knows a dark past, is bloody hard,' he says, sitting in a little café in Dili. 'I do have a few regrets, though. I love the police, and I'm proud of my service in the Northern Territory Police, and am proud of the men and women I've worked with throughout my career. But I feel I left Darwin perhaps a year early. I would have liked to have seen this case to its end. I feel I left some things undone. But it felt like the time was right to move on. I wasn't running away or trying to escape; the door was closing there, and another window opened here.'

He visited Darwin often and was in touch regularly with some of his colleages from Taskforce Regulus to keep apprised of the case. He felt he'd lived every day of the past three-and-a-half years trying to discover what had happened to Peter, and just couldn't let it drop. He was full of admiration for those colleagues who'd continued on, giving their all to the investigation. 'You know, people like David Chalker, Megan Rowe and Paula Dooley-McDonnell deserve commendations for the work they've done,' he says. 'They've worked so hard, and been so diligent and committed. The terrible thing is, if the trial ends in an acquittal, they'll be made to feel as if they've failed. If it ends in a conviction, at the very least, their contribution should be recognised.'

As for his own role in the case, he believes there were some mistakes, but he did the best he possibly could in the circumstances. 'My biggest regret was that I wasn't there when it first happened,' he says, looking off into the distance. 'Joanne should have been coerced into facing the press. The whole thing would then have played out so differently. I would have insisted she'd done it.'

OVER IN THE US, A NEW movie was premiering at Robert Redford's Sundance Film Festival. A small Australian horror film made on a miniscule $2 million budget, it was, however, making waves around the world. Called *Wolf Creek*, it was billed as loosely based on the stories of Peter Falconio and backpacker killer Ivan Milat. About three British tourists, two women and one man, travelling through the outback who tangle with an evil murderer played by John Jarratt, the film was so graphically violent, there were reports of members of audiences actually vomiting and others fainting as they watched.

First-time feature film director Greg McLean had himself been affected by the story of Peter's disappearance, Milat's gruesome toll and the horrific Snowtown killings. 'Australia, once the world's favourite beach, suddenly became a place where lonely, deranged men with murder on their minds stalked empty highways,' he says. 'Looking for vulnerable tourists a long way from home ...'

The film pays homage at various times to the Falconio case. At one point, an orange Kombi sits in a car park. At another, a man looking very like Murdoch grins in a bar towards the camera. And at another, the one tourist to survive the killing frenzy is actually accused of murdering his mates. Neither of the bodies of the dead are found, and the real murderer is left to roam free.

In the first press kit handed out at previews, Murdoch's name was used prominently in the notes. When the legal ramifications were pointed out, that was hurriedly changed.

*Wolf Creek* quickly became a massive hit around the world, and was due to open in Australia at about the time the trial was meant to start. The low-budget shocker was making a small fortune for its 'friends and family' backers. Years before one of the producers had approached an old schoolfriend to ask him if he'd like to invest in it. Mark Twiggs, as unaware of the movie's subject matter as he was of its commercial potential, declined.

BACK AT THE SPOT WHERE Peter vanished three-and-a-half years before, another man suddenly met a violent death. A thirty-one-year-old soldier lost control of his military truck after a tyre blew en route to a defence exercise 10 kilometres north of Barrow Creek. He was not wearing a seatbelt, and died soon after.

THE VOIR DIRE BEFORE Chief Justice Brian Martin QC was to last just ten days over two separate hearings. The prosecution would be laying some of its cards out on the table in terms of the evidence it was proposing to present before the jury; the defence would have its chance to challenge their plans.

Rex Wild QC explained that, in contrast with his case during the committal, he would be leading his case on the allegation that Murdoch had been running drugs between South Australia and Western Australia when he happened upon Peter and Joanne. Wild's deputy in the prosecution, Tony Elliott, then took over. Wild, with his full caseload, was needed elsewhere. He was running another murder case at the same time, against two teenagers accused of tying up two Thai-born sex workers and throwing them off a bridge, weighted down with car batteries. The boys hoped crocodiles would eat the prostitutes but 'salties' only attack living, moving prey. The womens' bloated bodies were spotted by tourists out on a crocodile-watching river trip.

In Wild's absence, Elliott told the court the prosecution in the Falconio case also wanted to talk about the guns Murdoch had in his possession when he was arrested in Port Augusta. Algie protested.

But it was when the DNA evidence was presented that Algie really saw red. Whitaker had been given the cable ties and, after carefully unwinding the black masking tape from around them, he'd diligently set about testing them with his LCN techniques. What he claimed he'd found had astounded Eckhoff. From the miniscule traces of cells he discovered inside the cable ties, he said he was able to identify one man: Murdoch.

The prosecution was triumphant – this was proof that Murdoch had not only handled the manacles but in all likelihood had made them. The defence were furious. They protested that this new development had been sprung on them at the last minute, when they'd had no time to independently verify Whitaker's results. Furthermore, the tests the scientist had carried out on the DNA from the Kombi gearstick and steering wheel had effectively destroyed the samples. Ian Barker made an immediate application to have the hearing stopped and the trial date put back to allow them to have their own DNA tests carried out on the cable ties.

When Whitaker came into the court, he was asked if it would be possible to do more tests in the UK for the defence to witness. He said it would. The judge then ruled that the trial be postponed until October 2005, to enable Murdoch's lawyers to examine fresh tests.

IN HIS CELL, MURDOCH WAS livid about the new 'evidence' that was now going to be put before the court, and angry that the case was being postponed yet again. In England, Joanne, despite her reluctance to step back into the spotlight, was distraught to get the last minute call to cancel her flight.

She had no idea that , in the small town of Wetherby, just 40 kilometres away from her hometown of Huddersfield, one of the last big battles over the truth about her ordeal and Peter's mysterious outback disappearance was finally being played out.

# CHAPTER FORTY-SEVEN

# The Final Reckoning

WHEN JOANNE LEES FLEW BACK into Australia on Friday 14 October 2005, no-one could quite believe their eyes. She was a different person.

For a start she looked stunning: she'd slimmed down markedly, losing at least 10 kilograms of weight, so her round, babyish face was now sharply defined with striking cheekbones, and she'd grown her dark hair long and straight, a fashionable fringe skimming her blue eyes. In place of the old T-shirts, comfy shorts and baggy jeans, she was stylishly elegant in a beige sleeveless wrap-around top, designer denims and gold sandals. Her attitude had changed too. In the past, she'd snuck into the airport at Darwin, doing her best to dodge the waiting press. This time, Joanne, now thirty-two, had let it be known she'd be prepared to have her dawn arrival filmed, photographed and reported on by a handful of journalists on condition that they would release their words and images to all the media, to avoid the kind of frenzied scrums that had greeted her in the past. Travelling with a family liaison officer from Sussex Police and childhood friend Martin Najan, she still refused to speak to, or even smile at, the little huddle awaiting her in the international airport arrivals hall, but at least she lingered long enough for them all to take photos and report on her demeanour.

The real surprise, however, was yet to be sprung. That came on the first day of the trial, on Monday October 17, at the Darwin Supreme Court. Whereas previously in the witness box during the committal, Joanne had been anxious, coy and evasive, this time she sat up straight, and answered questions directly in a much clearer, more confident voice. Dressed in a briskly businesslike white shirt and black skirt with her hair tied back in a neat ponytail, she was obviously still nervous, coughing constantly to clear her throat and sipping frequently from a glass of water beside her. But, for the first time in the four years and two months that had passed since that fateful event in the Northern Territory outback, she appeared in control, and determined to see out the whole thing to its end – whatever that might be.

'Don't forget, she's older now, and she's matured a lot,' said Police Superintendent Colleen Gwynne, who'd been in charge of the investigation into Peter Falconio's disappearance, and who, as a result, had got to know her well in the intervening years. 'People do change, and she's had a lot of time to think about this.' Doubtless her new appearance gave her more confidence, as well as the new relationship she'd started with thirty-one-year-old osteopath Miad Najafi who also happened to be a martial arts expert. Friends said he'd been teaching her self-defence.

A FEW METRES AWAY FROM HER, in the dock and flanked by two armed prison guards, sat Bradley Murdoch, who'd turned forty-seven just over a week before.

Dressed in his trademark pale blue shirt and stone-coloured trousers, with his glasses perched low on his nose, he stared at Joanne, then broke away to peer at the heavy folders and notepad he had balanced on his knees in front of him. With the police brief available to him in his cell, as well as access to a computer, he'd been working hard on his defence. He too looked nervous, but friends said he was quietly confident of an acquittal. 'He was depressed when the trial was adjourned before, because he just wants to get it over,' says one. 'He thinks he'll be fine.'

Occasionally, he glanced over at his girlfriend, Jan Pittman, sitting in the public gallery. Just as Joanne seemed to have slimmed down, she appeared to have bulked up, a heavy, tough-looking woman, her face set in a grim line of irritation that her boyfriend was having to go through all this iniquitous indignity. Her hair had recently returned from blonde to brunette and was cut into the nape of her neck, and she'd dressed conspicuously in a bright yellow top and white baggy knee-length shorts. She was heavily made up, with dark-varnished nails and diamond rings flashing on many of her fingers. Over her right arm, she carried a handbag bearing the photograph of a Dalmatian – a little signal of defiance for those in the know about her man and his 'mystery' dog.

ON THE OPPOSITE SIDE OF the public gallery the Falconio family sat in a tight huddle, Luciano with his hands clasped tightly in front of him, and his wife Joan, looking frail but determined on this, her first visit to the country where her son had vanished. She peered through tinted glasses intently, anxiously towards the judge. By their side sat Peter's brothers Paul, thirty-six, and Nick, thirty-seven, both also looking straight ahead, and both dressed in the aching black of mourning.

JOANNE SLOWLY, AND DELIBERATELY answered all the questions the prosecutor, Rex Wild QC, gently asked her. About the prospect she and Peter might have been going their separate ways towards the end of the trip, Joanne explained he was going to Papua New Guinea for a walking trip while she'd take a break in Sydney, and they planned to meet up again in Queensland before continuing on. About her dalliance with Nick Reilly, she said, 'He was a friend, a good friend and we became close and we were intimate at one time … we over-stretched the boundary of friendship but that ended and we became friends again.'

About her and Peter's last day together in Alice Springs, she talked about his trip to the tax advisor, her time on the internet, breakfast, the Camel Cup and lunch at the local Red Rooster fast food chicken restaurant. About their ill-fated drive up the Stuart Highway, she recounted the stop at Ti Tree, the sunset, the joint of marijuana, and then the darkness of an outback night. 'It began to get darker and darker until it was eventually pitch black,' she told the court. 'We were talking about where we would spend our birthdays. We were hoping that Peter's we'd spend in New Zealand, then we would be in Fiji for mine and then meet with some friends …' At the thought of their future plans, now never to be fulfilled, her voice eventually broke, and tears slid down her face.

Over the next couple of days, she continued to answer questions that had been asked many times before. She recalled once more being stopped by the man in the white four-wheel-drive, his description, the bang behind the Kombi which at first she thought might have been the exhaust back-firing but which she then believed could have been gunshot. She talked about being threatened at gunpoint, manacled and being pushed by the man out of the Kombi onto the gravel outside as she tasted blood in her mouth.

Wild seemed to gather himself to stand straighter. 'And do you see this man today?' he asked. Suddenly, the courtroom grew tense, and everyone leaned forward expectantly. Joanne didn't hesitate. 'Yes,' she said, staring straight at Murdoch. 'I'm looking at him.' Murdoch shook his head, as if he couldn't believe she'd got it so wrong. 'Oh, yes, it's you,' she mouthed angrily.

As she was asked to recount that night in closer and closer detail, Joanne slipped into the present tense. She sounded as though she was reliving the night. 'I'm moving my head around but he can't tape up my mouth,' she said. 'It gets all in my hair and around my neck but it doesn't go near my mouth. I'm just calling out for Pete … to come and help me.' When she talks of the sack being placed over her head, she says, 'I was screaming, "I can't breathe!"' Joanne's composure finally broke when she talked of lying in the back of her attacker's vehicle, wondering what he was doing. 'I just started thinking about Pete and wondering if he had shot Pete,' she said, her voice quaking as she battled to control the tears. 'I just kept asking what he'd done to Pete. It seemed a long time.'

Joanne talked of her escape from the back of the man's ute, hiding in the bushes, and her eventual rescue by road train driver Vince Millar. Her answers were characteristically slow, careful and matter-of-fact. At that point, however, the court judge, Chief Justice Brian Martin, intervened and asked if she could tell the court how she was actually *feeling* at various stages. Her eyes widened slightly, then she took a deep breath. It was the moment everyone had been waiting for: a real insight into this woman who'd apparently managed to surmount such incredible odds to get away from the gunman, yet who had seemed so reluctant, beyond reciting the facts, really to open up about the experience.

'I just kept thinking this isn't happening to me,' she said. 'I couldn't believe this is happening and I felt alone. I kept shouting for Peter. I thought I was going to die. Mainly, I just kept thinking I can't believe this is happening.

'It all happened quite quickly from being tied up to being on the ground. My main thoughts that I remember is just screaming out for Pete to come and help me. I was fighting so much I just had used all my energy and once he put me in the back of the vehicle, I thought, that's it. I'm definitely gong to die. I have no energy to get out of the situation. I just felt exhausted ...

'The next thing, emotion I can feel really strongly about, is when I asked him if he was going to rape me. I was so frightened. I was more scared of being raped than I was of dying and being shot by the man. And then when I asked him if he'd shot Pete. I kept asking, and he didn't give me an answer straight away.' She stopped and wiped her eyes. 'Just the realisation hit me that he might have killed Pete. After I had asked him if he was going to rape me and if he'd shot Pete, I just got some energy from somewhere, some inner strength. My focus was escaping, that's just what I concentrated on. Just getting out of there.'

IT WAS AT THAT POINT the popular image of Joanne as a so-called ice queen finally melted. By talking about how she felt during the attack, at last expressing that vulnerability she'd been so determined to hide, she suddenly appeared so much more human. The assembled journalists packed into the press room of the court, and spilling over into a jury room downstairs, scribbled furiously, knowing their headlines that evening were assured. They were still divided over whether to believe her version of events, but even the attitudes of her fiercest critics started to thaw. In the public gallery, Luciano Falconio nodded, as if he had really begun to understand for the first time. And on the benches in front of him, you could feel the jury warming to the young woman before them.

Joanne herself had relaxed. She'd relived the worst part of her ordeal, what else could there be? She opened up again when asked about how she felt after her escape. 'I didn't really sleep for days,' she said. '... I didn't feel utterly safe or secure. I felt vulnerable ... I was afraid of the dark, so I kept the light on. I didn't sleep for days. I just sort of rested.' She occasionally even allowed her sense of humour to sneak through. When she was asked if her attacker's four-wheel-drive looked new, she replied drily, 'Everything would seem new to my Kombi van.'

Gradually, she answered all the points on which she'd been criticised. She'd accepted 50,000 pounds for the Martin Bashir interview, she said, in order to keep the investigation alive when is seemed to have fizzled out. She'd said initially the dog was like a Blue Heeler – rather than a Dalmatian crossed with a heeler – because of the similar-sized Blue Heeler she'd seen at the Barrow Creek Roadhouse. 'I regard Dalmatians as friendly and floppy-eared … always reminds me of [the movie] *101 Dalmatians* and I don't think of that as an Australian dog. The dog the man had that night was clearly an Australian dog.' And, even though she'd always remained adamant that she'd been pushed from the front of the ute to the back, through an opening between them, she suddenly gave way on the point. It might have been a memory returning, or an eagerness to quash another well-publicised doubt clouding her story. 'It's possible he may have pushed me through the side,' she said.

GRANT ALGIE'S DEFENCE cross-examination started on the Wednesday, just before noon. He ran through the details of Joanne's story again. He quizzed her on her description of her attacker's vehicle, its bullbar, its size. He asked her about the man, and exactly what he looked like. He picked through the minutiae of her statements. He asked her again to run over the events of that evening. She volunteered the new information that, when she'd heard the bang from behind the Kombi, ironically, she'd thought at first she was to blame. 'I just remember thinking, looking straight ahead of me at first thinking, "Oh my God, what's happened to the vehicle, is it something that I've done to cause that?"' she said. Algie frowned. He then asked her about the man's stance, about how exactly he attacked her, about her injuries. It was then that Joanne's chin came up and, instead of playing the meek victim, she began to be more defiant. When Algie asked her if it was possible to sustain such injuries from lying on the ground as her assailant tried to tie her legs, Joanne replied coolly, 'It must because, because I suffered them.'

She was growing in confidence all the time. When she was asked why she didn't glance over to where she thought Peter might be lying, she frowned. When she was asked whether she perhaps wasn't concerned about his well-being, she actually bristled. 'I was concerned about my own life,' she replied. 'All I could see was darkness.'

On the subject of the front-to-back opening of the ute, she again reiterated her doubts. 'The police told me that there is no such vehicle that has front to rear access and that has put doubt in my mind and I looked at other possibilities that I got through,' she said. 'All I know is I got from the front to the back quite easily, I did not walk around a vehicle, so it is possible that the point where the man got the sack from where he lifted up the canvas, the canopy to get the canvas bag, is also a possibility of how I got in … I don't recollect it now. I just know that I got from the front to the rear, not by my own steam, I was put there forcibly by the man.'

Joanne grew positively bold, however, when the subject turned to her feat of moving her manacled hands from behind her back to her front. She told Algie she'd demonstrated it to the police, and then made an offer that stunned everyone. 'I think I kept my hands together, but if at any point the jury would like me to demonstrate that, just let me know,' she said. There was a murmur through the courtroom, a ripple of interest piqued.

Algie demurred quietly. His defence was based on chipping away at the credibility of the prosecution witnesses, especially Joanne. The last thing he needed was a vivid demonstration that what she said was true.

Chief Justice Martin, however, disagreed. The next day, he delivered his ruling: Joanne should indeed be taken up on her offer. Algie protested: he insisted he didn't plan to challenge her assertion that she'd managed to move her manacled hands. Martin wouldn't be moved. In a situation where the defence was questioning generally the reliability of her evidence, she should be allowed to prove the truth of her words in this instance.

As a result, during the break, Joanne changed into trousers and had her hands cuffed with a man's tie – to be tied with the cable ties once more would be too traumatic. Then, in front of the jury, she started the demonstration, the movement that journalist Richard Shears had said would be impossible even for a ballet dancer. With bated breath, the jury watched as she finally moved her hands deftly past the soles of her feet from back to front. It took her precisely a second and a half. In the press room later, everyone else had a try. Only two journalists were able to replicate the action successfully. Shears didn't even try.

The cross-examination finished abruptly without any of the grillings onlookers had expected about the couple's plans to part for a while, the dope they'd smoked together, and Joanne's affair with Reilly. It seemed as if Joanne's newfound confidence and her much more gentle and emotional presence, with all the fresh sympathy it was now evoking, had taken Algie by surprise, and knocked much of the stuffing out of Murdoch's men.

BEFORE JOANNE'S APPEARANCE IN court, the jury had been selected, painfully slowly as Murdoch came close to using up every single one of his challenges. At the start of the trial, eventually, Wild had laid out the prosecution's case, and both Paul Falconio and his father Luciano had testified. There was silence as Paul described their close-knit family of parents and four brothers, and said how Peter would always call home, no matter how far away he was. 'Has there ever been any period as long as this when you haven't heard from Peter whilst he was alive, to your knowledge?' Wild asked him finally. Paul's voice remained strong. 'No,' he replied, 'never.'

When Luciano took the stand, there was no-one who didn't feel for the heartbroken man who seemed to have shrunk over the past four years. In heavily Italian-accented English, he told how his son would try to ring home every week, without fail. 'The only time he's gone a fortnight without ringing anyone, on the beginning of the trip, when he was in Himalaya,' he told the court. 'Because there is no telephone up on the top of the Himalaya, you know.'

The last time he and his wife had ever heard from Peter had been the day before he'd gone missing. Luciano had answered the phone, but passed it on to Joan. 'I did speak very briefly but I always leave it to the mother because children like to speak to the mother more than the father,' he said. 'He was down in Sydney and Joanne had got a job in a bookshop and he was supplementing his income ...' By then, tears were flowing down his face so fast, he had to stop. In the public gallery, a few onlookers wiped their eyes. Peter's father eventually recovered enough to answer a couple more questions, then Wild left it. Algie decided not to cross-examine. It would have been too cruel.

At the end of that first week of the trial, Joanne and the Falconios emerged together on to the steps of the courts. Joanne looked quietly composed, plainly relieved to have finished giving her evidence, and pleasantly surprised by how cordial the press had been to her. Now she had shown something of the spirit that had allowed her to escape from her attacker in the outback, had at last shown some emotion, and was now giving them the opportunity for a photograph every day, instead of racing in a car through to the back entrance of the court, it was something of a redemption. Everyone had also remarked favourably on her transformation since her last appearance the year before. British commentators were busily comparing her to Victoria 'Posh Spice' Beckham; one Australian magazine printed her photograph next to one of Liz Hurley for comparison.

Joanne continued to ignore the assembled photographers, however, as she kissed each member of the family before climbing into the black Ford sedan with dark tinted windows that came for her every day. It was a rare show of togetherness from a woman who desperately needed to move on in her life, and a family still entrenched in their own sorrow and for whom, with no body to bury, true closure would be forever impossible.

# CHAPTER FORTY-EIGHT

# Judgment Day

OVER THE NEXT SIX WEEKS, eighty-two witnesses gave evidence, and more than 350 exhibits, including photographs, were shown to the jury. Many of the parade of men and women had already given evidence at the committal, and much of their testimony was exactly the same. Road train driver Vince Millar, on crutches after suffering a bad accident, talked of coming across Joanne in the middle of nowhere. His co-driver that night, Rodney Adams, described how their new passenger had been distraught and in a state of panic when they rescued her. Barrow Creek Roadhouse owner Les Pilton said she was on the verge of breaking down emotionally, but each time seemed to draw on some 'inner strength'. As he left the box, he smiled warmly at Joanne Lees and clasped both of his hands over Luciano Falconio's. Joanne smiled back, Luciano looked close to tears.

Police officers talked endlessly about their fruitless searches for Peter Falconio, their roadblocks that could easily have been avoided by someone who knew the back roads, the gathering of evidence, the crime scene itself, and Peter's St Christopher medallion which had, poignantly, never been found. They admitted that bungled communications between two groups of searchers meant that a second examination of the area where Joanne had hidden never took place, so that her tube of lip balm was not found until three months later – leading to defence accusations it had been planted there by police. One revealed that searches were still continuing for Peter with the last as recent as two months before. Joan Falconio sat steadfastly through all the evidence until she realised photographs of the pool of Peter's blood left on the roadside were about to be shown. Unable to bear that, she walked out.

It was the DNA evidence, however, that took up most of the time. Forensic biologist Carmen Eckhoff caused a sensation with her claim that the blood spot on Joanne's T-shirt contained DNA which was an exact match with that of Bradley Murdoch's. Pressed for a figure that expressed the likelihood it came from Murdoch, she announced it was '150 quadrillion times' more likely to belong to him than to any other person. Immediately, there was uproar in the press room as everyone raced around trying to work out what a quadrillion actually was. The figure turned out to be 150,000,000,000,000,000; with a quadrillion a million times a trillion. Frantic emails from UK newspapers came flooding in, demanding to know whether it was a British trillion or the different US trillion. Nobody stopped to wonder if it made any difference.

More figures came later from UK DNA expert Dr Jonathan Whitaker, who said DNA deep within the cable ties used to restrain Joanne, and isolated with his Low Copy Number (LCN) technique, was 100 million times more likely to have come from Murdoch. In addition, the DNA on the gearstick of the Kombi was 19,000 times more likely to be the defendant's, while his presence couldn't be excluded either from the DNA mix on the steering wheel. Murdoch rolled his eyes disparagingly. His counsel argued that some experts had concerns about the LCN technique, with any contamination likely to be magnified along with the small samples. Some contamination had indeed already taken place, with the director of the lab Dr Peter Thatcher's DNA being found on the cable ties. Defence lawyer Grant Algie put forward the proposition that the cigarette butts Murdoch's former drug-running partner James Hepi had been sent from his property could have been used by police to rub Murdoch's DNA on the cable ties. Whitaker disagreed. 'The reason why we've used LCN is that we have an expectation of finding the DNA profile [of the person] who has transferred DNA through handling and touch,' he explained. 'That contamination argument is a remote one.'

At this critical juncture, however, the case nearly came unhinged. One of the British journalists had asked a photographer for some photos of Murdoch's property seized in South Australia when he was arrested there, pictures that had been suppressed by the judge. The photographer mistakenly released the photos to the British media and another journalist wrote a story to go with them, which in turn was sent over to the Australian newspapers. One newspaper printed both the photos and a similar story. If the report had found its way into the Northern Territory, it would have been difficult to argue against the enormous prejudice it would cause in the minds of the jury. Thankfully, in the end, all copies were stopped coming into the Territory.

A few days later, the backpacker murder movie *Wolf Creek* opened around Australia, becoming the first local film to top the Australian box office chart in more than two years. Happily, distributors Roadshow Films agreed to a request from prosecutor Rex Wild QC that its Northern Territory release be delayed until after the trial.

But the case still wasn't out of the danger zone. Hepi, who claimed to police that Murdoch was the Barrow Creek killer, recounted their drug-running partnership and their drives through the outback, and Murdoch's alleged liking for wearing caps, and his 'scattered' demeanour when he returned from the July 2001 trip: 'He'd been on the gear for four or five days, racing around the country, he was fairly scattered … There had been a lot of gear taken to stay awake for those amount of hours, and like nervous tension, you know.' He claimed Murdoch had admitted he was the man pictured at the Shell Truckstop, but Hepi said he recognised him anyway. He also recited again the alleged conversation the pair had about burying bodies in spoon drains, and talked about the row that had finished their relationship in the Perth car park.

At that point, tensions between the two men exploded again in the courtroom, with the trading of insults between the pair. 'You're a f…ing liar,' growled Murdoch, while one heated claim Hepi made against Murdoch was immediately suppressed and struck from the record. Algie then said in a closed session of the court that his client had been hopelessly prejudiced in the eyes of the jury by Hepi's remark, and one TV network made an application to be allowed to report their words. Suddenly it seemed as if the case might again be derailed. But Chief Justice Brian Martin would have no truck with either.

Meanwhile, forensic anatomist Meiya Sutisno, who had compared the Truckstop video to TV footage of the defendant, claimed the man in the video was Murdoch. She was joined by an unlikely alliance of his friends trailing through the court, including Beverley Allan, who also testified it was him. 'He told me that it hadn't been a good trip,' said Allan. 'He said there'd been a few dramas, he suspected somebody had been following him on that occasion and that he'd had to deal with it.' She said Murdoch had denied his presence to his father too, and tapes were played of the two men's phone conversations while Murdoch was in Yatala Prison. 'They are trying to build a case up with all the lies and all the rest of it,' Murdoch told his dad, Colin. Murdoch left the court while the tape was being played, Algie saying he was still too upset over his father's recent death to listen.

He was upset too over the amount of food he was getting each day. His girlfriend Jan Pittman, sitting stony-faced through the parade of ex-friends, then complained to the lawyers about it, after she took note of the trolley stacked with sandwiches, chicken, sushi and fruit being trundled in to feed the jury each day. From that point on, Murdoch was given plenty to eat.

IT WAS THE CASE THAT HAD everything: love, sex, death, betrayal, drugs, travel, friendship ... and now the last drama: an earthquake. Just after court had begun for the day on Monday November 21, everyone in the courtroom felt a tremor. 'There's lots of history being made during this trial,' remarked Chief Justice Martin dryly.

BY THE SEVENTH WEEK OF the trial, the prosecution case had finished, yet no-one still knew what the defence case might entail. Algie had proved evasive. 'It could be a couple of weeks, then again it might not,' he said. 'You'll have to wait and see.' There'd been rumours that he was considering calling Murdoch to the stand, but most onlookers thought that unlikely. Whatever his innocence or guilt, Murdoch wasn't a particularly attractive-looking or articulate character, and his size and build could appear menacing to the jury. But by the end of the prosecution, Algie appeared to be on the back foot. He'd failed to make much headway with Joanne, his attack on the credibility of the DNA evidence had not dented Whitaker's confidence, and the line-up of Murdoch's friends prepared to say it was he on the Truckstop video and describe how he'd changed his appearance and four-wheel-drive after the July 2001 trip had proved overwhelming. So when Algie rose to his feet on the morning of Tuesday November 29, everyone expected a long list of witnesses he might be calling. Instead, he said just three words: 'Calling Bradley Murdoch.'

The effect was electric. Police Superintendent Colleen Gwynne raced outside to call Joanne who had decided to take a rare morning off sitting in court. Journalists ran from the press room to jostle for space in the courtroom. And Murdoch slowly, deliberately strolled up to the witness box, a faint smile playing around the corners of his mouth at the commotion he'd caused. Ten minutes later, there was a screech of brakes outside, a black sedan pulled up at the courthouse steps, and Joanne ran inside to take a seat in the second row behind the Falconios. It was the moment everyone had been waiting for and, now it was here, no-one could quite believe it.

For the defence, putting Murdoch in the stand was a huge gamble. Apart from his looks, he had a quick temper. He often spoke roughly too, swearing frequently, as had already been heard on the tape of his phone conversations. But while having Murdoch speak for himself was a risk, it was a calculated one. And, of course, if the case were lost, Murdoch might have no-one to blame but himself. His solicitor Mark Twiggs, however, saw it differently. 'It's the right thing to do,' he confided later. 'It gives him the opportunity to tell the jury he didn't do it. They've heard it from his lawyer, but they need to hear it from him.'

Algie led his client through his evidence, and their strategy became immediately clear. Murdoch admitted he was a drug-runner, heading a business with Hepi driving 9–11 kilograms (20–25 pounds) of cannabis at a time concealed in a long-range fuel tank from Sedan to Broome. He also conceded he always carried guns 'for protection' – his .357 Dirty Harry-style 10-inch barrelled revolver and a black .38 calibre Beretta pistol. During those long drives, he stayed awake with the help of lines of speed taken in cups of tea, and said he was obsessed with cars and changing them all the time to avoid police suspicion. But there he stopped.

He had eaten take-away from the Red Rooster chicken shop in Alice Springs on Saturday 14 July 2001, and had been in the Repco store opposite, but had never seen Joanne and Peter, he said. He had not followed them up past Barrow Creek, and had not stopped them. Instead, after he'd finished his business in Alice Springs that day, he'd turned off directly onto the Tanami Track and driven home to Broome towing his new camper trailer behind him, slowly and leisurely, just like a regular 'Tommy Tourist'.

His voice was gruff, but soft and, while he slouched back in the chair in the witness box, he was careful often to turn to the jury when he answered questions from Algie. It was obvious he was a man dedicated to his vehicles, going into minute loving detail, hopelessly over-technical for many to follow, about changes he'd made to them. 'Some people call it an obsession, I've sort of been lucky that I've been around people being able to pull spanners,' he said in his broad Australian accent, using his hands restlessly to illustrate each point. 'I've always mucked around with my vehicles, putting motors in and out of different four-wheel-drives.' As for guns, though, he denied he'd ever owned a silver revolver or had shown McPhail a gun as they drove through the desert in convoy, and said Hepi's old girlfriend Rachel Maxwell was wrong when she'd said she'd seen him with a silver gun. 'I never had a silver gun, so no,' he said.

When he'd left Broome for that July 2001 trip, he'd visited his parents, and bought a camper trailer in Adelaide in order to help his disguise. 'I'd been doing something illegal so I'd chop and change things around to look like Tommy Tourist, going down the road with a bit of a trailer on,' he explained. Then he left Sedan loaded up, arriving in Alice Springs at about 10.30 a.m. There, he called into Red Rooster. 'It's a bit of a spot that we always used to go to,' he said. 'I went into there and bought a chicken roll and a box of nuggets for Jack – he was a bit of a liker on nuggets – and a full chicken for the trip.' He called into Barbeques Galore, into Repco where he bought two jerry cans for water, a dash mat and new mudguards and then into a Bi-Lo supermarket where he stocked up with goods for his trip. He'd previously refuelled at a BP garage, so he had no reason to call into the Shell Truckstop. Then, about 20 kilometres outside of Alice, at about 3.30 p.m., he turned off on to the Tanami, where he took his time driving back, stopping off to camp, fixing problems with his car, and having breaks to allow Jack to run around. He knew nothing about the attack on the two British tourists until he was told about it later.

He said it wasn't him pictured at the Truckstop and any changes to his hair or moustache weren't significant as that happened all the time as part of his strategy to avoid suspicion while running drugs. 'I'll be clean-shaven, then you let it grow again,' he said. 'It's just another part of our appearances.

One minute you've got a beard, one minute you've got a mo, one minute you've got clean-shaven. One minute you've got a camper trailer on, one minute you've got a boat. When you're running drugs, you've sort of got to.'

As for the DNA, he suspected either Hepi or the police had set him up by putting his DNA on items. And the blood on Joanne's T-shirt? He didn't know how it had got there. 'I didn't know whether I crossed their paths or not,' he said.

USUALLY SO MILD-MANNERED; it was a shock when Wild stood up to start the cross-examination after lunch that day. In a scene that could have been straight out of the TV show *Law & Order*, 'Mr Murdoch,' he said, 'where did you bury Peter Falconio?' Algie leapt to his feet to object; Murdoch scowled and shook his head. But Wild continued, putting to him Hepi's account of the conversation about burying bodies, which Murdoch swiftly denied.

It was a bad-tempered session. When Wild queried how, on his timings, Murdoch had spent so long crossing the Tanami, Murdoch bit back at police officer Stephen Hall's previous evidence that it was quite possible at that time to travel at 100–120 kilometres per hour on stretches of the unmade road. He had, in contrast, driven at a safe 50–65 kilometres per hour, he said. 'I find that quite ridiculous if a police officer would stand up in this court and say that he'd do 120kph on a gravel road that changes all the time with his wife and his grandchildren in the back,' Murdoch hit back. 'I certainly wouldn't attempt anything like that.' He was also riled at the way Wild was asking him about all his previous drug runs. 'Are you trying to put me up over what, drug-running or something, or are you trying to mount up the amount of drugs that I was running?' he said.

By the next day, Murdoch had calmed down a little. Even when Wild continued to query how long it had taken him to get back to Broome – around 35 hours to drive the 1800 kilometres from Alice and taking five hours to drive one stretch of just 190 kilometres – Murdoch wasn't rattled. 'I was just plodding along,' he replied. 'I'm going home, I've got a trailer and no time that I wanted to be in Broome.'

He admitted his father had rung him to ask if it was him pictured in the Shell Truckstop video, but said he'd reassured him he was never there. The friends who thought the image looked like him were obviously wrong. While he did buy iced coffee, from time to time, he'd never buy single cartons, but five or six at a time, and he rarely wore caps. 'It wasn't me at Shell,' he protested. 'I keep saying that to you.'

Wild put, one by one, all the allegations to Murdoch: that it was him at the Truckstop, that he did stop the tourists, and that he shot Peter and tried to abduct Joanne. He denied them all. Then Wild accused him of souveniring Joanne's hairtie, and using her missing denim jacket to wrap Peter's head in to stop blood getting on his car. Murdoch said he did not. As he spoke, Joanne wiped a tear from her cheek.

ALGIE CALLED FOUR MORE DEFENCE witnesses: a salesman at Repco who claimed he'd served a 'clean-shaven' Murdoch; a DNA expert, Dr Katrin Both who said that she had strong reservations about the use of Low Copy Number testing as the risk of contamination was so high; biological anthropologist Professor Maciej Henneberg who said that Dr Meiya Sutisno couldn't possibly have accurately recognised Murdoch in the images from the Shell Truckstop as they plainly weren't him; and Professor Gale Spring who said magnifying the details would have distorted the detail too greatly to justify Dr Sutisno's claims.

THE DEFENCE AND PROSECUTION summings-up started on the eighth week of the trial, with Algie going first on Monday December 5. His case was simple enough: his client just wasn't the man who attacked Peter and Joanne that lonely night four years ago. Indeed, no-one could be sure Peter had even been killed: there had been sightings of him since, and there was no blood found in the Kombi. 'From time to time people do disappear themselves for reasons perhaps best known to them,' said Algie. 'Sometimes they turn up later, sometimes they don't. But the difficulty for you … you will be asked to convict my client of murder and there's no body.'

Moreover, he told the jury, there was no rational explanation why anyone would kill someone in such a remote spot and then move the body. 'Why would you possibly pick up a dead body, complete with blood presumably, and put it in your car?' said Algie. 'You would have to be nuts.' He said there was no evidence even that a gun had been fired, and questioned Joanne's version of events, and her identification of Murdoch as her attacker. As for the DNA evidence, he said police may have framed his client, a known drug-runner, planting his DNA on the cable ties which were already at high risk of contamination on their journey to South Australia and then to the UK. The blood on Joanne's T-shirt might have been left on a chair at the Red Rooster all three had visited earlier that same day. There were just too many holes in the prosecution's case to prove, beyond reasonable doubt, that Murdoch could be guilty of the charges. 'It's in the interests of the community in the broad sense that people are not found guilty of a serious crime unless there is a degree of proof and certainty,' he said. He reminded the jury of the Lindy Chamberlain case, where a similar reliance on 'experts' and no body led to a dreadful miscarriage of justice.

The prosecution case was similarly direct: Joanne had managed to survive the most terrifying experience of her life, Peter's parents and brothers 'a close and loving family' had been forced to endure the heartbreaking disappearance of a man with everything to live for, and Murdoch was a cunning and fastidious killer who'd gone out on a premeditated expedition with pre-made handcuffs. Wild said Murdoch may have murdered Peter because, fuelled with amphetamines, he'd come across the tourists' Kombi on his drug run and thought they were following him. He may also have thought Joanne was alone. Any discrepancies in her testimony, he said, as she wiped her eyes in the public gallery, had to be taken in this context. 'This has been a terrifying experience for her,' he told the jury. 'What we've got to remember is the agony of the moment – her focus is on the man, her focus is on where she finds herself, her focus is on escaping … This young woman is in a state of emergency. She is, in fact, fighting for her life.'

He said the DNA evidence 'especially the blood at 150 quadrillion times more likely to be Murdoch's' which linked him to the pair was indisputable. While the defence had claimed police set up their client, they'd offered no evidence for this suggestion. 'Corruption, conspiracy, this innuendo running through the case, there's not one bit of evidence to support it,' said Wild. 'Every time it's been put in this case, it's been denied,' he added. Finally, Peter did not stage his own vanishing: 'He's not disappeared himself, he's been disappeared by Bradley Murdoch.' And both Luciano and Joan Falconio wept as he said that, eventually, the young man's body might be found. 'But it might take some time,' he said.

As he spoke, Murdoch made faces, and mouthed obscenities, towards his girlfriend, Pittman.

AFTER THE JUDGE HAD ALSO summed up, the jury retired to consider their verdict. If they found Murdoch not guilty of the charges, he would obviously walk free that day. If they found him not guilty of some of the charges, he could still be released, since he'd already spent so long in prison awaiting trial. But if Murdoch were found guilty, the sentence would be automatic: life. The judge might then set a non-parole period of either twenty or twenty-five years depending on whether the crime was considered as 'aggravated' within the terms of the legislation, or might decline to set a non-parole period. In that case, Murdoch would be behind bars for the course of his natural life.

ON THE 37TH DAY OF THE TRIAL, on a dark, overcast day of driving rain and gusting winds in Darwin, the jury left the court at 12.50 p.m. to consider their verdict. Eight hours later, Chief Justice Brian Martin asked them to return to inform them they could deliver a 10–2 majority verdict if they couldn't reach a decision on which they were all agreed. In the middle of telling them this, however, he was interrupted by the court sheriff informing him they had, in fact, reached a unanimous verdict. He stopped his speech, startled, and a ripple ran around the courtroom. He then slowly asked the foreperson for their verdict on each of the counts.

Joanne's whole body started shaking, and she grabbed the arm of Paul Falconio sitting beside her. She then stared fixedly at the floor, waiting for the first verdict on the murder charge. And finally it came: Guilty. As the word echoed around the room, Joanne collapsed sobbing into Paul's arms. In front of her, Luciano Falconio put his arm around his wife Joan's shoulders, and she buried her face in his shirt. Bradley Murdoch gazed blankly, impassively, at the judge as he was, one by one, found guilty on every count. He continued to look straight ahead as Martin thanked the jury and then made the extraordinary admission: 'I utterly agree with your verdicts.' He then told Murdoch he would be sentenced to life imprisonment, and the prisoner was led away, as the Falconio family and Joanne embraced each other, the tears flowing freely.

It was a gripping finale to a tragic drama played out over four-and-a-half years. One life had been lost, several had been destroyed, and dozens more had been fractured forever by twenty seconds of madness on a lonely stretch of road in the Australian outback. And both Australia and Britain had become nations divided over the evidence of the lonely heroine, a woman treated in exactly the same way as Lindy Chamberlain twenty-five years before, another bruised survivor of a desert horror.

For Joanne, these verdicts had come as her final vindication, and she could hardly be blamed for savouring the moment. Later, on the steps of the court in front of a battery of cameras, she came out once more, flanked by the Falconio brothers, to face the press. She started to say something, but no words came out. She whispered to Paul to read her statement for her, but he told her it was time for her to speak up. She took a deep breath, and finally spoke.

'I am obviously delighted with the unanimous verdict given here today,' she said, softly. 'The past four years have been very traumatic for myself and the Falconio family and to see justice done here today eases a great burden for us all.'

Her relief at the verdicts, however, could not mask her distress at the continuing agony of not knowing where Peter Falconio lay. 'Finally, I would like Bradley John Murdoch to seriously consider telling me, Joan and Luciano and Pete's brothers what he has done with Pete. Today marks the conclusion of an intense period of distress for myself and the Falconio family that will enable us to take another step in the grieving process for Pete.'

Paul then stepped forward, echoing her concern about her lost boyfriend. 'The most important thing now is to find Pete's body,' he said. Nick too was sombre. 'Today isn't a celebration for us,' he said. 'We've waited for four years for this day. We are pleased with the verdict, but this will not bring Pete back.' Luciano fought back tears as he finally spoke too. 'I'm very, very happy – but my son is dead. There will not be any closure for us until we know where the body is.'

Friends say Joanne is unlikely ever to heal fully from the experience. She'll always be the woman who lived through a terrifying ordeal and staged an extraordinarily courageous escape – and then who came close to drowning in the doubts of a sceptical press and public. As for Murdoch, he's left a trail of destruction and despair as choking as the thick plume of red dust that billowed from his four-wheel-drive as he thundered through the desert with marijuana in the back, speed in his veins, and evil in his heart.

And for Joan and Luciano Falconio, his conviction brings no end to their nightmare. They know they'll never have any peace until the day they're able to bury their son. And that day, they know, might well never come.